Praise for *Letting Go*

"Whose voices get heard? Who gets ignored? Wrobel and Massey make a sharp and compelling case for shifting decision-making power – a must-read for the social sector.

— Ben Jealous, former President, NAACP

"This book is constructive, informed, comprehensive and above all, engrossing. An eye-opening and provocative read for those deploying capital to solve the world's big challenges."

— Tara Sabre Collier, Visiting Fellow, Skoll Centre for Social Entrepreneurship at the University of Oxford

"This insightful book shows why it is critical for philanthropy to incorporate insights from people with lived experience. Participatory funding can be a valuable tool for our giving – and our impact investing – as we seek to advance gender justice and open societies."

— Kavita Ramdas, Director of the Women's Rights Program, Open Society Foundations, and former President and CEO, Global Fund for Women

"How can we reimagine a more just world if we don't consider the redistribution of power as a key element to transformative change? In *Letting Go*, Ben Wrobel and Meg Massey address this question deeply in their sharp read with real world examples and solutions on how philanthropy and funders can step up by stepping down, and become better allies for the communities they seek to serve."

— Rodney Foxworth, CEO, Common Future

"Sharing power isn't just a concept, it's an action. We have to actually work differently as investors if we want to build community wealth and power, and truly realize the transformative potential of impact investing. This book provides an important roadmap from philosophy to action, and I hope the field will take its lessons to heart!"

— Morgan Simon, Founder, Candide Group and Author, *Real Impact: The New Economics of Social Change*

"Massey and Wrobel offer an important road map for turning statements of solidarity into meaningful action. Through their thoughtful and accessible framing of the history and principles of participatory funding, the authors outline a pathway forward for asset owners, foundation executives and community members. A critical read for critical times!"

— Jed Emerson, Founder, Blended Value and Author, *The Purpose of Capital*

"*Letting Go* is not just a rally cry for philanthropists and impact investors to rethink current funding paradigms. It fundamentally asks us to reckon with the haunting and personal question of 'what right do I have to do this work?' and, therefore, what actions must I take as a result."

— Nate Wong, Chief Strategy + Social Innovation Officer, Beeck Center for Social Impact at Georgetown University

"A beautifully written and engaging exploration into how philanthropic giving could and should be different. A great read for any funder wanting to understand how to shift power and let go, with some concrete examples of where this has worked and how we can follow their lead to make the world a more equitable place."

— Hannah Paterson, Portfolio Manager, National Lottery Community Fund

"It was a joy to read the stories behind some of the most innovative community-led projects operating today. Ben and Meg paint a picture of the growing movement to create new governance systems that engage community wisdom to create a more just and equitable world."

— Kelley Buhles Founder, Buhles Consulting, and former Senior Director, Philanthropic Services, RSF Social Finance

"If our ambition is justice, not charity, then the question of 'Who decides?' is key. By interrogating the usual ways we operate, and sharing stories of inspiring alternatives, Letting Go is the best introduction to the best ideas for social change."

— Rose Longhurst, Programme Officer, Open Society Initiative for Europe

"This is an exceptionally powerful book that will cause readers to ques-tion the fundamental process of how capital is allocated. Thankfully, it also offers insights into actionable solutions that can be taken to move towards a more equitable system. The concepts in this book will be abso-lutely essential in impact investing and philanthropy best practices in the future."

— Aunnie Patton Power, Founder, Intelligent Impact and Author, *(ad)Venture Finance: Creating An Epic Funding Journey That Blends Profit and Purpose*

"*Letting Go* is an essential read with advice, inspiration, and a call to ac-tion from passionate authors – to challenge how we think about philan-thropy and social impact and create systems that are collaborative and characterized by active participation of diverse voices, not just the wealthiest, as we strive to create a better world."

— Brandolon Barnett, Technologist and Author, *Dreams Deferred: Recession, Struggle, & the Quest for a Better World*

LETTING GO

How Philanthropists and Impact
Investors Can Do More Good by
Giving Up Control

BEN WROBEL AND MEG MASSEY
Foreword by Edgar Villanueva

To the ones letting go and the ones stepping up

CONTENTS

FOREWORD

Since 2018, I've been on a global crusade to engage philanthropists, wealth managers and others who control, manage and allocate money in a movement to decolonize wealth.

My travels led me to the Skoll World Forum in Oxford in 2019. I remember walking onto the magnificent stage of Oxford's New Theatre. I'd spoken across the United States to large audiences full of influential people, but this felt different. It *was* different. The previous year's keynote speaker had been Bono; they even gave me a makeup artist. I was going to speak in front of some of the most successful and influential people in philanthropy and impact investing—the people who objectively have a big say over the future of the world.

I wasn't sure how people were going to take my speech. Most conversations at Skoll are about solving social and economic problems on a global scale; I was telling the audience that *they* were actually part of the problem.

My book, *Decolonizing Wealth*, argues that what ails philanthropy at its core is colonialism. Almost without exception, funders reinforce the colonial division of Us vs Them, Haves vs Have Nots, and mostly-white saviors and experts vs poor, needy, urban, disadvantaged, marginalized, or at-risk people—often a euphemism for people of color. When it comes to getting or giving access to money, white men are usually in charge, and everyone else has to be twice as good (or more) to get half as much (or less).

Though my own experience is centered in philanthropy, the same dynamics hold true across what I call the loans-to-gifts spectrum. From bank loans and venture capital, to grantmaking and international development, the statistics are equally dismal.

What's needed is a massive dose of humility. The root of the word humility is related to the soil, like the word "humus." Humility literally means being close to the ground. This is where we find expertise and solutions, too: close to the ground, close to lived experience.

Ben and Meg's book is about humility. Specifically, it's about how to structuralize humility by shifting decision-making power in philanthropy and impact investing closer to the ground. It's premised around a big idea: that changing the way funders make decisions can not only lead to better decisions, but can also repair long-worn bonds of trust and start to take responsibility for the damage caused by well-intentioned altruism in the past.

In order for us to decolonize wealth, we need at least half of the people who make decisions about where money goes—at least fifty percent of staff, fifty percent of advisers, fifty percent of board members—to have intimate, authentic knowledge of the issues and communities involved. That means that some of the usual suspects will have to give up their seats; they'll have to take a step back.

Meg and Ben have conducted more than one hundred interviews with activists and altruists from around the world—even during a global pandemic—from Indigenous leaders in South America to community organizers in Boston. Their book is not about any single cause but about the entire spectrum of progressive causes; how the *way* we decide is just as important as *what* we decide. The process is indeed the point.

Shifting power like this will be an uphill battle, and it's going to require trust – trust that people in positions of power will be willing to give some of it up. There's plenty of reason for skepticism, but if ever there was a time for participatory decision-making to catch on, that time would be now. Our institutions are at a moment of reckoning; conversations about racial justice are happening in real time, out in the open. In Oxford, the audience at the Skoll World Forum accepted my speech thoughtfully, and I've been invited into even more conservative spaces because change makers everywhere know that we must do something different.

I wrote in my book that money is what we make it. Money can corrupt; it can be dirty; it can be, as the Bible says, the root of all evil if we love money more than people. But what is money but a way to measure value and to facilitate exchange? Money can also be a tool of love, a tool to facilitate relationships, to help us connect rather than to hurt and divide us. If it's used for sacred, life-giving, restorative purposes, it can be medicine.

Money, used as medicine, can help us decolonize wealth. And this book, in the right hands, can help get us there.

EDGAR VILLANUEVA

Principal, Decolonizing Wealth Project and
Liberated Capital
Author, *Decolonizing Wealth*

December 2020

INTRODUCTION

This book is about power—who has it, and how it's used.

The two of us work in a field that could be broadly defined as the "social sector": the foundations, impact investment funds and international aid organizations that collectively go about funding solutions to the world's thorniest problems, from economic inequality to climate change.

This kind of work can be very appealing, especially to a certain kind of young person trying to figure out how to use their privilege for good. Activist Courtney Martin has called it the "reductive seduction of other people's problems," writing that "if you're young, privileged, and interested in creating a life of meaning, of course you'd be attracted to solving problems that seem urgent and readily solvable." She notes that "There is a whole 'industry' set up to nurture these desires and delusions... encompassed so fully in the patronizing, dangerously simple phrase 'save the world.'"

But over the past few years, we, like many of our pedigreed peers, have become more critical of this industry, its power dynamics, and our own role in it. The social sector, like so many global institutions, is at a moment of reckoning. Books like Edgar Villanueva's *Decolonizing Wealth* and Anand Giridharadas's *Winners Take All* have punctured the air of righteousness around the architects of social change. Twenty years into philanthropy's so-called golden age, the unchecked rise of global inequality raises questions about just how effectively those trillions of dollars have been put to work.

For us, and for many of our peers, this reckoning boils down to a reckoning with our own egos. When you're watching a movie (particularly a bad one), you end up relying on a "suspension of disbelief" to get you through the plot. Some scenarios might seem like a stretch, but you're willing to hold back judgment in service of the larger story. Similarly, when you work in the social sector long enough, you learn to suspend disbelief about the power of your own judgment. If a problem is out there, it must be solvable. If it's solvable, then it must be within the reach of your own logic, reason and intellect. It's a perfect philosophy for a generation raised on the can-do idealism of "The West Wing" and the clean logic of *Freakonomics*.

For most of our careers, we've leaned into that suspension of disbelief. Between the two of us, we've developed what is sometimes incredibly shallow expertise on an incredibly wide variety of topics, from voting rights to vertical farming. We've frequently been positioned as experts on topics that six months prior we knew next to nothing about.

The idea for this book came out of a conversation we had at a conference for impact investors several months before the onset of the COVID-19 pandemic. The conference was about impact investing, which had grown from a niche topic into a field representing half a trillion dollars' worth of capital. It was held in an immense former stock exchange; the main hall was filled with investors from around the world who had paid upward of $1,500 to mingle and learn about the field.

The investors saw suffering in the world, and they nobly aimed to heal it. The ideas they were discussing—greenhouse gas reduction, microfinance, sustainable infrastructure—were all important. Still, the people in the room were mostly white, mostly male and almost entirely from the United States and wealthy European cities. Several times during the conference, investors (and, to their credit, the conference organizers) pointed out the lack of voices in the room from marginalized communities.

The investors were talking mostly to each other, about solutions to problems that many of them had never experienced. The setting of the stock exchange, with its cavernous ceilings that caused sound to bounce back, completed the picture of an echo chamber of privilege.

To change this dynamic, we need to change who has power. We need to challenge our assumptions about authority and expertise and rethink who has a voice in making decisions about our collective future. In short, we need an entirely different approach to the problem of problem-solving.

This book is about an approach to problem-solving that we call participatory funding. To steal a phrase, it's the biography of an idea. The idea is both simple and powerful: What if we shifted decision-making power away from expert grantmakers and investors? What if we gave that power to people with lived experience of the problems at hand?

You might be familiar with the idea of participatory funding in the context of local government. City budgets are essentially moral documents—setting the priorities for how tax dollars are spent. In the past few decades, cities from New York to Barcelona have experimented with handing over direct control of segments of city budgets to citizens, a process called participatory budgeting. In the summer of 2020, Black Lives Matter Los Angeles presented city leaders with a "people's budget" that included a plan to defund the police that was more substance than slogan—it called for cutting bloated police budgets and moving resources to needs like social workers, housing and education.

The operating philosophy behind participatory budgeting is that the best way to solve a problem is to follow the lead of the people who know it best. It narrows the distance that inevitably exists in any form of representative democracy: between mayor and citizen, federal and local, those who govern and those who are governed. Consigned to the margins of serious policy debate just a decade ago, participatory budgeting is now used in more than seven thousand municipalities around the world. Its rise has been a bright spot in an otherwise dismal decade for democracy; amid the rise of authoritarianism, it represents a return to democracy's roots.

Can this approach be applied to the social sector? As you might have guessed, grantmaking and impact investing are far from participatory as they are practiced today. Both fields are shaped and dominated by a homogenous group of decision-makers: mostly white, mostly men and mostly from the West. And both fields are distinctly undemocratic. The key point is a lack of accountability: although modern foundations and investors often perform the *functions* of government (public health, poverty alleviation), it's important to remember that these private-sector actors have none of the same democratic checks and balances.

Still, as we explored the history of participatory funding, we learned that there has been a decades-long debate about participatory decision-making in the social sector, and a legacy of effective experiments with philanthropic populism. That's what this book will be about.

The idea of "participatory grantmaking" had its first big moment in the 1970s, when a generation of trust funders, steeped in the civil rights and anti-war counterculture, pioneered the first wave of participatory foundations. These small "alternative" foundations were radically new for their time, and they were governed by residents who had final say over how grants would be distributed to their neighborhoods. We're currently riding a second wave in participatory grantmaking. This time it's being driven by human rights grantmakers like the Disability Rights Fund and FRIDA | The Young Feminist Fund that are inviting activists to set the agenda for social justice movements.

More recently, there's been a parallel conversation in the growing field of impact investing. A growing number of investment funds have started to rethink not just *what* investors should put their money behind, but *how* they make those decisions. Some of these funds operate on the neighborhood level, like the Boston Ujima Project, a community loan fund governed by residents of a working class neighborhood in Boston. Others operate on a global scale, like Village Capital, which uses a similar logic for investing in impact-driven tech startups. These funds are upending the idea that investment strategies and due diligence have to be driven by people with traditional backgrounds in finance.

A Call to Action

We've spent the past two years learning all we could about these emerging models for participatory funding. We've seen the incredible potential that they have to fix broken power dynamics in philanthropy and impact investing, and decouple the association of wealth with wisdom. And we're not the only ones. These models have started to get attention from mainstream funders. Participatory grantmaking was named "Most Promising Sector Reform Effort" by industry broadsheet Inside Philanthropy in 2018. Participatory investing was on the agenda of recent impact investing conferences, including SOCAP and the Mission Investors Exchange.

But the reality is that participatory funding still makes up a tiny percentage of all social sector funding. People in positions of power don't always welcome the idea of engaging outside voices, with reactions that range from skepticism to fear. Foundation boards, investment committees, and wealth advisers have an obligation to the money they manage—and can understandably feel that outsourcing the decision-making power would be an abdication of responsibility.

In the preface, Edgar Villanueva envisions a social sector where at least fifty percent of the people who make decisions about funding have direct lived experience of the problems they're trying to solve. We're a long way from that point. A growing number of funders are experimenting with participatory funding, but often warily, and with relatively small pots of money. There's an urgency in how funders talk about equity and inclusion that's not matched by the urgency of their actions.

This book is a call to action for the social sector. We've written it first and foremost for the people who make decisions about where money goes. But we also hope to engage and inspire anyone who cares about the major movements for equality and justice happening around the world today. As Edgar Villanueva wrote in the Foreword, this book is not about any single cause, but rather about the entire spectrum of progressive causes. It's critical to look at how these movements are funded.

In **Part One**, we'll set the stage by taking a snapshot of the social sector today, at a moment when capital is concentrated in fewer hands than at any moment in history. We'll look at the rise of "billionaire philanthropy," a new era of altruism that is often characterized by wealthy people parachuting into communities and trying to solve their problems, without asking first. Next, we'll explain how grantmaking and impact investing work in practice—both *who* is in the room, and *how* the people in that room engage with outside voices. Finally, we'll investigate a popular theory: that right now, in the wreckage of a global pandemic, is when big systemic change is truly possible.

In **Part Two**, we'll argue that participatory funding is a necessary ingredient in big systemic change. We'll explore the roots of modern participatory decision-making, with a focus on the past fifty years. Then we'll share examples of participatory grantmaking in action across the world, on issues from disability rights to sex work, before turning our attention to participatory models for impact investing on both a local and global scale.

In **Part Three**, we'll explore what it would take to reach the ambitious vision set out by Edgar Villanueva in this book's Foreword: a future where fifty percent of grantmakers and investors have intimate, authentic knowledge of the communities with which they work. This work is already being led by reformers at the highest levels of the social sector, who are engaged in a sustained campaign to chip away at outdated mindsets and habits. The ultimate goal for many of them is to make traditional philanthropy obsolete.

Finally, the **Afterword** will look at the potential for participatory decision-making in the public sector. Philanthropy plays such a large role in public affairs because public institutions around the world today are failing to meet basic needs. We aren't arguing that the social sector should replace government. Rather, we're arguing that it's possible to walk and chew gum at the same time: to both reform philanthropy and rebuild democratic institutions. In the Afterword we'll talk about the promise of participatory democracy—things like participatory budgeting, policy juries and other civic spaces that can allow people to have control over their own lives and feel more connected to democracy itself.

A note: we recognize that the story we tell will not be exhaustive. We spend most of the book examining the last fifty years, within the context of modern institutional funding in the West. There is a long history of participatory and communal practices in the African American community and Indigenous cultures worldwide that we only touch on only briefly. This is undoubtedly a reflection of our own implicit and internalized biases, as well as the demographics of our networks and the people we interviewed. We have done our best to tell all sides of this story; we also encourage our readers to follow the threads of other leaders and thinkers we write about, to learn about this subject from people with different perspectives and lived experience.

Letting Go

In 2011, Kristi Kimball and Malka Kopell, two grantmakers experienced in participatory funding, wrote an essay in the *Stanford Social Innovation Review* comparing grantmaking to surfing. "We would probably be better off as a society," they wrote, if the decision-makers in the nation's large private foundations took up surfing:

> "Why? Because surfing is about letting go....Surfing is incredibly humbling, an encounter with the enormous power, beauty, and unpredictability of the ocean. No surfer would attempt to change the shape of the waves or the schedule of the tides, because these forces are far beyond any one person's control.
>
> Just as men cannot control oceans, individual foundations cannot control social systems....Such an approach underestimates the vast power and complexity of the systems in which foundations are attempting to intervene."

The movement to scale participatory funding will be an uphill climb, but not for the reasons you might expect. The biggest obstacle won't be finding data to back up the theory, or detangling the complex logistics of gathering input from a wide group of people. Rather, it will be asking grantmakers and investors to embrace previously unthinkable levels of intellectual humility. In the words of Roxanne Nazir, a program officer at Open Society Foundations, the challenge will be to change "mindsets, identities, and learned behavior."

There are plenty of books about how to bring a strategic approach to grantmaking, or how to go about investing for good. What we're suggesting is something entirely different: that the best way to step up for social change is to step back, and that the best way to make an impact is to simply let go.

PART ONE

1

THE VIEW FROM THE TOP

On a late-September Friday in 2010, David Fincher's film *The Social Network* premiered at the New York Film Festival. Facebook was only six years old but already had six hundred million users. The much-anticipated film, based on the book *The Accidental Billionaires*, about the legal battles around Facebook's founding, was shaping up to be a damning portrait of the company's twenty-six-year-old CEO, Mark Zuckerberg.

Zuckerberg was nowhere to be found on the night of the glitzy Lincoln Center premiere, but he had a good reason to be out of town. He'd flown to Chicago the day before to appear on *The Oprah Winfrey Show*, along with two politicians with national ambitions: then-New Jersey Governor Chris Christie and then-Newark Mayor Cory Booker. They were there to make a big announcement: Zuckerberg was going to donate $100 million to Newark public schools.

According to Booker, this was not "some sort of elaborate publicity stunt" to distract from *The Social Network*'s release. Motivations aside, Newark's school system could certainly use the money. It was one of the lowest-performing school systems in the country at the time, with a high school graduation rate that hovered at around sixty percent—nineteen points below the national average. Most of Newark's school buildings were more than eighty years old, and nearly half of the district's students

3

lived below the poverty line. Zuckerberg was offering a massive cash transfusion and a promise to implement deep structural reform.

The Prize, a book-length postmortem of the project by Dale Russakoff, detailed how many Newark residents learned about the plan to shake up their school system the same way as the rest of America: by watching Oprah. Over the next few days Booker tried to make up for that with a call for grassroots community engagement, going on television again to say that "We have to let Newark lead and not let people drop in from outside and point the way." But that community engagement never materialized.

Early on, Zuckerberg's team launched a series of community forums, offering residents a "voice of influence" in the distribution of the $100 million. Residents showed up to community centers and school auditoriums to share what they were seeing in their neighborhoods, often stressing the importance of addressing children's social and emotional health alongside education reform. But the grassroots leaders who were hired to sell the plan to the community quickly grew disillusioned, and they abandoned a planned second phase of forums. One local foundation leader told Russakoff, "It wasn't real community engagement, it was public relations."

More than a decade later, the $100 million project to transform Newark's schools is widely regarded as a failure by Newark residents. The city got more than fifty new principals and four new public high schools, and schools saw some modest improvements. But the effort is mostly remembered for private-sector consultants from outside the city who were paid as much as $1,000 a day; for thousands of parents finding out without warning that their children would have to transfer to a different school; and for the dismissal of hundreds of support staff.

The project crawled to an ignominious end. In 2015, seventy-seven clergy members sent a letter to Christie requesting a moratorium on the plan, citing "venomous" public anger and "the moral imperative" that people have power over their own destiny. "My mom—she would've been fit to be tied with some of what happened," Cory Booker later told *The New Yorker*. A few years later, Newark Mayor Ras Baraka reflected back: "You can't just cobble up a bunch of money and drop it in the middle of the street and say, 'This is going to fix everything.' You have to engage with communities that already exist....To parachute folks in, it becomes problematic."

In His Judgment

The Newark school experiment is often cited as an example of the limitations of imposing philanthropy from the top down, dropping into a community without true engagement. It even caused a brief moment of reflection for the field. But the lessons have yet to fully sink in. Eleven years later, Zuckerberg's early brand of philanthropy—ambitious, outsider-led projects that take their cues from those at the top—remains the dominant model.

Of course, philanthropy has always been a rich man's game. Modern philanthropy dates back to America's "First Gilded Age," the period in the late nineteenth century following the Civil War. It was a time, much like today, defined by massive inequality, generated in part by brand-new industries that were still beyond the reach of government regulators (though back then, it was oil fields and railroads instead of tech start-ups). The lack of labor laws and income taxes allowed business tycoons like John D. Rockefeller, Andrew Carnegie, and J.P. Morgan to amass great fortunes; at the height of his power, Rockefeller's net worth was $400 billion in inflation-adjusted dollars, equivalent to two percent of the US economy.

This was unsustainable. In 1889, Andrew Carnegie wrote a now-famous essay, "The Gospel of Wealth," in which he laid out a philosophy that became the basis for modern philanthropy. "The man who dies thus rich dies disgraced," he wrote. A wealthy man, after providing for the basic needs of his family, should give away his surplus wealth "in the manner which, *in his judgment*, is best calculated to produce the most beneficial results for the community." His peers, including Rockefeller and Morgan, responded enthusiastically, creating the first formal foundations to govern how their money would be used to advance the public good after they passed away.

Their new philanthropic endeavors provoked concerns about the role of the rich in public affairs. In 1910, John D. Rockefeller made a pitch to Congress to give his new institution a public charter. The idea didn't go over well. Members of Congress called Rockefeller's new foundation a "deeply and fundamentally anti-democratic institution." One senator said the foundation, which would be controlled entirely by Rockefeller and his family, would be "unaccountable except to a hand-picked assemblage of trustees."

In the past twenty years, philanthropy has become ever more paternalistic. As global economic inequality has skyrocketed, and wealth increasingly concentrates at the top of the economic pyramid, philanthropy has gotten bigger, more ambitious and more top-down and donor-centric. Mark Zuckerberg's $100 million gift was a landmark moment in a new era of "billionaire philanthropy," a shorthand name for the modern era of giving and investing in which a handful of uber-wealthy individuals and institutions dominate the social sector landscape.

In this chapter, we'll look at the rise of donor-centric philanthropy. We'll also look at how a similar dynamic is playing out in the field of impact investing, where the story is less about a *devaluing* of wisdom from the ground and more about a failure of imagination; a missed opportunity to embed community voice in the design of new "double-bottom line" investment funds. As a result, investors who turn their attention to measuring social as well as financial returns often lack a compass for what social returns they should be focused on in the first place.

Billionaire Philanthropy

In May 2009, a year before Mark Zuckerberg's big announcement and in the midst of the Great Recession, Bill Gates and Warren Buffett invited Oprah Winfrey, Michael Bloomberg and several dozen other peers to a private dinner in New York City for a frank talk about philanthropy and the role of the rich in society. Just a few weeks earlier, Congress had passed a $787 billion stimulus bill that was already being criticized for not doing enough to address the growing economic inequality that had contributed to the recession and its slow recovery.

The meeting was described by the press as "clandestine" and "unprecedented." The point of the dinner, it soon emerged, was for Gates and Buffett to pitch a challenge to their peers: Join us in pledging to give half your fortune to charity during your lifetime.

This would be a major shift for the field of philanthropy. The model pioneered by Carnegie and Rockefeller involved setting up a charitable foundation near the end of your life; critics referred to this rather colorfully as the influence of "dead hands" over the affairs of future generations. Gates and Buffett were suggesting a more ambitious and urgent approach. They called their new commitment "the Giving Pledge." The press dubbed it "giving while living." Several dozen billionaires signed on to the pledge in the first year.

The Giving Pledge fundamentally reshaped philanthropy. As the rich started to give a greater proportion of charitable dollars, they started to remake philanthropy in their own self-image, skewing it toward their interests and toward elite institutions. In 2018, the *Chronicle of Philanthropy* put out a study on the winners and losers in philanthropy in the decade following the Great Recession. They found that the organizations with the biggest increases in revenue were the so-called "eds and meds"—hospitals and universities like the Mayo Clinic and Harvard. These are the large institutions that have the resources to wine and dine high-dollar donors and the capacity to quickly take on grants in the millions of dollars as Giving Pledgers ramped up their new foundations.

The losers, meanwhile, were "blue-collar nonprofits" that rely on small-dollar and grassroots donations. The United Way and the American Cancer Society both lost nearly a third of their revenue since the introduction of the Giving Pledge. This trend inspired Vox's Dylan Matthews to write a piece in 2015 titled, "For the love of God, rich people, stop giving Ivy League colleges money."

A decade later, The Giving Pledge has netted more than two hundred donors who have committed a total of $500 billion. The pledge spawned some of today's most influential and large-scale philanthropic projects, including Mark Zuckerberg's experiment in Newark and Jeff Bezos's $10 billion commitment to climate change.

But perhaps the biggest consequence of the pledge is how it has changed the *mechanics* of giving. By concentrating philanthropic power in fewer hands than ever before, it has incentivized the creation of a new, market-driven playbook for allocating resources from the top. Mark Zuckerberg's choices in Newark—to set a grand vision, hire thousand-dollar-a-day consultants and shake up dozens of schools in the course of a few years—marked a notable departure from how such a gift might have been handled 20 years earlier, or how it might be handled by a regional community foundation. But to Zuckerberg, a tech entrepreneur who grew a dorm room hustle into a global disruptor, it came naturally.

This gets to the lasting legacy of the Giving Pledge: ushering in a new era of business leaders who take lessons from their former lives. Liesel Pritzker Simmons, an impact investor and philanthropist who co-founded Blue Haven Initiative, told us that many of her peers take the "move fast and break things" mentality they learned in Silicon Valley and apply it to their giving. "Imagine you're a tech CEO," she says. "You grew your company to a global scale, and you're a billionaire by the age of 40. Now you see your next job as saving the world. And you're going to approach that new job in a very similar way to how you approached the old one."

The Moneyball Playbook

When Giving Pledgers turned their attention to their new job of saving the world, they found they had a clear playbook to follow. The playbook was written not by philanthropists, but by economists.

In the late 1990s, Michael Porter, an economist favored by Wall Street CEOs for his theories of market competition, argued in the *Harvard Business Review* that foundations should approach decision-making like any business. In his landmark article *Philanthropy's New Agenda: Creating Value*, he laid out a market-based approach to grantmaking.

> "In business, a company's strategy lays out how it will create value for its customers by serving a specific set of needs better than any of its competitors. A company must either produce equivalent value at a lower cost than rivals or produce greater value for comparable cost.
>
> ...The goals of philanthropy may be different, but the underlying logic of strategy is still the same. Instead of competing in markets, foundations are in the business of contributing to society by using scarce philanthropic resources to their maximum potential. A foundation creates value when it achieves an equivalent social benefit with fewer dollars or creates greater social benefit for comparable cost."

Benjamin Soskis, a historian of philanthropy, has argued that Porter's call to action played a major role in normalizing a market-based model of philanthropy. "Business enterprise had long served as a model for philanthropy," he said, "But the association between the two was now expressed even more concretely and instrumentally, the stuff of bullet-points and not merely casual metaphors."

Market-based philanthropy (also known as strategic philanthropy, or philanthrocapitalism) has been enormously popular with Giving Pledgers and legacy foundations over the past twenty years. But many critics argue that this business-oriented approach is at the heart of what's wrong with philanthropy today. They argue that the model encourages grant-makers to act like CEOs who set priorities at the top—treating non-profits like contractors whose job is to see their vision through. It also encourages a dry, dispassionate, technocratic approach to fixing complex and messy human problems.

One nonprofit leader, Rob Meiksins, summed up the problem elegantly when he coined the term "Moneyball Philanthropy." It's a reference to the Michael Lewis book, *Moneyball*, about using data to build a championship-winning baseball team. He wrote:

> "The Moneyball Philanthropy approach argues that donations should be made to organizations that are the most effective, [leaving] all the others behind. It is based on a belief in empirical data showing that if a certain amount of money is invested, there will be a predictable and positive impact on a social ill."

But philanthropy, it turns out, is not like baseball. "Baseball is played with very strict boundaries, rules and systems," he wrote. "The results are predictable, and immediate. Life, in general, is not quite so neat and tidy, riddled with variables of human personality, politics and other pressures that can change at a moments' notice."

Still, market-based philanthropy doesn't seem to be going away. Instead, today's philanthropists are keeping ever-tightening control over how their money is spent. Bill Gates set a precedent when he decided that the Gates Foundation's resources would be allocated at the discretion of just four board members: himself, his wife Melinda, his father and the billionaire Warren Buffett. In the twenty years since, donors have begun shifting their money away from community foundations, which are accountable to a broader set of stakeholders, and creating private foundations or donor-advised funds that give them even tighter control.

Today's grantmakers are also more likely to restrict who they will even consider for an open grant. In 1994, only six percent of large foundations had invitation-only policies in place, meaning they would share grant applications with a pre-selected group of nonprofits. By 2008, the percentage had increased to twenty-nine percent. Proponents argue that this cuts down on the administrative burden of applications—some receive thousands of applications for a dozen grants—but in practice, it often keeps money flowing within the same circles.

Finally, today's grantmakers are more likely to issue grants with strings attached, known as "restricted grants." These grants can only be spent on uses approved by the funder or within a narrow scope of purposes. In theory, restricted grants are a way to better track how money is spent and calculate its impact. In practice, small nonprofits get saddled with running high-profile campaigns on behalf of wealthy foundations and reporting back with detailed metrics while they struggle to pay for staff salaries or office supplies.

Restrictions and reporting requirements can make winning a grant a pyrrhic victory, especially for smaller nonprofits. "Getting a grant these days can be more trouble than it's worth," one activist told us. "It's like the time that Oprah handed out a Pontiac G6 to every member of her audience—and then those people were saddled with $6,000 in taxes. You end up spending as much time trying to please the foundation as you do solving the problem at hand."

The Moneyball Playbook is bad for all small nonprofits, but it's been worse for some than for others. Several studies have found that Black-led nonprofits in the United States are more likely to receive restricted grants than their white peers and that they "lack the networks and resources to engage deeply with donors," whether that's the cost of a conference ticket or the ability to get invited to a conference in the first place. This cycle of disinvestment creates a catch-22, in which many Black-led organizations are considered "too small to fund." Today, only eight percent of grant funding goes to nonprofits with a Black leader.

It's worth pausing here to note that there is nothing *inherently* wrong with a metric-based approach to problem-solving. In moderation, data is quite important—especially for interventions that require longitudinal data or have a scientific bent, like climate change mitigation or vaccine distribution. There are also countless examples of nonprofit service providers and social entrepreneurs changing their approach for the better because data revealed something that the people involved missed, such as a gap in services or an ineffective tactic.

But relying solely on numbers at the exclusion of people's stories, feelings and lived experience can risk simplifying complex human processes into a series of spreadsheets devoid of nuance. And the result is philanthropy that can be out of touch—sometimes comically so.

Out of Touch

Fade in: It's a snowy evening in Norway. A blond mother and her two children sit huddled around a fire, warming themselves against the frost as saccharine violin music swells in the background.

Outside, a Nigerian man turns toward the camera. "Breaks your heart, doesn't it?" he asks. "As an African, you may think, 'What can I do to help?' Well, the answer is very simple." Inside the cabin, the man pops out from behind a Christmas tree, smiling and lugging a bulky radiator. "As Africans, we need to remember that being warm makes people happy. So let's donate our radiators and deliver the gift of warmth to Norway this Christmas."

The closing line: "Give a girl a match; she'll stay warm for a day. Give a girl a radiator, and she'll stay warm for a lifetime."

This satirical infomercial for a fake campaign called "Radi-Aid" was produced by a group of students in Norway who were seeking to raise awareness about out-of-touch philanthropy and international aid. By flipping the familiar dynamic between countries in the West and emerging markets (referred to as the "Global North" and "Global South"), the video highlighted the absurdity of someone from a far-away country purporting to know what people in need truly need. The students even give out a Razzie-style award each year, the "Rusty Radiator," for the most egregious examples of out-of-touch charitable ad campaigns.

There are, unfortunately, an abundance of examples of out-of-touch campaigns to choose from. The donor-centric approach to grantmaking has frequently produced interventions that ultimately have a huge opportunity cost, given the alternatives for how the money could be spent. Indeed, it's been the driving force behind some of the biggest public missteps in philanthropy in recent years.

One famous example is the Global Alliance for Clean Cookstoves, a public-private partnership launched in 2010 to tackle the threats posed by wood-burning stoves, which contribute to respiratory illnesses as well as climate change. This real-life Radi-Aid had all the hallmarks of a philanthropic campaign du jour: deep-pocketed donors, a big announcement at the Clinton Global Initiative and the audacious, headline-grabbing goal of distributing one hundred million stoves to poor households around the globe. *The New Yorker* called the project "the quest for a stove that can save the world."

Eight years and $75 million later, however, the alliance announced that it had fallen well short of its goals. They had built and distributed the stoves on schedule, but there was an unexpected hitch: People didn't want to use them. In one village southeast of Mumbai where five hundred stoves had been installed, ProPublica interviewed a woman whose stove sat abandoned in a corner of her kitchen. She told the reporter that the "clean" stove simply didn't cook food like she wanted it to. "'This one does things fast,' she said in Hindi...nudging a handful of twigs further into the family's age-old chulha, a hand-sculpted open-topped clay perch for a pot or two. 'That one does it too slowly.'"

In the United States, any conversation around philanthropic missteps inevitably comes back to public education. Mark Zuckerberg's experiment in Newark was only one failed big-dollar campaign to attempt to fix America's public schools. The Gates Foundation has spent hundreds of millions of dollars on ambitious and well-intentioned but ultimately donor-centric projects, including a massive effort to break large high schools into smaller ones. But each one failed to achieve the desired results.

Of course, it's easy to criticize the big strikeouts in philanthropy. But an honest accounting of billionaire philanthropy would also need to question the more successful efforts.

The Gates Foundation, for instance, has donated $5 billion to fighting malaria and seen incredible success. But critics point out that this work has drawn dollars away from more basic and vital investments in health systems and primary care—like pandemic prep—in emerging markets. Professor Katharyne Mitchell has written that the foundation's anti-malaria campaign created solutions in "vertical silos...while horizontal systems of basic care, coordinated by local or national governments, are sidelined or even undermined." In other words, Bill Gates has made progress with malaria, but his institution chose not to invest in self-sustaining, public health systems that could continue the fight.

Sometimes the billionaire's touch is not so much good or bad as it is *apparent*. In 2019, Jeff Bezos made a big announcement: He was creating a new $10 billion organization to fight climate, called the Jeff Bezos Earth Fund. Inside Philanthropy founder David Callahan compared this announcement to a nine-hundred-pound gorilla emerging on the scene. "Bezos may soon be giving more for climate annually than the next top five funders combined," he wrote, noting that Bezos could "radically reorder the funding landscape," imposing his will on the climate change conversation and setting priorities for the movement—priorities over which thousands of activists have spent years debating.

Teddy Schiefler, a writer for Recode, summed it up like this: "Jeff Bezos is going to have a ton of influence over the world's response on climate. Maybe he'll have good ideas. Maybe he won't. But should any single, non-elected person have so much power in determining society's response to a crisis that affects all of us?"

We think not, and for the rest of this book, we'll explore ideas about shifting philanthropy away from a donor-centric approach. But before we do that, let's turn our attention to impact investing. The growing field is sometimes called a "cousin" to philanthropy, and often has parallel goals—as well as a similarly funder-centric approach.

The Rise of Impact Investing

After the Giving Pledge was announced, the pledgers started meeting once a year to check on progress and share what they were learning. In May 2012, several Giving Pledgers, including Warren Buffett and Bill Gates, flew to Santa Barbara for a private meeting with a group that included Elon Musk and Steve and Jean Case, the founders of AOL and the Case Foundation.

On the agenda: a new trending topic called impact investing. The term had been coined a few years earlier by the Rockefeller Foundation's Antony Bugg-Levine at an elite gathering at the foundation's lakeside retreat center in Italy. It was a new way to brand an old idea: using your money to invest with an altruistic intent in social entrepreneurs, community development projects and the like, with the intention of generating positive social or environmental impact beyond turning a profit. For the Cases and other early adopters, impact investing was a way to augment the goals of traditional philanthropy by putting to work investments that had previously been agnostic to (or actively working against) the public good.

Impact investments can take a variety of forms, from venture capital gambles to small-dollar community loans. Venture capital investors purchase an equity stake in a social enterprise and fund its growth, with the expectation of significant returns if the company succeeds. Community loans are exactly what they sound like: loans to small businesses, housing developments, and other projects intended to strengthen local economies. Either way, the goal is to fill gaps in the capital markets by funding projects that support marginalized communities or tackle issues like financial inclusion and climate change.

It didn't take long for impact investing to catch on with the donor set. *The Economist* reported that Warren Buffett was skeptical about the idea coming out of the Santa Barbara meeting, but "many of the other attendees were so gripped that they plan to convene a follow-up discussion on it." It was appealing on a number of levels. Wealthy individuals saw a way to advance their favorite cause while still making a reasonable return on their money, and foundations saw the model as a way to put their hefty endowments to work on the same issues as their grants.

Indeed, several years after the Santa Barbara meeting, impact investing now accounts for an estimated $700 billion in investments around the world. The Ford Foundation recently committed to investing $1 billion of its $12 billion endowment in funds that align with its mission, and it is one of more than two hundred foundations in a network called the Mission Investors Exchange that made such commitments. And nearly every big-name philanthropist has staked a claim in the impact investing space. In 2019, as part of his gorilla-sized push to fund climate change solutions, Jeff Bezos joined Bill Gates, Alibaba founder Jack Ma and dozens of others to launch a billion-dollar investment fund called Breakthrough Energy Ventures, which funds cleantech startups with investments as large as $20 million.

We have both spent the past few years of our careers working primarily in impact investing, and we believe fully in its potential. In the words of Jacqueline Novogratz, an early impact investor, these investments "dare to go where markets have failed and aid has fallen short." The United Nations estimates that there's a $2 trillion financing gap standing in the way of reaching the UN's widely-accepted Sustainable Development Goals by 2030, and philanthropy alone won't get us there in time. (We think that governments should be playing more of a role, but that's a subject for a different book.) However, there's a fundamental misconception about impact investing that stands in the way of the field reaching its full potential.

The popular story about impact investing is that it's derived from *philanthropy*: an attempt to apply market-based processes to achieve altruistic goals. But the real story is a bit different. Impact funds, on a practical level, are derived from *finance*. They are modeled on the same financial vehicles used by oil companies or hedge funds. This might seem like a minor distinction, but it's an important one.

Here's what we mean. In the first few years after that Santa Barbara meeting, hundreds of impact investment funds sprouted up around the world. These funds generally originated in one of two ways. Some were built from scratch by philanthropists or their money managers and were modeled on Wall Street investment firms or Silicon Valley venture capital funds. Others were spin-offs from major financial institutions, like Bain Capital's Double Impact fund or Goldman Sachs' Urban Investment Group.

Either way, the result was the same: The vast majority of impact funds have operating models that closely mimic those of traditional investment firms, which are notoriously insular, secretive and unaccountable to anyone besides shareholders.

This is reflected in how most impact fund managers make decisions. Power typically sits with a small and exclusive set of decision-makers at every step of the funding process, from building a theory of change, to performing due diligence on potential investments, to making final calls on where to invest. While impact investors aim to solve problems for a broader-than-normal set of stakeholders, often those from marginalized communities, on a practical level they are only accountable to a narrow set of wealthy shareholders.

Rodney Foxworth, CEO of Common Future and a prominent impact investor, spoke to us about how the first meetings of wealthy impact investors had long repercussions. "Impact investing's 'original sin' began at its inception," he told us. "Early impact investors focused their principles on *what* they were investing in, as opposed to *how* they were investing. It created a disconnect."

Indeed, after a decade of mainstream impact investing, there are already several data points that speak to the downsides of this "investor-centric" approach.

We've seen what happens when communities aren't involved in the due diligence process. You get failed investments along the lines of the Clean Cookstoves project, where big ideas do not get off the ground because of a fundamental misunderstanding of local culture. One frequently cited example is the PlayPump, a social enterprise that was supposed to bring drinking water to thousands of African communities by "harnessing the power of children at play." The PlayPump was a merry-go-round type device that pumped drinking water into a storage tank as the children played on it. The startup generated a lot of attention and excitement in 2005, including support from then-First Lady Laura Bush. But a few years into the PlayPump's rollout, "Frontline" released a report revealing that the device did not address a major underlying problem—water scarcity—and, ironically, children found the PlayPump to be too much work. By 2010, virtually all of the PlayPumps had been replaced with traditional hand pumps.

We've also seen what happens when impact investors have full control over what counts as "impact," a broad and fuzzy definition that sometimes reaches comical proportions. You may know the story of Juicero, the Silicon Valley tech startup that promised to "hack" healthy eating with WiFi-enabled juicing machines that squeezed individually packed bags of pulp. The company had all the raw ingredients for success: a founder with deep experience in the food industry, a designer who had worked with Steve Jobs and more than $100 million in venture capital funding. But it was soon revealed that their flagship product cost $400— and that it was essentially useless. When reporters at Bloomberg tested a Juicero device, they found that squeezing the bags by hand yielded about the same amount of juice just as quickly as using the device. The company shut down within weeks.

Juicero is a fun punch line for how out of touch Silicon Valley can be. But what most people forget about the story is that Juicero marketed itself as an impact-driven startup. In breathless press releases and marketing materials, the company's leadership gushed about the power of "raw, plant-based nutrition," and their excitement in "solving some of our nation's nutrition and obesity challenges." And several of Juicero's financial backers marketed themselves as impact investors.

Perhaps the most damning indictment of impact investing has less to do with individual investments and more to do with broad demographic trends. Nearly eight in ten employees at impact funds in the United States are white; more than half are white men. In the United Kingdom, ninety-eight percent of board directors at impact funds are men. This plays out in who gets funding; women are still far less likely to receive funding from impact investors. And in Africa, a favored region for American and European impact investors, more than half of impact investing dollars flowed to social enterprises that had only white founders.

The broadest concerns are that impact investing, for all its good intentions, will end up replicating the unjust power dynamics of the global financial system—and that the world's biggest investors, unconstrained by accountability to anyone but their shareholders, will use the brand of impact to increase their stranglehold on the direction of the global economy.

The Never-Ending Pledge

There's a funny phenomenon with Giving Pledgers: They can't seem to stop getting richer, no matter how hard they try.

The world's richest people continue to see their net worth grow at a rapid pace, despite the increasing amounts that they give away. By all indications, the coronavirus pandemic exacerbated this trend. In the first four months of the pandemic, the top one hundred living Giving Pledgers saw their combined wealth increase by twenty-eight percent. In a September 2020 blog post, Anand Giridharadas calculated that if Jeff Bezos gave all eight hundred seventy-six thousand Amazon employees a $105,000 bonus, he'd be left with exactly as much money as he had at the start of the pandemic.

That means that the "social sector" is only going to get bigger and more influential. In 2020, several major foundations took out bonds totaling $1 billion as the pandemic spread, signaling a new era of mega- giving by traditional conservative institutions. Around the same time, a number of powerful investors announced a new $500 million impact fund at the 2020 Davos World Economic Forum. The impact investing market is expected to hit $1 trillion in assets under management in the next few years, and it could very well overtake philanthropic spending soon.

For better or worse, the social sector has increasingly become a place to look for moral leadership on addressing the world's biggest problems. Five years ago, neither of us would have written this book. We're both policy wonks who moved to Washington, DC, with high-minded ideas about public service, inspired by the civic experiments of the Obama administration. After Donald Trump became president, we were suddenly staring down a very different future, one when meaningful progress often felt hopeless. Even after he has left office, undoing the damage done can feel like an overwhelming task.

That's why it's so important to confront the social sector's top-down nature. While there's no doubt that a lot of good has come out of the era of billionaire philanthropy and impact investing, it's also clear that the direction of the social sector is taking some concerning turns, and that good intentions cannot make up for disproportionate power. As wealth continues to concentrate at the top, fewer and fewer people will decide the direction of our collective future.

That's also why it's so important to approach criticism of the social sector in a balanced way. It's not productive to simply villainize well-meaning elites or write funders off as beyond reform. These funders play a big and growing role in our everyday lives, and they are not necessarily ill-intentioned; they are working in an imperfect system, using tools and structures they borrowed from their predecessors.

Rather, it's important to remember that philanthropy has changed dramatically in the past two decades, and that it will change again; the only questions are how, and in what direction. The two of us tend to approach criticism of philanthropy and impact investing the same way we approach criticism of the tech companies that many of these philanthropists came from. You can appreciate Facebook for connecting you with friends while simultaneously holding it accountable for privacy concerns. You can appreciate Amazon's convenience—especially while ordering home supplies under quarantine—while challenging the idea that any single company should have such dominant power over e-commerce.

And you can encourage these powerful people and institutions to get better. That's what we'll be doing for the rest of this book.

2

THE ROOM WHERE IT HAPPENS

In his book *From Generosity to Justice*, Ford Foundation president Darren Walker told a story about a time he made a mistake.

The Ford Foundation, with its $12 billion endowment, is among the wealthiest and most influential foundations in the world, and also considered among the most progressive. Most years, they give out more than $500 million in grants. Founded nearly a century ago by Henry and Edsel Ford, it built a reputation as a progressive and thoughtful foundation. Ford grants supported artists during the Red Scare, launched some of the first legal aid clinics at law schools, underwrote civil rights litigation, publicly supported early efforts to fight HIV/AIDS, and provided one of the first investments in what would become the field of microfinance.

When Walker was named Ford's tenth president in 2013, his election made waves in the foundation world. As a gay Black man who grew up on food stamps, he was a fresh face on the roster of mostly white foundation executives. He used his new platform as a mandate to galvanize not just Ford, but philanthropy as a whole, in service of a more hands-on, justice-oriented approach. Early in his tenure, he was named by Elton John as one of *TIME*'s 100 most influential people, cited for "changing the language of philanthropy from 'them' and 'they' to 'us' and 'we.'"

In his first two years as president, Walker led an internal effort to sharpen the foundation's focus. Ford had become known as a "peanut butter" funder, meaning their strategy was to spread a little bit of money over a lot of different types of projects. Soon after taking office, Walker kicked off a strategic planning process with the foundation's staff to build a vision for a narrower, more tightly focused and responsive vision. In 2015, he held a press conference to announce the results of the shakeup: Ford would reorient all its programming around the problem of "inequality in all of its forms."

The timing was certainly appropriate. With the world still reeling from the global financial crisis, it was becoming abundantly obvious that the post-crisis economy would be shaped by profound global inequality. The rich, buttressed by golden parachutes and in control of the response to the crisis, would come out of it more or less all right. Banks would be bailed out. Lehman Brothers traders would find new jobs. Recent Ivy League grads would take a "gap year" while the job market sorted itself out. But the rest of the world would feel the brunt of it.

Walker believed that philanthropy needed to respond accordingly. "Philanthropy can no longer grapple simply with *what* is happening in the world, but also with *how* and *why*," he wrote in a *New York Times* op-ed. Ford's new model would focus on solving the *root causes* of inequality rather than just addressing the symptoms. "Feeding the hungry is among our society's most fundamental obligations, but we should also question why our neighbors are without nutritious food to eat," he wrote. "Housing the homeless is an imperative, but we should also question why our housing markets are so distorted." Ford would redirect its funding toward advocacy, social justice and human rights: for instance, litigation on behalf of immigrants, and advocacy campaigns to protect voting rights. He called this approach a "new gospel of wealth."

In the week after making the announcement, Walker received dozens of voicemails, emails, and questions at public forums about the strategy. One of them was from Diana Samarasan, a woman who ran a small, public foundation in Boston called the Disability Rights Fund. On a

Facebook Live chat hosted by Walker and watched by hundreds of people, Samarasan told Walker that he had made a major omission: Not once, in laying out their vision of a world without inequality, did the Ford Foundation mention disabled people.

Nothing About Us Without Us

This was a big omission, to put it lightly. About fifteen percent of the world's population has some kind of disability—including more than three hundred million who experience "serious difficulties in functioning." And they suffer deep systemic inequality, no matter where they live.

More than seventy percent of people with disabilities around the world are unemployed, and their poverty rate is more than double that of the general population. They are often structurally excluded from civic engagement and political power by inaccessibility and outdated attitudes. In the 2012 US presidential election, a third of voters with disabilities experienced problems at the voting booth. It's far worse in the Global South, where few countries have national legislation on par with the Americans with Disabilities Act. (For instance, in Indonesia, which we'll talk about later, only three percent of disabled people voted in a recent presidential election.)

Samarasan was familiar with these challenges as the founder of the Disability Rights Fund. As the name implies, the fund gives grants to grassroots activists and nonprofits engaging in political advocacy for the rights of the disabled. When she reached out to Walker, the fund had recently finished deciding on its previous round of grant recipients, which included a Haitian nonprofit lobbying for the rights of children with disabilities and a Micronesian activist group pushing the government to adopt a disability-inclusive disaster plan. When she read Ford's announcement she worried that once again, the biggest foundations were giving short shrift to the most urgent work in the disability community.

Philanthropy has consistently underfunded the disabled community. One study from 2008 found that less than three percent of total global grant dollars went to disability organizations. A more recent study found that aid projects targeting disability inclusion represent less than one percent of international aid, equivalent to less than one dollar per person with disabilities.

But the sheer numbers are only part of the problem. The larger issue is that historically, philanthropic projects for disabled people have tended to take a paternalistic approach. To wit: The majority of grants for disabled people are for care and medical research or, as one disability rights activist put it, "either fixing or caring for us...it often seeks to change people with disabilities rather than addressing and helping to eliminate the systemic forces that marginalize those with disabilities."

This paternalism has encouraged the disability rights movement to adopt an unofficial slogan: "nothing about us without us." The slogan is a rallying cry for participation, popularized by disability rights activists fighting apartheid in South Africa. It also has an interesting history. The original Latin version of the phrase, *Nihil de nobis, sine nobis*, was coined in sixteenth century Poland. Back then, it was a rallying cry for anti-monarchists who were trying to overthrow their king and create a more democratic system. Two hundred and fifty years later, anti-monarchists in the British colonies took inspiration from the Polish struggle, coining their own translation of the Latin antecedent: 'No taxation without representation.'"

How could the Ford Foundation have left this entire community out of their strategy to fight inequality? Four years after the incident, Darren Walker would devote a section early in his autobiography to this question, writing that the omission of disabled people was a low point in his career. The emails, voicemails and text messages from Samarasan and other disability rights advocates wracked him for days. He kept asking himself, "How could I have overlooked this critical dimension of inequality? How could our entire organization have overlooked it?"

He reflected that in retrospect, the answer was obvious: When Ford was building out its new vision and strategy, no one in the room represented the voices of people with disabilities. As he wrote in a mea culpa blog post:

> "Those who courageously—and correctly—raised this complicated set of issues pointed out that the Ford Foundation does not have a person with visible disabilities on our leadership team; takes no affirmative effort to hire people with disabilities; does not consider them in our strategy; and does not even provide those with physical disabilities with adequate access to our website, events, social media, or building. Our 50-year-old headquarters is currently not compliant with the Americans with Disabilities Act—landmark legislation that celebrated its 26th anniversary this summer. It should go without saying: All of this is at odds with our mission."

Walker's response—listening and taking action—was laudable. But his initial mistake speaks to two fundamental problems with decision-making in philanthropy today. Both problems fall under the category of "representation." The first problem is the consistent lack of diversity in the rooms where funding decisions are made. The second important problem is equally important but tends to get less attention than staff or board diversity: a lack of engagement with, or accountability to, the larger world *outside* that room.

From Diversity to Accountability

In philanthropy, there's a tendency when talking about representation to start and end the conversation with staff and board diversity. In politics, business or any other field, the demographic makeup of the room—the all-white board, or the all-male panel—is a justifiable flashpoint for activists. But the issue of diversity (*who* is in the room) only addresses one part of the equation. The other part is accountability, or *how* the people in that room consult with those outside it.

If diversity is about demographics, then accountability is about process. What checks and balances are there on any given decision? Who defines what success looks like? For the purposes of this book, the most important question is: Whose opinion is consulted beyond the room where the decision is made?

Accountability is always an important part of the conversation. On the level of city politics, diversity is about whether the city council members look and sound like their constituents; accountability is about whether they hold open town meetings or make important decisions behind closed doors. In business, diversity is about scrutinizing the demographic makeup of the board or C-Suite management, while accountability is about challenging a corporation to commit to involving external stakeholders in governance.

Diversity has certainly been a hot topic in philanthropy in recent years, and for a good reason. Every one of the top fifteen donors in the United States is a white man, reflecting the homogeneity at the top of the economic pyramid. But that's just the tip of the iceberg. The diversity stats get more concerning as you get further away from the source of money.

Foundation board members (sometimes called trustees) have wide latitude in decision-making and can often veto grant decisions—or put in a good word for a friend. A 2017 survey of the top foundations in the United States found that seventy-two percent of board members are white and sixty-three percent are male; half graduated from an Ivy League university. Only one survey respondent out of 200 lived in a state with a poverty rate among the five highest in the country, and he was a celebrity: Bryan Stevenson, the famous Alabama civil rights lawyer who was portrayed in the film *Just Mercy* by Michael B. Jordan.

Take one step further away from the source of the money, and you arrive at foundation staff: the grant managers and young associates who do the day-to-day work of reviewing proposals and interacting with grantees. In theory, there's no reason why this group should suffer from the same diversity deficit as board members. But they are also homogenous, particularly when it comes to class. Many entry-level roles at foundations require elite college degrees, which in turn often necessitate access to SAT tutors; not to mention a working knowledge of how to dress, what names to drop and other cultural signifiers.

This has all led to a conversation within philanthropy about the "like funds like" phenomenon. To put it simply, grantmakers tend to give to who they know and what they know. They tend to favor projects, bids and proposals that reflect their identities—their demographics, outlooks and worldviews. From a social science perspective, this is not particularly surprising. We're all shaped by our limited view of the world; our empathy is constrained by the contours of our lived experience. But for a major industry that hands out hundreds of millions of dollars a year, it's problematic.

This phenomenon is supported by a growing body of research. Black people represent eight percent of foundation CEOs in the United States...and eight percent of grant funding ends up going to nonprofits with a Black leader. Transgender people represent two percent of board members and staff at American foundations...and transgender advocacy receives less than a penny of every dollar granted. There are similar mirror-image numbers for the Native American community (fewer than forty Native people in the United States serve in key leadership roles at private foundations), the Latinx community and more.

This "like funds like" problem applies to the disabled community. Darren Walker's Ford Foundation was hardly alone in under-indexing on disabled decision-makers. Fewer than a quarter of foundations in the United States have a board member with a disability, despite good-faith efforts to improve representation. One grantmaker, responding anonymously to a survey by the disability rights group RespectAbility, said that they had seen their foundation's leadership "pat themselves on the back for hiring a person with a disability—to our buildings and grounds department to work as a day porter." Another described an "unconscious attitude that a [staff member] with a disability is a goodwill project, not a peer or a colleague."

The debate about representation at the Ford Foundation could have ended with a simple commitment to hire more people with disabilities at their New York headquarters. But by the time Walker heard the feedback, there was a growing acknowledgment inside philanthropy that simply improving diversity among staff was both necessary and not sufficient.

The fact is that diversity alone is an imperfect metric for progress. There are entire books written about how diversity metrics can obscure more than they reveal. For example, women represent three quarters of foundation staff after years of advocacy for gender equity, but still only represent forty percent of decision-makers. There's also the danger of tokenizing diverse hires, regardless of their role, by asking one person to shoulder the burden of an entire race, gender or sexual orientation.

But even when diversity commitments are truly successful, they only result in bringing in new perspectives *inside* an institution. They don't actively address how to engage people *outside*—those who are not professional grant managers. It's a crisis of participation.

The Ladder of Participation

The concept of participation is a little bit like the concept of democracy: vague, abstract, and easy to co-opt.

Most philanthropists, if asked, would probably say that they make an intentional effort to engage people with lived experience. They could probably point to specific examples—a site visit, community panel or feedback survey. As one grantmaker told us, "No one in philanthropy has anything bad to say about participation."

But what does authentic participation actually *look* like? And how can we measure it? Edgar Villanueva is one of many critics pointing out that grantmakers tend to talk a bigger participation game than they practice. Authentic knowledge, he writes, can't come from "a site visit to the community or interviewing someone from the affected community. It comes from living inside that community and experiencing that issue for oneself. Period."

Fortunately, there's a framework for measuring participation that comes in handy: the Ladder of Citizen Participation. The framework comes from the world of public policy. In 1967, US President Lyndon B. Johnson tasked a policy analyst named Sherry Arnstein with developing a strategy to integrate citizen feedback into a new program for revitalizing slums and blighted neighborhoods. Local officials were given primary control over how funds were spent, but not all were committed to engaging residents. To the extent that town hall meetings or surveys were used at all, they were viewed as a necessary evil rather than as an opportunity to gather meaningful information. As Arnstein met with local officials, she saw repeatedly how decision-makers dismissed residentconcerns, even ones they'd solicited, as ill-informed or just plain wrong.

This experience led Arnstein to publish an eight-page treatise in the academic *Journal of the American Planning Association* laying out her ladder of participation. The ladder was a visual framework to illustrate how decision-makers can engage community members in any civic process.

The lowest rung is *nonparticipation*. This refers to any time where power holders make decisions with minimal input: a one-way information flow with no feedback channels. An example of this might be a government office that holds a monthly press conference to share what they've been working on but takes no questions.

The next rung up is *tokenism*. The most common example of tokenism is the dreaded feedback survey. People may have the opportunity to fill it out and share their opinion, but there's no way of knowing whether it's going to be seriously considered or put straight into the recycling bin.

But Arnstein was more than just a critic; she wanted to offer a positive vision for how to authentically engage people whose lives will be affected by decisions you make. The highest rung on her Ladder of Participation is *citizen power*. This refers to processes that authentically engage the community, whether it's inviting citizens onto a budget committee or handing the entire job of planning and managing a revitalization project over to a neighborhood group.

Arnstein's ladder is a useful framework for quantifying the level of authentic engagement between a decision-making body and the general public. As one contemporary example, consider civilian review boards, a mechanism that's become increasingly popular for holding city police departments to account. In theory, a review board is a powerful way to hold officers and political appointees accountable for abuse and brutality. But in practice, some boards have more power—more "teeth"—than others. There are nearly 150 oversight boards in the United States; the ones that have some sort of formal enforcement power get high marks from criminal justice reform advocates, while others are clearly designed to be little more than democratic window dressing.

With this framework at our disposal, we can speak more directly about decision-making at most foundations. But first let's take a step back to talk about the funding *process*. This gets to the *how* of philanthropy—how money moves from the grantmaker to the nonprofit.

The Funding Process

We like to talk about funding in the context of *design* because it's a good reminder that grantmaking is essentially problem-solving. The whole process is a flowchart, a series of decision points that, hopefully, yield the best results. And despite a huge amount of variety from grantmakers to grantmaker, most funders design their processes around three key decision points.

The first decision point involves developing a hypothesis, or a *theory of change*. A theory of change is a mini-manifesto that lays out what the grantmaker thinks is wrong with the world and how they want to go about solving it. It might sit on a foundation's website or in its marketing materials. It can get revisited every year or stay the same for a century. Either way, a theory of change defines the foundation's values, priorities and vision for the future. Ford's new strategic vision was a new theory of change: it reflected Darren Walker's belief that moving from a "peanut butter" approach to targeted funding around inequality could be more effective in the post-recession context.

With the theory of change in hand, the next step in the funding process is to build a *pipeline* of ideas. The grantmaker will usually post a call for applications to solve a problem aligned with its theory of change. It's a lot like a job application, with specifics about location and past experience, and a request for a well-written cover letter. Some grantmakers receive hundreds of applications in their pipeline.

Finally, there is the all-important stage of *vetting* options and deciding who to fund. This vetting process can be as simple or complex as the grantmaker wants it to be. Many foundations have long lists of criteria and multi-stage approval processes; on the other hand, an individual donor might decide who to fund based on nothing more than their gut. We'll spend the most time on this step in this book: it's the final yes or no, the stage when a board of directors will get involved, not to mention the lawyers.

Every one of these decision points offers an opportunity for grantmakers to engage people outside of their organization. But most of the time, that doesn't happen. Grantmaking processes across the industry tend to sit low on Arnstein's ladder. We spoke about this with a former grantmaking consultant who wished to remain anonymous. We'll call him Joshua.

Joshua has a profile that makes him typical for a young aspiring do-gooder. He graduated with honors from an Ivy League college, and then joined a major consulting firm that followed the model of market-based philanthropy popularized by Harvard Business School professor Michael Porter in the 1990s. The firm works with dozens of foundations and donors, including Ford, to improve their strategies and outcomes.

Joshua told us about a particular project a few years back that made him rethink his interest in philanthropy. His team, based in a major coastal city, was hired by a large Texas foundation working on criminal justice reform. The foundation wanted to improve the life outcomes of young people who had experience in the juvenile justice system. They wanted to engage the community; to "do something different than the top-down model of philanthropy," according to Joshua. So they hired his team to run a series of convenings with local stakeholders to "get input from the grassroots."

The experience was demoralizing. "There was almost no effort made to incorporate the opinion of young people or people who actually had experience in the juvenile justice system," he told us. "When we organized our convening, the people in the room were government leaders, corporate social responsibility directors from big local businesses, and a few nonprofit CEOs. It was all grasstops." The one exception was a single focus group with a dozen local kids who had interacted with the juvenile justice system. But "it ran about ninety minutes, in a project that cost several hundred thousand dollars."

Joshua was disheartened that the stakeholder meetings turned out to be democratic window dressing, giving community members the "illusion of choice"—something the Texas funder bluntly acknowledged. At the final convening, there was a big decision to make about which local stakeholder would lead the group after Joshua's consulting team left town. "I remember meeting with the funder before we gathered the group to make that decision," Joshua said. "My boss told us, 'We want them to think they have a choice, when really we already know which choice we're going to make.'"

Joshua left the consulting firm shortly after this project. He told us that "the model we used was an improvement on the top-down model—but it wasn't one in which power was equally shared, by any means." In other words, it was what Sherry Arnstein might call *tokenism*. "There were a lot of ways that behind the scenes we were still allowing the foundation to set the agenda and set the table, even though on paper it wasn't advertised as such."

This story gets to the heart of Sherry Arnstein's ladder—and speaks to a problem Arnstein foresaw forty years earlier. Arnstein wrote that one of the most persistent dangers for any citizen was that a process that sits near the bottom of the ladder could be disguised as one that sits at the top. "There is a critical difference between going through the empty ritual of participation and having the real power needed to affect the outcome of the process," Arnstein wrote in 1969. Participation without redistribution of power "allows the power holders to claim that all sides were considered, but makes it possible for only some of those sides to benefit." For the powerless, it is an "empty and frustrating process."

Participation and Impact Investing

In the ten short years since impact investing became mainstream, it's become clear that the field has many of the same decision-making flaws as philanthropy.

For one thing, impact investing has a diversity problem. There is no comprehensive source of demographic data about *impact* fund managers. (We've heard more than one investor mention under their breath that it's because no one wants to know just how bad the numbers are.) But assuming that the numbers are analogous to the broader investing industry, the picture is pretty dismal. There has only ever been one woman or person of color as CEO of a major Wall Street investment bank, and she assumed her position in December 2020. Women manage less than ten percent of global assets; Black people manage less than three percent. This lack of diversity perpetuates the "like funds like" problem; multiple studies show that investors are less likely to invest in people who don't look like them.

But as with philanthropy, the second and deeper problem with the field has to do with accountability—*how* decisions are made.

Impact investors use a funding process that is broadly similar to that of philanthropy. It can also be broken down into three decision points when an investor or investment committee reaches a conclusion that has financial consequences. First, investors *develop a theory of change* for their fund, signaling to the rest of the world the types of investments they want to make. Next, they build a *pipeline* of possible deals. Finally, they *vet* those deals, analyzing their ability to deliver financial and social returns.

And as with philanthropy, each of these decisions tends to be made in an opaque and insular way.

When impact investors talk about their *theory of change*, they use a term borrowed from finance: "investment thesis." Jeff Bezos's impact fund has a thesis that consumers will choose clean energy options as long as they are competitively priced, and so the fund invests in cleantech start-ups. Many funds have an investment thesis that is based around a specific place (what journalist Amy Cortese calls "locavesting"). That might mean investing in small businesses owned by people of color, or it might mean building affordable housing in a low-income neighborhood based on the theory that these investments will lead to economic growth.

While there are some examples of impact funds engaging outside stakeholders as they develop their investment thesis, it's not yet a widely adopted practice. This can create perverse incentives; an investment thesis is often tied to a desired rate of return or social outcome, and setting an imperfect north star can cause a fund to veer off course.

Next up is building a *pipeline* (or "deal flow")—looking for potential investment opportunities. Some leads are inbound, but the best investors build deal flow by finding hidden gems that others haven't caught onto yet.

This setup is ripe for implicit bias; investors inevitably tap into their network to find deals, which can be incredibly limiting. One study of social networks found that the average white person's social network is ninety-three percent white. Another common tactic is to attend pitch competitions where social entrepreneurs present their ideas in under five minutes, which is also less than ideal. Wharton professor Laura Huang found that in this setting, there's a statistical advantage to being tall, attractive and male.

Finally, there's the all-important step of *vetting* deals to decide where to invest their money. This includes the process of due diligence, or reviewing past financial statements and generally doing some sleuthing to make sure the deals are all they're cracked up to be. The average venture capital firm reviews more than a thousand companies in order to make ten investments.

There's a level of celebrity and respect bestowed on investors who know how to pick 'em; it's often attributed to an almost mystical gut instinct. (Warren Buffett is known as the "Oracle of Omaha.") Very few impact funds open up the due diligence process in any way; it all comes down to the judgment of a small group of people making decisions behind closed doors.

What Does Structural Reform Look Like?

We've just laid out a number of endemic problems with the design of philanthropy and impact investing. We know that many readers of this book are likely deeply skeptical, if not cynical, about the idea that powerful people might be open to meaningful structural reform. As activist Audre Lorde famously said, "The master's tools cannot dismantle the master's house."

But as we'll explore in the next chapter, there are reasons to check that cynicism. We're optimistic about the potential for philanthropy to reform and for impact investing to mature into a more equitable field. That's because a growing number of foundations and impact investors are exploring *participatory funding* models that shift decision-making power to people with lived experience of the problem at hand.

For a simple illustration of participatory funding, let's look at the ending to the Ford Foundation story that started this chapter.

After Darren Walker heard from activists about Ford's erasure of disability rights, he made a public apology in which he acknowledged the foundation's history of "ableism." Then, he set about addressing it. The following summer, Walker's chief of staff, Noorain Khan, convened a "learning group" for program staff at Ford. The group hosted a series of meetings over the following months, featuring disability rights activists from organizations like RespectAbility USA and the National Association of the Deaf who were invited to speak about any aspect of their work.

One of those speakers was Catherine Hyde Townsend, a recognized thought leader on disability inclusion and rights and board co-chair at the Disability Rights Fund. She spoke to the group about disability and intersectionality and noted that Ford could not succeed in revolutionary social change without seeing how disability discrimination is intertwined and multiplied for so many of the world's most marginalized.

"It felt like such a pivotal moment for all of us," recalls Townsend. "There were a ton of diverse people with disabilities in the building. People at Ford had never seen that before. We'd been trying to knock on the door at Ford for years, but until then, we didn't have access to the most powerful people."

Townsend is now Darren Walker's Senior Advisor for Disability Inclusion, and under her tenure, Ford made some major steps forward on inclusion of disabled people. Following a yearlong audit of their existing engagement with the disabled community, Ford developed a training to help their staff integrate disability inclusion into their work. In 2018, they hosted the Disability Rights Fund's tenth anniversary celebration, welcoming hundreds of diverse disabled activists into its space. They held it at their temporary offices, since their permanent headquarters was being refitted with wheelchair ramps, a "sensory garden" designed for people with sight impairments, and other renovations to improve accessibility.

But the most substantial piece of course correction was the creation of a new, experimental grantmaking vehicle that would bring disabled activists directly into the room where decisions are made. In 2019, Walker teamed up with fifteen other foundation presidents to launch the Disability Inclusion Fund, a $10 million participatory grantmaking fund that supports the disability rights movement in the United States.

The structure of the fund is notable. Decisions about funding are made by a committee that is split evenly between disabled people and foundation staff to "ensure that a range of experiences, perspectives, identities, and geographies go into all grantmaking decisions."

A few weeks after the COVID-19 pandemic hit the United States, the Disability Inclusion Fund launched a $200,000 rapid response vehicle to support the needs of people with disabilities, from transportation to culturally competent healthcare. "COVID-19 lays bare what the disability community has been telling us all along—that our social systems fail to include them," Walker said when the vehicle was announced. "We must seek out and support the disability community's voices, actions and innovative solutions."

The Ford Foundation's story is important because it speaks to the moment we're in: a moment when funders are listening and adapting. Diana Samarasan and other activists challenged a titan of modern philanthropy on how his institution was engaging the outside world, and they got results. It was a victory for the idea of *nothing about us without us*. In the next chapter we'll look at why timing may have played a key role.

3

A MOMENT OF RECKONING

The Skoll World Forum on Social Entrepreneurship, created by eBay founder Jeff Skoll, is one of the premiere conferences for philanthropists and impact investors. Every year, more than a thousand people travel from all over the world to the gothic university town of Oxford, England, paying upward of $1,300 for a ticket to hobnob with fellow funders: foundation presidents, tech billionaires and strategy consultants like Joshua. The theme of the conference changes each year, but the broad purpose remains the same: deciding how to tackle some of the world's thorniest problems.

On a crisp spring day in April 2019, a grantmaker from a small public foundation took the stage of the downtown New Oxford Theatre to deliver the conference's keynote remarks. Edgar Villanueva was in many ways an outlier at Skoll. He grew up poor outside Raleigh and comes from a Native American community, and he was the first in his family to graduate high school. He landed his first foundation job in 2005, working at a North Carolina foundation focused on health equity, and continued under the radar at multiple foundations until 2018, when he took a major career risk by writing a first-person, tell-all book about his deep discomfort with the philanthropic community of which he was a part.

Villanueva is a calm and steady presence on stage; he speaks bluntly. As he always does at gatherings of wealthy philanthropists and impact investors—he spoke at more than a hundred that year alone—he started by interrogating the source of their money. Much of the money that is distributed by grantmakers and investors today can be traced back to a history of exploitation and colonization. That includes the theft of Indigenous land, the kidnapping and enslavement of African people and the systemic undervaluing of "women's work." The present value of labor extracted from enslaved Black people in the United States, for example, is estimated between $5 trillion and $14 trillion dollars.

That history isn't so easy to shake off. Philanthropy is infected with what he calls a "colonizing virus," a regressive mentality that reinforces the colonial division of "us versus them," with white saviors and people of color who need saving. It manifests itself in the lack of diversity among foundation leadership, in the paternalism of strings-attached restricted grants, and in the failure of funders to listen, engage or make themselves accountable to the communities they serve.

Philanthropy, Villanueva told the crowd, had long ignored these questions. "It's an acrid history... a dark history that folks don't want to revisit often." But the industry needed to address these questions now.

Just a decade ago, this kind of speech would have been unthinkable at the Skoll Forum. The conference is normally a place of heady optimism; *Forbes* described it as a celebration of "people on a mission to make a positive change in areas that governments and for-profit businesses have overlooked." But times had changed. Shortly after his provocative keynote speech, Villanueva stepped back out on stage for a panel titled, "Is Philanthropy Part of the Solution or the Problem?" The moderator began by asking the roughly two hundred fifty people in the audience if they agreed with the statement that "philanthropy is at a moment of reckoning." Nearly everyone raised their hand.

It was a reflection of the moment in history when Villanueva spoke. Around the time that philanthropy leaders descended on Oxford's pubs and bookstores for the Skoll Forum, students at the university were petitioning for the removal of a statue of Cecil Rhodes—the namesake of Oxford's elite Rhodes Scholarship—

because of his well-documented embrace of racism and imperialism. They were initially met with resistance, as the school's leaders cited Rhodes's history of charity and benevolence. But a few months later, in the midst of global Black Lives Matter protests, the leaders relented and agreed to place the statue in a museum, where it could be presented in context.

Femi Nylander, one of the student activists, told a reporter that the governors' change in heart was because of the change in public consciousness, "We are seeing a paradigm shift," he said. "You can see that everywhere."

Philanthropy's "Brief, Balmy Season"

For a short window of time at the end of the twentieth century, philanthropy was insulated from the kind of scrutiny, criticism and suspicion that it had received since Congress's grilling of John D. Rockefeller in 1910.

Many people who started their grantmaking careers in the late 1990s, and who now work at the industry's highest levels, came of age during what philanthropy historian Benjamin Soskis calls a "brief, balmy season at the closing decades of the century and at the opening of the new one." In the prosperous '90s up through the Great Recession, there was a short period where the general public had a "largely celebratory" attitude toward the rich and the generous. This was the era of the celebrity philanthropist, of Bono at the Oscars and hagiographic biographies of people like Bill Gates. The rich were giving away more money than ever before, and there was an air of excitement about the whole endeavor. Soskis wrote that for the first time since Rockefeller, "philanthropy began to enjoy the benefit of the doubt."

Those years were a good time to work in the industry. Graduates from Harvard Business School and top public policy schools flocked to places like the Gates and Omidyar foundations that were "disrupting" legacy foundations. The Obama White House launched an Office of Social Innovation and Civic Participation to liaise with foundations and impact investors, imbuing the Obama brand on the industry. Gara LaMarche, president of the powerful donor collective Democracy Alliance, has written that just before the economic collapse, philanthropy was "the place to be if you wanted to actually bring about social change."

That all changed with the financial crisis in 2008, when the world's mood turned decidedly anti-elite. This might sound like a cliche, but it's actually measurable. In the first two decades of the twenty-first century, poll after poll showed a precipitous decline in public trust in the world's largest democracies. The Edelman Trust Barometer, an annual study that spans twenty-eight countries, has shown steadily declining levels of trust in government, nongovernmental organizations (NGOs) and other elite institutions. More than half of respondents globally agreed that "capitalism as it exists today does more harm than good in the world."

This trust deficit turned the spotlight onto leaders of virtually all major institutions, and grantmakers and investors have been no exception. In the first few years of the economic recovery, a number of books came out that, in the words of LaMarche, "trained a critical eye on donors long accustomed to basking in the glow of their largesse."

Of course, people have trained a critical eye on institutional philanthropy since its formation, from Congress's grilling of John D. Rockefeller to the grassroots perspective of civil rights leader Ella Baker. But after the Great Recession, the criticism grew to a crescendo it had never before reached. In 2013, David Callahan founded the industry news site Inside Philanthropy to cover the day-to-day actions of major donors and foundations, in an effort to increase oversight and transparency. Two years later, sociology professor Linsey McGoey published *No Such Thing as a Free Gift*, a critique of the Gates Foundation that put the term "philanthrocapitalism" into popular circulation.

The conversation arguably hit the mainstream thanks to a charismatic *New York Times* journalist named Anand Giridharadas, who had covered education for much of his early career. In 2015, Giridharadas landed a fellowship at the Aspen Institute, a clubby think tank in Washington, DC, that holds a stable of well-connected policy wonks. In a now-famous speech, he stood up in front of his peers and, as *New York Magazine* reported,

> "broke with protocol, accusing his audience of perpetuating the very social problems they thought they were solving through philanthropy. He described what he called the Aspen Consensus: 'The winners of our age must be challenged to do more good, but never, ever tell them to do less harm.' The response, he said, was mixed. One private-equity figure called him an 'asshole' that evening, but another investor said he'd voiced the struggle of her life."

The speech landed him a book deal, and in 2018, he published *Winners Take All: The Elite Charade of Changing the World*, which became one of the year's most discussed books and a *New York Times* bestseller. The book went after the "global corporate class" who "grow wealthy through the exaltation of markets and then turn their attention to ameliorating some of the consequences." Giridharadas questioned why we should trust these elites to fix a broken system that had served them so well. His public persona was smart, antagonistic and sharp; he went on television and accused philanthropists and impact investors like Bill Gates, Bono and Jeff Bezos of "enabling inequality."

Giridharadas has inspired a passionate and devoted following, including his very own folk song. Jonathan Mann, a YouTuber who has written a song a day for four thousand days, chose to write one of those songs about the author. Over a breezy rock beat, he sings about how Giridharadas inspired him, as well as his suave persona:

"At the Aspen Institute
He made himself clear
In a room full of billionaires
He held up a mirror
...Speaking truth to power
Time to ban those billionaires
And he wears a cool blue suit
And he's got really cool hair"

Giradharadas's book was followed a few months later by another major release: *Just Giving: Why Philanthropy Is Failing Democracy and How It Can Do Better.* This was a more scholarly critique, written by Stanford University professor Rob Reich. In it, he questioned why American foundations receive copious tax breaks (more than $50 billion a year in aggregate) despite their lack of public accountability. In an echo of the congressmen who criticized John D. Rockefeller, Reich called philanthropy a "deeply and fundamentally antidemocratic institution."

Impact Investing in the Spotlight

Several of philanthropy's biggest critics have also written about impact investing. Giridharadas has tweeted that impact investing "gives [the investor class] more influence and the moral glow to continue practicing pillage economics elsewhere." Edgar Villanueva has argued that the colonizing virus affects funding across the "loans-to-gifts spectrum" and points to the lack of diversity at banks and investment firms.

Still, the most powerful critiques of impact investing have come from investors and social entrepreneurs themselves. A recurring theme is that mainstream impact investing does not go far enough to address the problems with traditional finance. "Impact investors have adopted the stance of venture capital," social entrepreneur Astrid Scholz told us. On

Valentine's Day 2016, Scholz and three other female entrepreneurs wrote an article about their experience with venture investors. It started with the line, "Startups, like the male anatomy, are designed for liquidity events." It was a clear-eyed critique of most investors' relentless push for billion-dollar valuations at the expense of any other size or style of growth.

Scholz has a solution in mind. A follow-up manifesto in 2017 announced that "Zebras fix what unicorns break," coining a new term for the startups that neither wanted or needed to be the next Uber or Airbnb. "When VC firms prize time on site over truth, a lucky few may profit, but civil society suffers," it read. "The capital system is failing society in part because it is failing zebra companies: profitable businesses that solve real, meaningful problems and in the process repair existing social systems."

One outspoken investor is Rodney Foxworth, CEO of the non-profit Common Future, who was up on stage with Villanueva during his Skoll panel. Foxworth grew up in a working-class Baltimore neighborhood. As a child, his grandfather told him the story of Black Wall Street, a neighborhood in Tulsa, Oklahoma in the early twentieth century that was home to more than three hundred Black-owned businesses and financial institutions, until it was burned to the ground by white domestic terrorists aided by the National Guard.

Foxworth began his career as a community organizer and journalist in Baltimore. Later, he started his own impact fund to connect social entrepreneurs of color with big-money funders. In 2015, when Freddie Gray was shot and killed by police officers just miles from his office, Foxworth found himself sitting on countless panels with wealthy individuals and investors who were ostensibly shocked by what had happened, yet refused to acknowledge their complicity in the divestment of neighborhoods like the one where Gray lived.

On stage at Skoll, Foxworth argued that even well-intentioned impact investors have blind spots for social entrepreneurs who don't look like them. "Martin Luther King's assassination was fifty years ago," he told the audience. "People sometimes use him as an example of a social entrepreneur. But I don't think Martin Luther King would have gotten capital today." King had gone to historically-Black Morehouse College, not an Ivy League School; he had never run an organization before. He would not have been trusted by funders looking for someone who looked more like Mark Zuckerberg.

In his writing, Foxworth argues that impact investing needs to get past the conventions and paradigms of traditional investing: "If we're truly motivated to deconstruct the enormous wealth inequalities that have ravaged and extracted wealth from rural, indigenous, and majority communities of color, we must rid ourselves of the power dynamics, biases, and culture that got us here in the first place."

All of this criticism had clearly gotten through to the grantmakers and investors at the Skoll Forum by 2019. By responding affirmatively to the question "Is philanthropy at a moment of reckoning?" they were acknowledging that their industry needed to account for itself.

That's what the crowd seemed to be saying, at least. But would a group of insiders raising their hand about a "reckoning" actually translate into structural reform?

For the first few years after the criticism began, it was hard to tell what was just talk and what was real. The message was certainly being heard at the top. Bill Gates wrote a blurb for *Winners Take All* that called the book "thought-provoking," and Darren Walker wrote in his 2019 book that Giridharadas, Villanueva, Reich and others highlighted a "very real danger: the way we work can easily mirror the imperfect systems that created us." But it wasn't until the coronavirus pandemic rocked the world that it became clear that this reckoning might actually lead to actual reform—to real structural change.

Can the World Be Reprogrammed?

When we started researching this book in the summer of 2019, around the time Villanueva spoke at Skoll, we had our doubts about whether moments like the keynote would actually add up to much. There's a long history of elite audiences politely tolerating progressive speakers, only to keep doing whatever it was they were going to do anyway.

Then a pandemic stopped the world in its tracks—and suddenly, all of the frayed threads of injustice hidden behind a more-or-less functioning fabric of society were out in the open. The rollout of the Paycheck Protection Program, which excluded ninety-five percent of Black-owned businesses in the United States, revealed that the financial system was every bit as unjust and broken as its most vocal critics had long declared. Companies that six months earlier had signed onto the Business Roundtable's endorsement of "stakeholder capitalism" were now raking in record profits as their front-line employees served the public without hazard pay or expanded sick leave.

We also saw how long-held assumptions about the rules of the economy could quickly be broken. The United States Congress passed massive economic stimulus bills and paused payroll taxes, issues that progressives had been pushing for years, and the country didn't fall apart. Canada began giving its residents $2,000 per month in what amounted to a wide-scale experiment with universal basic income. Some large employers started offering dependent care and flexible hours for their workers, and they didn't go bankrupt. These were all choices that had apparently always been on the table, waiting for those in power to summon the will to make them.

The same dynamic has played out in philanthropy. In the first several months of the pandemic, major foundations adopted structural changes that reformers had been pushing for decades. Over the summer of 2020, more than seven hundred fifty foundations, including Ford, signed on to a Council on Foundations pledge to convert their "restricted" grants into "general operating support." It was a significant shift that immediately loosened the strings attached to tens of millions of dollars in funding. Six out of ten foundations reported that they decreased reporting requirements to reduce the burden on grantees.

Impact investing also has seen some structural reform. A number of foundations that invest their endowment in mission-aligned portfolios began to delay interest payments and suspend loan payments. The Kresge Foundation suspended interest payments on its program-related investments for six months, which saved loan recipients about $1 million; the John D. and Catherine T. MacArthur Foundation announced a plan to forgive or defer as much as $25 million in its impact investment program.

Dana Kawaoka-Chen, co-director of the donor network Justice Funders, calls this philanthropy's "matrix moment." In a blog post calling for deep structural reforms, she asked, "Can the world—as it currently is—be reprogrammed?" It's the right question for the moment.

When Edgar Villanueva stepped onto the stage at Skoll, this breaking point was still a few months away. But Villanueva, like his peers, was helping to seed ideas that would later grow. Unlike some of the other sharper-tongued critics, he did it in a way that was constructive rather than accusatory.

On stage at Oxford that day, he didn't excoriate his audience; he offered a model for how to be better. He admitted that as a Native American working in a white foundation world, he often found himself caught between competing priorities: philanthropy's "bubble of privilege" on one side, and his Indigenous community on the other. "This is complicated work," he said. "There are a lot of contradictions."

He talked, as he often does, about money as a type of "medicine."

"Money has been used wrong in the past: to dominate, separate, divide," he said as his keynote wound down. "But it can be used to facilitate healing, connection, belonging." He encouraged the audience to start their journey to using money as medicine by honestly confronting power dynamics in their everyday work. "The dynamics of colonization, the dynamics of white supremacy…show up in who gets to be a leader, who is esteemed as an expert, who gets to control, allocate and manage wealth," he said, urging funders to rethink the mechanisms of how they allocated resources and the *design* of their funding process.

Villanueva also pointed out that there's plenty of precedent for these ideas. Indigenous cultures, including his Lumbee Tribe of North Carolina, have long practiced forms of shared gifting. In West Africa, "tontines" have brought small groups of people together to contribute fixed sums to a common pot and take turns collecting the money. Mutual aid societies in the United States can be traced to the free Black people who pooled resources to support people escaping enslavement and create an economic infrastructure for their communities. These practices all share a key principle: centering the people who need resources, rather than the people providing them.

In *Decolonizing Wealth*, Villanueva lays out seven principles to use as a framework for this essential redesign. The broad concepts are aspirational—relate; listen; represent—but the specific details are nothing short of a fundamental rethinking of the structural design of contemporary philanthropy and impact investing. In the book and in many of his talks, he recommends that funders find ways to shift decision-making power in their funding processes to the people and communities most impacted by funding decisions. Shifting power means going a step beyond simply institutionalizing the act of *listening*, which is how most funders approach community engagement. Instead, it requires making a structural change to give outsiders a voice in the process.

At a time when many grantees and social entrepreneurs are feeling disconnected from and disrespected by the institutions that fund them, and when massive inequality is creating a chasm of lived experience between people with money and people with ideas, Villanueva's proposed treatment is an injection of participation.

Participatory funding is the process of shifting decision-making power over grantmaking or investing to the very communities most affected by them. It's a structural fix to the broken power dynamics in traditional funding—a way to change philanthropy and impact investing from closed, opaque and expert-driven to open, transparent and community-driven.

We wrote earlier that any funding process, at its most basic, has three broad decision points: creating a theory of change, building a pipeline and deciding who should get funding. Participatory funding boils down to a series of choices that grantmakers or investors can make at each of those decision points to systematically incorporate community voice. They can invite affected communities to come up with priorities for a given year; they can tap into outside networks to build a more inclusive pipeline; or they can create external decision-making committees to review applications and vote on who gets funded.

The key element behind any participatory funding process is that the funder gives a voice to people who don't usually get a say in the decision, voluntarily letting go of power in the process. Above all, it requires a deep dose of humility, an acknowledgment by the funder that they do not have all the answers.

To tell the story of participatory funding, we'll start with the story of participatory grantmaking, a concept that dates back to time immemorial but more recently has a fifty-year history in modern philanthropy. It all began with a group of young heirs of great fortunes who wanted to do philanthropy differently than their parents—and were labeled "traitors to their class" for their efforts.

PART TWO

4

THE ROOTS OF
PARTICIPATORY FUNDING

On a quiet morning in the spring of 1969, a Yale student named George Pillsbury walked from his dorm room on campus to the local headquarters of the Black Panthers in the gritty heart of New Haven, Connecticut. He dropped a brown paper bag on the front step and snuck out of sight, unseen. The bag contained $200 in cash – about $1,500 in today's money.

George Pillsbury was the heir to a well-known family business, the Pillsbury Company, based out of Minneapolis. They produced refrigerated biscuits and dinner rolls, and had recently rolled out a new ad campaign featuring a "dough boy" who chuckled when poked in the stomach. His family had a history of high-profile philanthropy, including a building at the University of Minnesota named after his great-grandfather.

George was expected to follow in those footsteps. But when he arrived at Yale, he found the transition out of his Minneapolis bubble to be a shock after eighteen years of "private schools and debutante parties." He had his first encounter with inner-city poverty, and became involved in anti-war and women's rights protests. He began supporting local grassroots organizers like the Black Panthers with a few hundred dollars here and there, an amount that could make a big difference to activists trying to print fliers or order meals. But he never let anyone know he was rich. He made his donations anonymously.

George went on to co-found one of the first participatory grant-making funds in modern history: the Haymarket People's Fund. It was a radically new kind of foundation in both function and form. While his parents' generation donated to museums and the Boy Scouts, Haymarket gave to social justice groups. And while his parents' generation made decisions about their giving from the gut, the Haymarket Fund entrusted funding decisions to community leaders and grassroots activists. As Pillsbury told us, "We couldn't move forward with social change philanthropy and have the donors make all the decisions."

There are several eras where we could start the conversation about participatory funding's roots. The question itself is fraught with questions of power and privilege. We could begin in the agoras of ancient Athens, where republicans led the first formal experiments in making democratic decisions about community resources. Or we could talk about the communal giving practices woven through the history of inidigenous cultures in West Africa and the Caribbean. Not to mention the mutual aid societies in freedman communities after the first American civil war, built by people who had escaped enslavement and were trying to build a life.

Each of those histories is worthy of several books of their own, and we don't want to downplay their significance. But this book is about the movement to democratize the *modern* institutions of philanthropy and impact investing. That's why we're starting our history in the 1970s, with the first big disruption of institutional philanthropy since Andrew Carnegie wrote the *Gospel of Wealth*.

For the first fifty years or so after John D. Rockefeller created his eponymous foundation, few philanthropists strayed far from his example. Most wealthy people set up foundations at the end of their life; the bulk of their giving went to mainstream civic institutions, like museums.

Although the grassroots protests for civil rights and peace were the biggest news stories of the day, records show that only a few small private foundations at the time (including the Ford Foundation) supported social justice activists. Few donors got their hands dirty with social change. They succeeded *in spite* of institutional philanthropy, not because of it.

The social revolutions of the 1960s changed the profiles of young people of wealth. A decade earlier, Pillsbury and his Ivy League-educated friends might have sought to join the Kiwanis Club after graduating and enjoy the benefits of postwar American largesse. Instead, they looked up to contemporaries like John Lewis, Abbie Hoffman and Angela Davis, and spent their time planning rallies and launching antiwar magazines. For the first time in American history, there was a generation of young people publicly expressing discomfort with their privilege and wealth.

Pillsbury moved to Boston after graduation, where he met several other young progressive activists of wealth: heirs to fortunes like Sears, DuPont and IBM. They knew that they wanted to do something about the state of the world, but they weren't satisfied with their parents' model of giving. They started to gather at each other's houses and talk about how to do things differently.

In 1974, Pillsbury and his friends pooled together some money to start a new "alternative foundation." They would call it the Haymarket People's Fund, named after a famous labor strike in the 1800s that laid the groundwork for the eight-hour work day. The fund's first innovation was to provide seed funding for grassroots activists agitating for social justice and civil rights. They were often the first money in—venture capital for the grassroots, paying for things like fax machines and postage. "Our parents give to the symphony," Pillsbury said at the time. "We give to the Symphony Tenant's Organizing Project."

Many newspapers at the time focused on this element of Haymarket's work – *who* they funded. (The *New York Times* in 1977: "Reluctantly wealthy, they give to radical groups.") But Pillsbury and his friends took the mission to transform philanthropy one step further. Many of them were uncomfortable with their wealth and didn't want to flaunt it through public donations—which was why George dropped cash anonymously outside the Black Panthers headquarters. In a decision inspired by local Black churches, Haymarket's founders decided that the fund would have a participatory grantmaking model.

Here's how it worked. Like any other foundation, Haymarket accepted applications and gave away grants. The fund invited activists to submit applications to the small Haymarket staff, which worked out of a Cambridge, Massachusetts office littered with old furniture and political posters. The staff screened those applications and ultimately accepted about three-quarters of them. They then sent the list to eight regional "community boards" across New England made up of local activists. Those boards deliberated and made a final decision over which groups would receive funding.

According to a 1977 *New York Times* article, the Haymarket People's Fund's early grantees included radical community newspapers, tenants' unions, and "a group of woodcutters in rural Maine who are trying to unionize." In 1979, the fund helped organize an anti-apartheid benefit concert for racial justice groups in Boston and South Africa, with Bob Marley as the headliner.

Haymarket became a blueprint for other participatory grantmaking funds launched by young people of wealth. By the early 1980s, there were sixteen community funds around the country that invited local boards to make grantmaking decisions; they banded together to form a network called the Funding Exchange. In Los Angeles, Pillsbury's sister Sarah created the Liberty Hill Fund, which, among other things, helped a small anti-nuclear activist group organize a major protest that filled up the Hollywood Bowl. In New York, the Funding Exchange-connected North Star Fund used community panels to bankroll housing advocates on the Lower East Side.

Many of these funds are still around, and we'll talk about the Funding Exchange's lasting influence later in the book. But for our purposes, let's skip to the second wave of participatory funding, at the turn of the twenty-first century, when the internet hit the mass market.

Open-Sourced Altruism

The funds in the Funding Exchange were incredibly influential, but they were limited in scope and geography by the technological limits of their age. There was no Zoom or even email; meetings were limited by the turtle-like speed of landlines, printed fliers and (eventually) fax machines and pagers. Participatory grantmaking remained largely local.

The internet changed all that. It can be easy to forget how much of a revolution the early internet was. For better and often worse, the internet democratized where, how and with whom we share information. Long before the term "Zoom call" entered the popular lexicon, it was becoming easier and easier to communicate and cooperate across borders, languages and cultures. So it's no coincidence that one of the first participatory grantmaking projects on an international scale was run by the early internet's best-known platform for democratized information: Wikipedia.

Jimmy Wales founded Wikipedia in 2001. From the start, Wales saw the online encyclopedia as an experiment in democratic governance, testing the notion that a far-flung group of writers and editors could co-create information that was up to date and accurate. Within a few years, Wikipedia volunteers were adding or editing 50,000 articles a month.

But within a few years, Wales and his team noticed a major flaw in their editing community, one that might sound familiar by this point in the book. Eighty percent of Wikipedia's writers and editors lived in the Global North (which, for reference, is home to just twenty percent of the world's population). Nine out of ten contributors were men. In 2017, Wales acknowledged these disparities and wrote that "for the largest free knowledge platform in the world, this implies a significant set of knowledge gaps."

As part of the solution, the team turned to their philanthropic counterpart, the Wikimedia Foundation. The foundation started handing out grants to advance knowledge equity. Several of the funded projects were live "edit-a-thons": events where members of an underrepresented community could come together to add cultural context to Wikipedia pages.

According to Katy Love, who led the foundation's grantmaking from 2016–2019, the early process for selecting these grantees was "very informal and ad hoc." "Back then, grant decisions were being made by San Franciscans in Wikipedia's headquarters," Love told us. "And we knew that wasn't the right way to achieve the mission, to share the sum of human knowledge."

So the foundation's team decided to address the problem by doubling down on Wikipedia's core values of democracy and transparency. They built an open-source grantmaking platform on Wikipedia itself. On this platform, anyone could start a Wikipedia page that served as a grant proposal, and other members of the community could weigh in with comments, suggestions, and edits. Ultimate funding decisions were made by volunteer committees from the global Wikipedia community that represented a wide range of lived experience.

As more grants went out the door, more people began participating in this open-source process. Within a few years the Wikimedia Foundation became the largest participatory grantmaker in the world, giving out more than seven million dollars a year and engaging as many as 1,500 people annually in the process. The foundation has now given out more than $35 million to grantees in over eighty countries to advance knowledge equity and other causes.

Another early experiment with online participatory philanthropy was led by future Giving Pledgers Jean and Steve Case—two of the leaders of America Online, the defining company of the internet age.

In the late 1990s, Jean Case was Director of Marketing at AOL, which meant she had a bird's-eye view into the power of the early internet, from the organizing ability of MoveOn.org to the grassroots listservs that would become the Occupy Wall Street movement. In 2006, she enlisted civic engagement expert Cynthia Gibson to create a nationwide grantmaking project, dubbed Make It Your Own.

The process was run by the Case Foundation and involved several "citizen-centered" phases. (The term "citizen" was meant to include immigrants who lacked legal status.) First, the foundation brought together people from around the country to collectively write a rough draft of the grant guidelines. Next, it built a pipeline of ideas by inviting anyone with internet access to submit ideas for civic renewal through the Case Foundation website. Finally, the foundation recruited several dozen people around the country to help narrow the list from five thousand applications to just one hundred, before asking a small group of leaders in the civic engagement field to pick twenty finalists.

The project was a success. The *Financial Times* likened it to "open source" software, comparing it favorably with the then-ultramodern Linux operating system. One philanthropic leader used a similar analogy when he contrasted the model with the "closed circuit" of traditional grantmaking. It started to open people's minds to the idea that grantmaking could be done in a radically different way.

Over the next decade, grantmakers around the world continued to create new participatory grantmaking funds on a local, national and global scale. That included several outside the United States; for instance, UHAI ESRAI was created in 2009 to fund advocacy for LGBTQ+ people in Eastern Africa and was led entirely by African activists. We'll explore more of those funds in the next chapter. But first, let's look at a similar evolution happening around the same time in the nascent field of impact investing.

Democratizing Finance

The idea of democratizing investment has a long intellectual history, but it wasn't until after the Great Recession that it started to enter mainstream financial discourse.

If you're going to understand one core principle behind democracy and finance, it might as well be the solidarity economy. It's an economic philosophy born out of the grisly factories of Great Britain in the early nineteenth century. Factory workers, covered in soot and tired of oppressive working conditions, wrote down a series of principles centered around democratic decision-making and cooperation. The core element was something they called non-extraction—the idea that an investor shouldn't make more money out of an investment than he puts in.

The concept kicked around academic circles for more than a century, largely remaining on the margins of mainstream economic thought. But in the 1980s the Solidarity Economy movement experienced something of a revival in Brazil. In the aftermath of a brutal military dictatorship, a new leftist party took power and launched a historic wave of worker-owned cooperatives and successful experiments in direct democracy.

Word spread, and a decade later thirty economists gathered in Peru to discuss what a non-extractive economic system could look like in a modern context.

By the time the Great Recession hit in 2008, the intellectual ground had been laid. In Zuccotti Park, Occupy Wall Street protestors frequently spoke about a 'solidarity economy' as they made the case for a just transition to a new economy. They painted a vision of a post-capitalist world, where leaders would put people and planet front and center, rather than the pursuit of blind growth and profit maximization. In this world, businesses would be managed by workers, banks would be responsible to public stakeholders, and city budgets would be decided by the people.

Of course, this vision never quite materialized. Capitalism, and for that matter capital, have proved to have significant staying power. Instead, something interesting happened. A generation of activists, investors and young philanthropists have borrowed principles from the solidarity economy to build new systems inside capitalism that model solidarity and democratic principles.

Some of these systems operate on the local level: neighborhood loan funds, built by grassroots activists who wanted to develop alternative economies when mainstream capitalism wasn't working for them. Take the Southern Reparations Loan Fund, created in 2015 by activists of color as an answer to the deep racial wealth gap in the United States South, where slavery gave white Americans a two hundred-year head start on building wealth. The fund lends to worker-owned businesses that support Black and immigrant communities, along with poor white people. The board and staff are all local, and most are people of color or immigrants themselves.

Other participatory loan funds created around this time include the Baltimore Roundtable on Economic Democracy and the L.A. Co-op Lab. Several of them came together to form a national network called Seed Commons, which we'll talk more about later in this book.

Other systems operate in the context of big finance and venture capital. In just the past decade, VC has transformed from a stodgy industry to a driver of the global economy and culture. Facebook, Google and Uber all used VC funding to fuel their meteoric rises—and there are hundreds more companies that have followed the hyper-growth strategy that tens of millions of dollars in capital can buy. There are now more than 350 "unicorn" companies around the world, or private startups worth more than one billion dollars, and many of these companies have monopolized industries and crowded out public services. More and more, decisions made in VC boardrooms define the way we live.

But it's become apparent to anyone paying attention that the VC industry has what investor Ross Baird calls "blind spots." The vast majority of investment funds are just as white and male as foundations, and just like foundations they tend to fund what and who they know. Around the world, female entrepreneurs receive less than 15 percent of venture capital funding. More than half of all venture funding globally goes to startups headquartered in San Francisco, Boston or New York.

In September 2009, three impact investors decided to try and create a better system. Bob Pattillo, Ross Baird and Victoria Fram were early impact investors. They were frustrated with the homogeneity of VC culture, and the end result: instead of the world-saving innovations that Silicon Valley promised, money was being wasted on food delivery apps and valet services for the rich.

They created an organization called Village Capital that would apply a solidarity economy lens to VC investing: What would it look like to flip the power dynamics of VC investing and entrust due diligence and investment decisions to groups of social entrepreneurs?

They ran their first test in New Orleans in September 2009. At the time, the city was deep in recovery mode from Hurricane Katrina. Families who evacuated were returning to their homes to find that there was nowhere to shop or grab a cup of coffee, let alone work. Village Capital gathered twelve entrepreneurs starting businesses in the city, based on ideas ranging from a New Orleans-inspired clothing line to a renewable energy consulting firm. The entrepreneurs collectively chose an education technology company, Kickboard, to receive investment.

Over the next decade, Village Capital ran this "peer-selected investment" more than sixty times around the world and built a portfolio of more than one hundred seed-stage startups. In 2019, Emory University ran an independent audit of the process and found that female entrepreneurs dramatically overperformed: forty-six percent of Village Capital's portfolio companies have a female founder or co-founder, compared with fifteen percent industry-wide.

They also found that the collaborative vetting process was slightly *better* at picking successful startups than traditional investors. These are data points that have helped Village Capital's leaders and other reformers make the case for participatory funding.

The Case for Participatory Funding

In funding, as in any industry, there are good ideas that never make it into the boardroom and bad ones that still get adopted.

Case in point: When the *New York Times* wrote about the Make It Your Own project in 2007, the article included references to other experiments in "open source philanthropy." One of the stories was about the MacArthur Foundation's investment in hosting events on the online virtual world Second Life, which was briefly believed to be the future of gaming.

Participatory funding is a good idea that still hasn't penetrated most boardrooms in mainstream philanthropy or impact investing. It has its zealous supporters, but there are also a fair share of skeptics. This shouldn't be a surprise. Participatory funding challenges long-held, implicit assumptions that professionals and insiders are most qualified to call the shots, and it lies directly in the face of the prevailing logic of market-based thinking that still has a strong grasp on the social sector.

That means that advocates of participatory funding need to make a strong case; they need to build an intellectual framework, then advocate forcefully for that framework in front of people in positions of power. For the rest of this chapter we'll explore the two big arguments that advocates use in those conversations. We'll call them the inside argument and the outside argument.

The inside argument focuses on efficacy and outcomes. It makes the case that shifting decision-making power will result in better decisions and that there is a quantitative value to tapping into perspectives beyond the ivory tower. This is the line of thinking favored by adherents of strategic philanthropy and those focused on double or triple bottom lines. It's used by consultants and academics who are trying to persuade old-guard foundations and investors to adopt participatory methods.

The outside argument focuses on the moral dimension of participatory decision-making. This line of thinking ties participatory funding to broader movements for justice and equity. It places philanthropy in the broader context of a society that values efficiency over equity, of failing democratic institutions and ongoing oppression and colonization. Although it's not always the first point that advocates of participatory funding will make, we've found that it's what motivates them to keep going despite the odds.

Advocates for participatory funding know that they need to be armed with both arguments, inside and outside, if they want to make their best case. Let's examine both arguments more deeply.

The Inside Argument: Tapping into the Value of Lived Experience

The first argument goes like this: Bringing in more perspectives, beyond those of "experts" and professionals will lead to more effective and responsive decisions. This argument is built on the premise that there are multiple types of expertise.

The social sector thinks about "expertise" in a limited way. Funders tend to place a high value on what we'll call white-collar expertise, the kind that comes with a diploma and fancy title. Anyone who lives in think tank-heavy Washington, DC knows that it's not uncommon to attend a panel about healthcare in sub-Saharan Africa or economic revival in Detroit and see a lineup of mostly white, mostly male researchers who have spent years studying the issue from afar. They can cite statistics and explain the macro view of the problem, but rarely speak from a place of lived experience.

The two of us fall into this category of white-collar experts. We both studied history and political science at liberal arts universities; we both have worked at think tanks and nonprofits working on problems that we have never lived through but that we genuinely want to see solved. As we advanced in our careers, we both started to feel uncomfortable with the level of authority that our pedigrees gave us. We regularly found that our voices were louder and more likely to be listened to than those of activists of color or community members with first-person stories.

And it's those missing voices—the ones that speak from experience in the world, not the classroom or office—that can add the most valuable perspective. There is significant quantitative evidence that bringing in the perspective of people with lived experience leads to better and more informed decisions. People often point to participatory budgeting—which involves giving residents of cities, districts and other municipalities the chance to vote directly on how public budgets will be spent—as an example.

Participatory budgeting, which dates back to ancient Greece, was revived in Brazil in the late 1980s as part of the same populist movement that created the solidarity economy. The city of Porto Alegre, a coastal capital on the country's southern tip, was part of Brazil's miraculous eco-nomic expansion in the second half of the twentieth century. After gaining attention on the international stage when it hosted the World University Games in 1963, Porto Alegre became a hotspot for wealthy European immigrants who bought prime property and priced out long-time residents (not dissimilar to Russian and Chinese oligarchs buying mega-million-dollar apartments in Manhattan). By the late 1980s, after Brazil's economic collapse, the city had developed a wealthy urban core surrounded by poor settlements called *vilas*.

In 1990, the *vilas* residents organized to elect a far-left Workers' Party to run the city's government. A succession of mayors developed a participatory budgeting process that, according to one article, "inverted the decision-making process so that citizens decided how a portion of a city's budget was spent. The process gave a voice to the poor whose interests were usually ignored. They now had a say in which projects should be funded and built."

Porto Alegre was a social scientist's dream: a decade-long controlled experiment in participatory decision-making. Participation in budgeting meetings started slowly, with about a thousand people attending in the first year, but it exploded to forty thousand people a decade later. And the results were astonishing. According to data from the World Bank, the process led to a more equitable distribution of city services. By 1997, sewer and water connections increased from seventy-five percent to ninety-eight percent, health and education budgets tripled, and the number of schools quadrupled.

That data was a game changer. Over the next twenty years, advocates of participatory budgeting cited those numbers when making the case to bring the process to their city. By 2013, more than seven thousand governments around the world had implemented some version of partic-ipatory budgeting, including in New York City, Paris and even rural vil-lages in China. Fourteen countries use participatory budgeting on the national level, including South Korea and Portugal. Almost a million people globally have participated in their local process, and these pro-cesses taken together have allocated $350 million.

Our favorite example is Youth Lead the Change, a participatory budgeting project run by the city of Boston that allowed middle and high school students to vote on how they wanted to spend $1 million of the city's education budget. Youth Lead the Change incorporated young people's voices into each stage of the decision-making process.

The first step of the process was creating a steering committee com-posed of student volunteers to determine how the rest of the process would work, and by what rules. Next, the steering committee members went back to their communities to develop a pipeline of ideas through "idea collection assemblies" at Boston public schools. The members then worked with city leaders to vet the ideas and put them into the language of government-speak (for example, by using terms like "feasibility" and "projected impact"). Fourteen potential projects made the final ballot, and several thousand students voted at "Vote Fest" events around the city that featured barbecue, performances and raffles.

What we love about this project is the wisdom reflected in the results. The students didn't vote for better food in the cafeterias or more sports equipment; they voted for things like capital investments in heating systems and industrial fans. Boston is a city of extreme temperatures, and many schools are housed in old buildings that lack central air conditioning or heating. It's hard to learn when it's too hot or cold to focus.

Social scientists tend to get excited about the data they see in studies of participatory budgeting. One paper tied Brazil's use of participatory budgeting to an eleven percent decrease in infant mortality and an uptick in spending on health and sanitation. A Harvard study on Youth Lead the Change found that the project resulted in heightened sense of awareness about government among young people in Boston, as well as a greater feeling of empowerment.

Can this logic translate to philanthropy and impact investing? Josh Lerner says that it can. Lerner is the executive director at People Powered: Global Hub for Participatory Democracy, a nonprofit pushing for participatory budgeting and other democratic processes. He sees a direct parallel between his work and participatory funding in private sector altruism.

"The experience of participatory budgeting shows that funding deci-sions are generally better when they're made by and with communities," Lerner told us. "Community members have invaluable expertise in their own lives and realities. When institutions combine their technical expertise with this lived community expertise, money is more likely to go to the greatest needs. Perhaps even more importantly, sharing real power over real money builds people's long-term capacity to take action together and create lasting change."

Ultimately, the best argument for participatory funding's efficacy might be its intuitiveness. One researcher at the Baring Foundation studied a participatory grantmaking process for LGBTQ+ people in South Africa. His conclusion? "[The idea] that involving beneficiaries in defining and coming up with solutions to the problems will result in better intelligence and, ultimately, investment—is instinctively right."

The Outside Argument: Decolonizing Wealth

If the inside argument focuses on efficacy, the outside argument focuses on equity.

It may be helpful to define equity; it's a term that's thrown around a lot, and it's often misused. The biggest confusion might be the difference between equity and equality; both terms are about promoting fairness. But equality is about giving everyone the exact same resources, regardless of need, whereas equity is about distributing resources based on the needs of the recipients. So participatory funding isn't about redistributing resources to ensure everyone is treated equally; rather, it's about making sure ideas from everywhere have a fair shot at success.

Right now, the playing field is uneven. To recap: Most wealth is still controlled by white men in the Global North. Philanthropy boards are more than sixty percent male, and seventy-two percent are white, as are eight in ten employees at impact investment funds. These numbers are reflected in the lack of diversity in who receives funding. There have been loud calls to improve equity in the social sector from within and from outside major institutions.

Participatory funding is a rare thing; it's a concrete structural reform that can make a meaningful difference in conversations about diversity, equity and inclusion. Bringing in outside voices improves equity in several ways.

First, it drives funding to groups that wouldn't normally get funded, leveling the playing field for small organizations. Funding is a competitive space. Vu Le, editor of the website Nonprofit AF, compares it to the Hunger Games: a field of organizations "fighting against each other to win any substantial funding." But this isn't Hollywood, and the winners aren't the underdogs. Instead, the ones who emerge victorious tend to be well-funded and well-connected, with highly paid development directors and the inside scoop on new opportunities.

Participatory funding gives smaller organizations more of a shot by neutralizing the advantage of money and connection. Many of the participatory funds we spoke with tell us they often are the first to put money into the nonprofits or social entrepreneurs they fund.

Second, participatory funding democratizes access to the skills needed to raise money from funders, breaking down false barriers of language and culture. There is a language of funding that is largely made up and exclusionary. The world of investing, for instance, is full of terminology like "product-market fit" and "cap tables" that obfuscate what is often, at least with early-stage investing, a gut decision.

In a participatory process, however, the nonprofit leader or social entrepreneur gets to put herself in the shoes of a funder for a period of time, learning how funders talk and how they make decisions. Ultimately, this recenters philanthropy toward the kinds of grant applicants who know more about how to talk to their neighbors than how to talk to foundation leaders, and it recenters social entrepreneurship away from Harvard Business School graduates and toward entrepreneurs who sit in investor blind spots.

Finally, participatory funding fundamentally changes power dynamics by changing the role of funders from givers and deciders to supporters and connectors. Reimagining their role is a big psychic leap for many funders, but the ones who have made it find the new equilibrium liberating and fulfilling. As we'll explore in the next two chapters, the practical challenges with making that change are real, but so are the benefits— including a glimpse into what a more equitable future actually looks like.

That's not to downplay the importance of "traditional" experts in participatory processes. Grant managers, investment analysts and board members all have something to bring to the table; it just needs to be balanced by other kinds of expertise. As Lerner likes to put it, in participatory processes, traditional funders become a "new kind of hero."

"When you share power, people step up," he told us. "But if you don't support them they'll fall right back down."

5

GRASSROOTS GRANTMAKING

In the early hours of May 26, 2006, an earthquake measuring 6.2 on the Richter scale struck the Indonesian island of Java. The shockwave caused catastrophic water damage to cities and small towns on the coast. Yogyakarta, home to Indonesia's largest university, received the worst damage: thirty-five thousand houses destroyed, and two hundred thousand people left homeless, at the mercy of torrential rain and aftershocks.

Dwi Ariyani felt the shock of the earthquake a few minutes later. She lived in a town a few miles inland from Yogyakarta, also heavily affected by the quake. Over the next several days, she watched as her town began the rebuilding process in what seemed to her like a tragic succession of missteps. Aid workers from other Indonesian islands arrived without maps of the neighborhood and always seemed one step behind; aid workers from Europe seemed to be applying a by-the-numbers approach to a very nuanced situation.

Above all, Ariyani saw that the disabled community was not being invited to the table. She has used a wheelchair from a young age, a major disadvantage for a young woman in Indonesia. As a teenager, she persuaded her school to build a wheelchair ramp and became the only woman in her university class to study computer technology. After graduation, she persevered as employer after employer refused to hire her because of her disability *and* her gender, and she ended up working at a disability charity organization doing database management.

In the days after the earthquake, Ariyani put her data skills to use. She set up an office in the backyard of a village leader with a table, some chairs and a computer. When her mother visited Ariyani's work space, she cried when she saw the conditions her daughter was working in. But Ariyani was thrilled. After just a few weeks, she had eighteen volunteers working with her to design a disability-inclusive response, including the launch of a children's center to provide psychosocial support to children with disabilities and connect them with relief services from humanitarian NGOs.

With her bootstrapped approach, Ariyani had achieved results that most grantmakers would be thrilled to see—at least on paper. But as she set out to raise formal funding for her project, she realized that she faced some significant structural limitations.

First, Ariyani lived in a small rural town. Most grantmakers were centralized in cities like Jakarta, where Indonesia's disability rights movement had started.

Second, Ariyani was running a new and very informal operation, with her outdoor backyard "office" and a small band of dedicated volunteers. Many large grantmakers had application processes that were designed for bigger and more established nonprofits. They would ask for complex financial statements or include catch-22 requirements like requiring Ariyani to prove she had five years of management experience or a ten- person staff.

But most crucially, many grantmakers who expressed interest in disabled communities were wary of supporting political advocacy work. For instance, some of the largest foundations were created by business leaders who had close relationships with the Indonesian government. They had calculated that they could get more done if they stayed out of politics and instead focused on funding charity or aid work.

Ariyani knew her experience with philanthropy was one shared by thousands of disability rights activists around the world. That's why in 2012 she was thrilled to join the team of a new foundation, one that put voices like hers at the center.

The Disability Rights Fund

The design for the Disability Rights Fund was inspired by a successful experiment in participation on one of the world's biggest stages: the United Nations.

In December 2006, the UN met in its home in midtown Manhattan for a ceremony adopting a new treaty: the Convention on the Rights of Persons with Disabilities (or CRPD). The meeting was a big moment for the UN and for human rights. The UN is a big, bulky, slow organization. It's hard to get its members to agree on pretty much anything; the UN passes about one treaty a decade. This particular treaty had been the subject of discussion for more than a decade. Over the previous three years, every last one of its fifty articles had been drafted line by line by a working group and debated in ad hoc committee sessions.

But what was most remarkable was the process that UN leaders decided to use for the development of the treaty. The UN made the historic move of reserving one-third of the seats of the working group drafting the treaty text for activists from the global disability community in addition to the traditional government representatives. This was a far more participatory and open process for civil society leaders than had ever been conducted at the UN.

The treaty that ultimately passed was seen as a landmark victory for human rights; it included more robust protections for disabled people than the Americans with Disabilities Act. Tonally, it constantly emphasized that people with disabilities were capable of making decisions about their own lives, not mere objects for charity, medical treatment or protection. It defined their existence as one of inherent power and humanity rather than as something to pity.

Having those outside voices in the room had made a difference. Partway through drafting the treaty, the UN working group came to a difficult topic: guardianship. Many governments still have legal mechanisms that allow for disabled people to be put under guardianship against their will, stripping away their autonomy and appointing someone else to make personal decisions on their behalf. This often leads to forced detention and mental health treatment. This kind of unequal treatment in the eyes of the law was at the heart of what activists were fighting against.

One of the activists at the UN working group meeting was Tina Minkowitz. Minkowitz is herself a survivor of involuntary psychiatric treatment and has become a renowned human rights lawyer; she has written that she would "prefer death to another round of forced psychiatry." She is credited with pushing for unprecedented strong language protecting disabled people's rights. The final treaty read: "States parties reaffirm that persons with disabilities have the right to recognition everywhere as persons before the law"—a glorious statement of victory for the disability rights community.

Diana Samarasan, the disability rights activist from Chapter 2, was working in Budapest at the time of the UN treaty, taking former Soviet Bloc governments to court for the abuse of people with disabilities. Samarasan saw the horrors of forced guardianship firsthand; at one mental health institution in the Balkans, she saw people "tied to beds and crammed in small rooms with broken windows." The staff told her that "it was OK because the people living there 'don't have the same feelings that we do.'"

When the treaty passed, activists and donors had the same thought: "Now what?" The treaty still had to be ratified by each of the member countries in the United Nations. It was a massive undertaking that would require resources to match: sustained funding for grassroots activists and community organizers in countries around the world, many of which had governments that offered virtually no protection for disabled people. The Fund for Global Human Rights, with capital from an anonymous donor, decided to hire a consultant to come up with a strategy to fund this rights-based work. Samarasan was that consultant.

Samarasan brought together other activists and donors, many of whom were skeptical that foundations would be up to the challenge, given their paternalistic record on funding disability rights. The discussion kept coming back to the UN treaty process. What if all decisions about resources for disabled people could be made by disabled people? What if philanthropy gave disabled people a vote when making funding decisions aimed at them?

Samarasan and her team found examples of this participatory approach in campaigns on behalf of people with HIV/AIDS and foundations like the Global Greengrants Fund. The consistent theme was the use of lived experience activists as advisors to recommend and decide on grants. They decided to create a fund based on the same principle, with Wellspring Philanthropic Fund putting up the seed money.

Who Decides Who Decides?

In 2007, Samarasan—who had never been a grantmaker—began a yearlong dialogue with many different disability activists and donors who had been involved in the CRPD process about how the new fund would look. The first question to answer was a meta one. As part of the fund's structure, disabled people would pick which organizations would receive funding. But how would that process work, exactly? What would be the "rules of the game"?

We call this the "Who decides who decides?" question. Technically, Samarasan could have just developed her own funding model or outsourced fund design to a company like consulting firm FSG. But that would go against the whole ethos of "nothing about us without us." So she used the activists and donors who were already part of the dialogue to create the structure for what would eventually become the Disability Rights Fund.

There are a range of models for designing a participatory grantmaking fund varying in extent and nature of participation. (See the Resources section at the back of this book for more on these models.) For instance, there are "open collective" models like Make It Your Own and the Wikimedia Foundation, in which decisions are entirely open-sourced and anyone in the world can weigh in. There are also "closed collective" models, which bring together several individuals and organization representatives working in a particular field to make decisions as a group.

At the first fund design meeting, in March 2008, Samarasan and the other participants defined the priority areas to be funded, as well as the first target countries for funding, the size of the grants and how to make the grantmaking process accessible to everyone. All of these questions fed into the biggest one: what kind of participatory grantmaking model would govern the new fund.

After much research and debate, the group chose a representative participation model. The core decision-making body is the grantmaking committee, composed of an equal number of institutional donors and activists who serve four-year terms. Each year, the grantmaking committee meets in June to discuss grant applications and make recommendations. Their decisions get passed along to a board committee, also composed of fifty percent disabled people, who give final approval to the grants.

A key early question was who should be on the Grantmaking Committee – or rather, how that decision should be made. Samarasan built a partnership with the International Disability Alliance, an umbrella network of global and disability organizations with a wide and diverse reach. Whenever a new seat or seats open up on the committee, Samarasan and her team reach out to the IDA and ask for nominations, with context about what characteristics they are looking for, always making sure to strive for parity across gender, geography, race, indigeneity, type of disability and more.

The first round of peer review and grant funding for the Disability Rights Fund ran in 2008. The fund has since run its participatory process nearly a dozen times and distributed more than $37 million in grants to more than three hundred organizations and activists in Africa, Asia, the Pacific Islands and the Caribbean. In that time, the structure of the fund has been in a state of constant, intentional—if often frustrating—evolution.

The Process is the Point

The Disability Rights Fund could still be considered in "beta" mode; Samarasan, like many participatory grantmakers, is constantly iterating on the fund's model. The purpose is to hone the rough edges and make things run more smoothly. But ultimately, the real reason is so Samarasan and her team can constantly check and recheck their own assumptions, privilege and bias.

Over the course of co-designing the fund, Samarasan, her staff and stakeholders in the disability movement have sat through hours and hours of meetings, heard both constructive feedback and frustrating non-sequiturs, and had to refine and refine all over again. She believes that these long hours have been well spent and indeed created the solid foundation from which to continue to expand DRF's work. As she is fond of saying, "The process is the point."

One example of the never-ending "process" for any participatory grantmaker is constantly challenging assumptions around what true representation looks like. Cynthia Gibson has written that research about participatory practices, from city budgeting to healthcare, shows that one of the most important factors in success is to be proactive and intentional about involving people from all parts of a community or constituency—"not just those who may be more inclined to participate or are automatically invited because of their titles, financial status, or social capital."

Over the course of the first round of funding, Samarasan learned a number of nuances about hierarchies in the disability rights movement. "Disabled people are incredibly heterogenous," she said. "People who are deaf will have a different life experience and perspective than people who are blind, or people with Down syndrome, or people who became disabled instead of being born with a disability." She learned, for instance, that people with a disability that is less limiting of their mobility and communication will be louder advocates. But more broadly, any movement has activists who we've heard described as "familiar faces." Maybe they're the ones who always speak at conferences. Maybe their English is better. Or maybe they fit into grantmakers' expectations of the kind of people they expected to work with.

Only recently, in its twelfth year of grantmaking, has the fund started intentionally seeking reviewers (and grantees) who are working at the intersection of LGBTQ+ issues and disability rights. "You need to constantly ask who is *not* at the table," Samarasan said, "and be willing to identify and reach out to people who are missing."

Participation also cannot be conflated with free labor or feedback. Samarasan made sure that the committee members who were ultimately selected were given honorariums for their time and were provided with appropriate accommodations like personal assistants, sign language interpreters, Braille documents, and accessible hotels and meeting spaces. "If we don't pay them, or provide for their needs," Samarasan said, "we could exclude people who can't take unpaid days from work but [who] would otherwise provide significant value to the process."

The expenses of honorariums and accommodations may seem extraneous, but they're not. "You're paying for expertise," Samarasan said. "People think, 'oh, they're giving us their thoughts.' No; they're experts."

Another major question in the never-ending iteration of the Disability Rights Fund is the staff makeup. The fund's staff members are ultimately the ones who "decide who decides," and Samarasan has made a point of ensuring that her team is representative of the disability activist community. She told us one story about a perspective that Dwi Ariyani brought to her role as a program officer: she suggested that the DRF team translate their grant application into Bahasa, the official language of Indonesia. That change alone doubled the amount of applicants from the island nation.

Over the past decade, as the Disability Rights Fund has honed and re-honed their model, the field of participatory grantmaking has experienced something of a renaissance, gaining the largest wave of new participatory funds since the creation of the Funding Exchange. By our rough count, there are now at least forty funds that are wholly participatory. These funds can be global or local; some are large and some are small. There are two broad types that we'll explore in this chapter.

The first type is what we'll call *movement builders*. The Disability Rights Fund is one example. These funds seek to reorient philanthropy away from a mindset of "fixing" marginalized communities, and toward supporting their grassroots organizing and advocacy work. Their leaders use participatory models as a blunt tool to encourage philanthropy to be more responsive to and inclusive of activists on the ground.

The second type of participatory funders are what we'll call *community builders*. These are "place-based" funds that center on a geographic community, usually a city, town or neighborhood. The Haymarket People's Fund and all of the other Funding Exchange funds were com-munity builders. Leaders of these funds seek to develop a comprehensive, long-term set of strategies to address the social, health and economic needs of marginalized people in their corner of the world—and to make sure that the most marginalized voices are at the table when that strategy is developed.

In the next few pages, we'll take a look at a few examples of funds in both categories. We'll start with movement builders, and the movement that offers the most potential to be transformed in the long run by participatory grantmaking: women's rights.

Gender and Justice

The pattern should be clear at this point, but it's still worth spelling out: Men, and mostly white men at that, dominate philanthropy. Men outnumber women on foundation boards, foundation executive teams and lists of individual givers. (The original Giving Pledge list included only one woman who was not part of a couple.) Women may make up seventy-six percent of foundation staff after decades of advocacy, but they still represent only forty percent of decision-makers.

It also should be no surprise at this point that this male perspective influences what gets funded. Only five percent of global philanthropic funding goes to organizations specifically serving women and girls. Just one percent of international aid that does have a gender focus actually reaches feminist organizations on the ground. The remaining ninety-nine percent goes straight into the hands of large international NGOs, often paying for expansive development projects that treat women's issues as a secondary or tertiary priority. One study found that more than half of women's rights organizations have never received multi-year funding from an institutional donor.

Over the past forty years, a shadow philanthropy industry has developed to fill that gap: a network of alternative "women's funds" that operate parallel to mainstream foundations and donors. Many of the earliest funds were bankrolled by the first generation of women to rise to the top ranks of Wall Street banks and white-shoe law firms, and focused on addressing issues that mainstream philanthropy had avoided. The Ms. Foundation for Women, founded in 1973 by Gloria Steinem and others, was the first major fund dedicated to issues like abortion access and sexual assault prevention. Mama Cash in Amsterdam and the Global Fund for Women followed shortly after. By the turn of the twenty-first century, more than one hundred forty-five women's funds were operating around the world, and collaborating through hubs like Prospera and the Women's Funding Network.

Most of these women's funds were not created to be explicitly participatory, but on the whole they do take a remarkably inclusive approach. In 2018, the Women's Funding Network found, incredibly, that seventy-five percent of women's funds invite people with lived experience to read over grant applications or make funding recommendations. Several early influential women's funds were designed to be participatory, like Fondo Semillas in Mexico and Fondo Centroamericano de Mujeres (Central American Women's Fund) in Central America.

In the past decade, the women's funding space has embraced "formal" participatory grantmaking in a remarkable way. Rather than a single funder pioneering the way, like the Disability Rights Fund has done, there have instead been numerous women's funds testing out variations on participatory models, often while working together—a feature of these funds' inclination for collaboration.

One of the most influential participatory women's funds of the past decade has been FRIDA | The Young Feminist Fund. FRIDA was dreamed up in 2009 by a global group of young feminist activists who met up at a conference in Marrakech, Morocco. They shared their frustrations with traditional philanthropy: they ran up against many of the same barriers to entry Dwi Ariyani encountered. In the words of one activist: "We had to present this really perfect English and this perfect organization that had everything in terms of finances and legal registration to compete for funding with large, Western NGOs."

FRIDA uses an "open collective" grantmaking model inspired by the Fondo Centroamericano de Mujeres, which incubated the fund. Every year, FRIDA puts out a call for applications from women and transgender activists under the age of thirty who live in the Global South.

Anyone who submits an idea receives back an anonymized list of applications from peer activists in their region of the world and votes on who should receive funding. (They cannot vote for themselves.) This ensures that young feminist activists are setting the priorities for their own movements.

FRIDA's leaders argue that feminist movements are most effective when led by people who understand local context. "The movement to end gender-based violence needs to be complicated, contextualized and decolonized for it to resonate on a global level," wrote FRIDA staffer Deepa Ranganathan.

Take the #MeToo movement. While the hashtag might resonate with Western audiences and appeal to Western funders, in other cultures, it can actually undermine the work of local activists. In Thailand, while some traditional grantmakers were encouraging activists to use the #MeToo brand, FRIDA was busy funding Thaiconsent. Ranganathan wrote:

> Thai culture isn't very confrontational. The way they are trying to break free of a slut-shaming society is [by] creating viral hashtags of their own. The hashtag #donttellmehowtodress which went viral in Thailand last year, was particularly aimed at changing perceptions around survivors and perpetrators of sexual assault. Wipaphan Wongsawang, founder of Thaiconsent, explains, "The whole movement [of #MeToo] was in English; this language barrier is a huge thing."

Ten years in, FRIDA has awarded around $7 million in grants to more than two hundred fifty initiatives in one hundred fifteen countries in the Global South. In total, hundreds of young activists have reviewed grants and gained insight into how funding works. But FRIDA's larger legacy might be how it has inspired other major women's funds to experiment with participatory grantmaking.

Case in point: shortly after Malala Yousafzai won the Nobel Peace Prize as a high schooler, she and her father created the Malala Fund to fight for twelve years of free education for girls around the world—and almost immediately, the fund joined the With and For Girls Collective, a donor collaborative launched in 2014 and inspired by FRIDA. The members include other funds in the Women's Funding Network, as well as mainstream foundations like the Nike Foundation and the Global Fund for Children.

The With and For Girls Collective models its approach after FRIDA's. The collective funds girl-led and girl-centered organizations working on issues like reproductive rights, child marriage and racial justice. Applications are initially screened by the collective's staff, but final decisions are made by regional panels of adolescent girls, who interview local applicants to determine who should receive funding.

FRIDA's legacy also extends to second-generation funds—that is, participatory funds launched by their FRIDA alumni. Magda Pochec, a young activist in Poland, reached out to FRIDA in 2016 at a moment of crisis for her country. A new far-right political party, Law and Justice, had recently come to power on the promise to restrict women's rights by tightening abortion laws, promoting traditional gender roles and banning gender studies in schools. The election had inspired a budding protest movement, with hundreds of thousands of protestors taking to the streets. But Pochec's experience raising money from traditional grantmakers convinced her that they were not up to the task of supporting this momentum. "I was writing proposals in a language that is not my language about priorities that are not my priorities," she told us.

Her experience reviewing peer grants for FRIDA broadened her outlook on what philanthropy could be. "It wasn't just the experience of being part of the participatory grantmaking process, but rather being exposed to the narrative that FRIDA created," she said. "The language they used was revolutionary. They created this new approach that was mind-blowing. They were doing things my way."

In 2018, Pochec launched FemFund, modeled directly after FRIDA, to resource small, informal feminist groups in Poland. One of their grantees, the Abortion Dream Team, travels around Poland in a van teaching women and allies how to perform abortions in settings as diverse as a barn on the edge of the Carpathian Mountains and office buildings in Gdańsk. "We build connections between diverse communities—this is more important than the money," Pochec told us. "Money is just a tool for us to build this connection."

FRIDA can now even claim a third-generation descendant. One of FemFund's first peer reviewers, Ola Muzinska, has followed in Magda's footsteps and begun fundraising for her own participatory fund for LGBTQ+ youth in Poland.

Women's funds often take on issues, from abortion rights to period poverty, that are outside the comfort zones of traditional funders. For our next example of a movement builder, let's look at a participatory grantmaker working on a cause that until very recently was still on the fringes of mainstream feminism: the Red Umbrella Fund.

From Rescue to Rights

As the most-visited city in the world's fifth most popular travel destination, Venice welcomes nearly thirty million foreign visitors every year. In June 2001, many of them were clogging the narrow streets between the city's canals to see the installations for the forty-ninth Biennale Arte.

Among the featured contemporary artists was Tadej Pogačar, a forty-one-year-old Slovenian who had made a name for himself as the founder of the P.A.R.A.S.I.T.E. Museum of Contemporary Art, known for disruptive public exhibits. The museum's website explains that "In the same way as a parasite in nature, which as a rule fulfils its life conditions only in a direct relation to its host...the museum takes over territories, chooses spaces, interrupts relations and gets fed by the juices of institutions."

Pogačar didn't disappoint. Few were prepared for what greeted them at the site of his installation, CODE:RED: thousands of sex workers carrying red umbrellas. Pogačar had collaborated with them to amplify their protest of poor treatment and human rights abuses through a march that wound its way from the "Prostitute Pavilion" through the landmarks of Venice's history of courtesans, brothels and other sex work. The red umbrella quickly became a symbol of activism for sex workers' rights.

There are an estimated forty million sex workers in the world, but the world's oldest profession is a dangerous one, with risks ranging from sexually transmitted diseases to violent assaults at the hands of clients. Treatment for the mental and physical impact of that violence is often inaccessible, or, when it's provided by state health clinics, conditioned on giving up sex work.

For many sex workers, including the ones who marched in Venice that summer, there is a clear solution: decriminalization. Sex work is illegal in most countries around the world, and arrests and fines perpetuate the trade's cycle of poverty. Governments that ban brothels put sex workers at increased risk of violence from their clients because they are forced to operate in isolation. Fear of arrest also discourages sex workers from contacting authorities about potential trafficking victims. Recognition of the profession as an honest job would go a long way; indeed, one recent study published by the National Institutes of Health in the US found that decriminalization, as implemented by New Zealand and a handful of other countries, reduced violence against sex workers and even increased the likelihood that they would report potential trafficking victims to law enforcement.

But philanthropy has been intensely reluctant to support advocacy for decriminalization. By the latest count, less than one percent of global human rights funding—already a small corner of overall philanthropy—went to support sex workers' rights. Even mainstream feminist funders avoided the issue; as recently as 2013, Ms. Foundation founder Gloria

Steinem equated decriminalization to an endorsement of sex trafficking. Foundations that do direct money toward the sex worker community tend to take an approach that Paul-Gilbert Colletaz, a former sex worker and current participatory grantmaker, calls "rescue not rights."

"To access funds [as a sex worker], you have to say you're not going to do sex work, or you need to say you've been trafficked," he told us. In 2006, the Gates Foundation became one inadvertent catalyst for this new approach. The foundation gave a $5 million human rights grant in 2006 for Project Lantern, an anti-trafficking initiative from the International Justice Mission that publicly conflated consensual sex work with slavery and human trafficking. Sex workers' rights activists were livid.

"Some of [the funders] will say that they don't have a position on sex work, but they have a position on human rights, they have a position on labor rights," Colletaz explained. "And I think most of the game is making them see that sex workers are humans and that makes them part of human rights. If you work on human rights or labor rights, you need to work with sex worker-led organizations."

Two years after Project Lantern was announced, the Open Society Foundations and two activist organizations—CREA and the Global Network of Sex Work Projects—began a "donor dialogue" on sex work and human trafficking. That several-year process led to the launch in 2012 of the Red Umbrella Fund, named after the movement inspired by the Venice march.

The Red Umbrella Fund is participatory to its core. Activists from around the world—primarily current and former sex workers like Colletaz—form committees to set membership, criteria and budgets. A "program advisory committee," made up of a diverse group of activists selected for three-year terms, is responsible for funding decisions. Each year, the fund gives out a maximum of thirty flexible grants to sex worker-led networks and organizations. As one woman involved in the peer review process said, "We understand which projects or groups will really be effective towards positive change. Bottom line, it's our bodies, our lives, and we should be at the forefront of all decisions affecting us."

Colletaz emphasized that the Red Umbrella Fund can, on a very practical level, reach people that most institutional donors cannot. Sex work is still illegal in most of the countries where the fund works, and punishment for breaking the law can be severe. This means sex workers are often afraid of getting involved in advocacy for fear of retaliation. The Red Umbrella Fund sets up particular precautions to ensure the safety of peer reviewers.

In 2018, when India's lower house of government passed a bill that would conflate consensual sex work with human trafficking, two Red Umbrella Fund grantees (ADARSHA and the All India Network of Sex Workers) mobilized their network to oppose it. Like the intersectional network of Polish feminists convened by FemFund, these groups partnered with India's disability community and advocates for an end to caste-based discrimination to lobby policy makers and host educational workshops for sex workers about the bill. The strategy worked, and by July 2018, the Indian government agreed to withdraw the proposal.

Community Builders

Place-based grantmaking is not new; arguably, it's the oldest form of grantmaking. But in the past three decades, it's become a growing trend among foundations and donors who believe the way to be most effective is to stay focused and hyperlocal: to develop a comprehensive, long-term set of strategies to address the social, health and economic needs of a neighborhood, city or region. Place-based strategies now account for $5 billion in grantmaking each year.

This work is by nature dependent on cooperation and collaboration with many different stakeholders. Any neighborhood or city is a living, evolving organism. According to the Milken Institute, place-based philanthropy needs to be "genuinely embedded within the [community]" to be effective; that means "fostering relationships with those who have directly experienced the challenges at hand." This is no easy task. More than half of community foundations have fewer than six paid employees, and these foundations serve an average population of one hundred eighty thousand people.

This makes community builders particularly fertile ground for participatory grantmaking. Every single one of the sixteen original Funding Exchange funds were place-based. Particularly in the past decade, place-based participatory grantmaking has become more popular as a model around the world. We'll look at two participatory funding organizations operating locally in two very different parts of the world. One is in the Palestinian territories, where decades of international aid have fragmented a once-strong social fabric. The other is in Brooklyn, New York, where long-time residents facing gentrification are struggling to hold on to the community that they know and love.

Rawa: Creative Palestinian Communities Fund

In 1993, Palestinians became some of the largest recipients of international aid in the world, virtually overnight.

That was the year that Israel and the Palestinian Liberation Organization agreed to the Oslo Accords, which created the new government of the Palestinian Authority. The authority's initial revenues would come entirely from Israel and from foreign aid. Nearly three decades later, many Palestinians felt that their proud society, with its centuries-long history, had grown dependent on foreign aid and philanthropy.

We sat down with Moukhtar Kocache, an outspoken critic of philanthropy in the region. In 2011, Kocache was working as a program officer at the Cairo office of the Ford Foundation focusing on arts and human rights in Palestine, when the Ford Foundation pulled all its funding from the region. This forced him to quickly end decades-old relationships between the foundation and the museums and universities that anchored

Palestinian culture. "In some cases grantees had to spend down funds within a few months," he told us. "It was traumatizing."

According to Kocache, international aid has broken down the social fabric of the Palestinian people. People who used to be leaders in their community are now on the payroll of global NGOs, advancing foreign agendas that do not necessarily align with the will of the people living there. "When you create a massive administrative system that is vital to people's livelihood, they will become passive," Kocache told us. "If you tell someone they don't know how to make decisions and they need hand-holding, they will internalize that. It's a sterilization of grassroots organizing and community development on many levels."

This is particularly problematic in the tense geopolitical environment of Palestine, where locals are constantly having to defend their land against settlers and their rights against an aggressive Israeli state. "In moments of political urgency," Kocache said, "grassroots groups are the first to lead community mobilization."

Since leaving his role at the Ford Foundation, Kocache has been part of a revival of locally led foundations in Palestine. In 2007, he helped create the Dalia Association, the first ever community foundation in Palestine. (Dalia means "grapevine" in Arabic.) The founding charter reads, "We are diverse in terms of age, gender, religion and politics, yet we are united by our vision—to realize our rights as Palestinians to control our resources and sustain our own development for generations to come."

A few years later, Kocache helped convene a meeting of philanthropy and development professionals to discuss how philanthropy could organically grow an alternative to donor-driven development and aid. That meeting led to five years of co-design with Palestinian leaders of what ultimately became Rawa: Creative Palestinian Communities Fund.

"Rawa was built on the premise that if we are to end cycles of dependence on foreign aid and liberate ourselves from conditional funding, dishonest brokers, and imposed solutions, communities must have decision-making power," Kocache said.

Rawa uses a participatory grantmaking model that cedes grant-making to leaders in four geographic "clusters." Some of these clusters are in the West Bank and Gaza, while others are in Jerusalem and other parts of Israel. Local leaders in the clusters seek out grassroots development projects for Rawa to fund; their 2019 grant cohort included a community strawberry farm in Beit Hanoun that offers job training, and a group in Gaza working to preserve and promote Palestinian filmmaking.

In February 2019, Rawa launched its grant cycle and held its first community forum, where cluster leaders come together to debate priorities and grants. This gathering raised several challenges, including Israeli-imposed restrictions on people's movements. They ultimately decided to hold the event in the West Bank town of Jericho and had the cluster in Gaza connect via video.

Kocache told us that like the Disability Rights Fund, Rawa is constantly iterating. "We're always worried," he reflected. "We're always asking, 'Are we doing things in a more participatory manner today than a year ago?' We just have to be able to say yes. We have an ideal and we hope to be able to move toward that."

Brooklyn Community Foundation

On the other side of the world, people living in Brooklyn are dealing with very different issues of displacement. Crown Heights, a Brooklyn neighborhood of brownstones and parks a short subway ride from downtown Manhattan, is one of the most historically diverse neighborhoods in one of the most diverse cities in the world. Hasidic Jews live just blocks away from West Indian immigrants; more than a third of its residents were born outside the United States.

But this diversity has been waning. Between 2000 and 2010, Crown Heights lost between ten and fourteen percent percent of its Black population. A quarter of residents who currently live in the neighborhood have moved there since 2010; most of these newcomers are young white people who were pushed out of Manhattan and even Williamsburg by rising rent. This has made Crown Heights a very visible example of what New York City Mayor Bill de Blasio famously referred to as a "tale of two cities."

Amid all this gentrification, a local Brooklyn foundation decided it needed to change as well. For years, the Brooklyn Community Foundation had been sponsored entirely by a private bank. In 2009, when the bank went under, the foundation decided to convert to a public community foundation. Cecilia Clarke, a longtime Brooklynite and nonprofit leader who had never worked in philanthropy, took over the presidency of the reconstructed foundation in 2013. "They had done a fantastic job as a bank foundation, mind you, but the board was the bank board, it was bank officers," she told a local paper.

In Clarke's first months in office, she launched what is now considered to be one the broadest community-engagement efforts in the recent history of philanthropy: the Brooklyn Insights project. The foundation interviewed a thousand community residents, ranging from owners of brownstones to families renting apartments in impoverished projects. As Clarke told a board member two weeks into her tenure, "This is not going to be a strategic-planning session where we close the doors and shut down our website and say, 'See you in a year.'"

The message that came out of those conversations was clear: Longtime Crown Heights residents felt that decisions about the neighborhood's development were entirely out of their hands. Clarke and her team took that message to heart. In 2015, the foundation launched a resident-led grantmaking model in Crown Heights called the Neighborhood Strength Initiative.

The first step of the initiative was to hold three public visioning sessions, during which the foundation would ask Crown Heights community members to identify top concerns and possible solutions for their neighborhood, starting with the simple question: "What is your vision for Crown Heights?" At these sessions, residents shared concerns including displacement of longtime residents, police brutality and the proliferation of real estate developments that did not reflect community history or culture.

Next, the foundation connected seventeen residents from Crown Heights to form an advisory council and narrow the ideas into one focus area that the foundation should support. One video of a council meeting shows a young Black mother, a white activist and a Hasidic Jew debating productively—and respectfully—about the merits of various priorities.

The group wanted to focus on reclaiming public spaces for the community, such as playgrounds and parks. At the council's recommendation, the Brooklyn Community Foundation sought proposal ideas from nonprofits and community groups to make existing space more accessible to Crown Heights residents. The council reviewed the proposals that came in and made a recommendation to the foundation's board.

The now-annual Neighborhood Strength Initiative is not fully participatory; the board retains ultimate authority to reject any proposal. But so far, it hasn't rejected any, even when it could have been financially advantageous. In 2017, the board approved a grant to the political advocacy group New York Communities for Change to push for more affordable housing in the proposed redevelopment of the Bedford Union Armory. A Brooklyn Community Foundation donor and personal friend of the board chair was in charge of the redevelopment that the activists were targeting. But, true to their commitment to community voice, the advocacy project was approved without a hitch.

Place-based funds like Rawa and the Brooklyn Community Foundation are focused on providing grants to nonprofits. But communities need more than nonprofits to thrive; any strategy to revive a neighborhood or city cannot ignore the pivotal role of small businesses and local economies.

In the next chapter, we'll look at community-driven impact investing. Impact investing, as we've discussed, suffers from many of the same biases as traditional philanthropy. The people making decisions tend to be white, male, from backgrounds of privilege and living far away from the communities they are trying to help. And the processes for making decisions tend to be top-down, closed off and driven by wealthy invest-ors. But new models for investing are emerging that thoroughly upend those power dynamics.

6

DECOLONIZING CAPITAL

Every Wednesday evening for the past few years—at least, before the pandemic—a group of Boston residents from the working class neighborhoods of Dorchester, Roxbury and Mattapan meet to plan for the future of their neighborhood. They gather in the partitioned conference room of City Life/Vida Urbana, a nonprofit that lets other organizations meet in its space on the third floor of a rehabbed Samuel Adams brewery.

For most of the week, the space is a meeting center for community organizers fighting for housing justice in the surrounding neighborhoods. Stacks of cardboard signs around the perimeter of the room read, "Stand Up! Fight Back" and "We Will Not Be Moved;" a papier-mâché model of Dracula labeled "Count Bankula" sits perched atop a filing cabinet. The latest battle for the City Life/Vida Urbana organizers has been a fight against the redevelopment of a former racetrack into luxury condos with minimal affordable housing at a time when one in three renters in the state is at risk of eviction.

But during these weekly meetings of the Ujima Fund, the topic is not how to influence the city's major developers; it's how to build a new, resident-driven model for community investment.

The Ujima Fund, part of the Boston Ujima Project, is the first "democratic investment fund" in the United States. The fund's model gives residents of Boston's working class communities of color total control over the direction of economic development in their neighborhood. The Ujima Fund has been described as "a little alien in the belly of capitalism," but it's only one of several community-driven investment models that give residents or specific communities power throughout the funding process, from building a theory of change to vetting ideas. These models help investors tap into a broad range of perspectives outside of their own lived experience and give community members and entrepreneurs a say in the direction of the local or even global economy.

The Ujima Fund is a community loan fund with a twist. The fund has four hundred investors, ranging from low-income residents to wealthy donors and impact investors. It also has members, who must live in Boston proper or identify as having been displaced from their homes by rising rents. Members can join for as little as five dollars a year, which goes toward the fund's loan loss reserve, and each member gets one vote on how the Ujima Fund invests its money. Investors who are not residents—for instance, Harvard students, foundations investing their endowments, or churches, mosques and synagogues in the greater Boston region—can become "solidarity members," but they do not get to vote.

This is, needless to say, not the norm for Boston. Outside the meeting room is a diorama exhibit about redlining, the systematic denial of mortgages to people of color in urban areas to prevent them from buying a home in certain neighborhoods or getting a loan to renovate their house. One of the diorama's features is a blown-up map from the 1930s with detailed instructions from the Federal Housing Authority to local lenders, warning them of neighborhood "infiltration" by "Italians...negroes" and other "detrimental influences." In his landmark article "The Case for Reparations," Ta-Nehisi Coates wrote about redlining that "across the country, whites looking to achieve the American dream could rely on a legitimate credit system backed by the government. Blacks were herded into the sights of unscrupulous lenders who took them for money and for sport."

The defining political battle for many older residents of these neighborhoods was the I-70 crisis in the 1970s. As Boston's suburbs began to grow, developers proposed an "Inner Belt" into downtown that would ease rush-hour traffic. The proposed road would have gone right through Roxbury; blueprints showed homes and gardens sliced in half. Roxbury residents, led by future city council member Chuck Turner, worked together to prevent the plan from going through. The momentum from the I-70 fight launched a number of grassroots activist organizations, including Ujima's host for their weekly meetings, City Life/Vida Urbana.

This history of redlining and top-down city politics—not to mention blockbusting and other quasi-legal tools for segregation—created a city with deep divisions around race and wealth. Today, Boston's one hundred eighty thousand Black residents have a median net worth of $8. The lifespan of a resident of Roxbury is thirty-three years lower than that of someone living in the tony community of Back Bay two miles away. These inequities have created deep distrust between residents and city leaders; more than one person we spoke to called the city's development arm, the Boston Planning & Development Agency, the "Black People Displacement Agency."

The Ujima Fund was created in the context of the latest racial divide: tech-driven gentrification. In the past decade, Boston has grown into a hub for biotech startups; it was considered a serious candidate for Amazon's second headquarters. And once again, those with the biggest checkbooks in the city—the investors—are pushing a development agenda that favors young, wealthy, mostly white tech workers and threatens to displace longtime residents of places like South Boston.

Opting Out

The day that Nia Evans realized she needed to build a new model for economic development from scratch was in 2015, when she learned about Boston's surprise bid to host the 2024 Olympics.

At the time, Evans chaired the Boston NAACP's economic development committee. A tireless organizer, she had spent the early part of her career helping parents at under-resourced Boston schools fight for a larger share of the city budget. She later became the executive director of the Boston NAACP with a mandate to focus on issues like education and criminal justice reform. But she soon realized that economic development was never far removed from either conversation.

Evans and other organizers learned about the plan for an Olympics bid from an article in the *Boston Globe*, which said that the Boston 2024 Partnership—a private group of wealthy individuals—already had buy-in from the city to pursue the bid. The Boston City Council had even hired a well-connected consulting group to do it, and the work was already well underway.

"It was a provocation," Evans recalls. "The city didn't consult the NAACP; they didn't consult the Urban League or Lawyers for Civil Rights; they didn't call any of the Indigenous organizations in Boston. We all heard about it in the newspaper after the city decided to bid."

The Olympic bid set off a wave of protest in Boston. Hosting the Olympics is a big decision; it's a multibillion-dollar enterprise that can reshape a city, often at the expense of already-marginalized neighborhoods. In advance of the 2012 Summer Olympics in London, for instance, developers razed an East London low-income housing neighborhood and left its longtime residents struggling to make ends meet. Though some members of the Boston NAACP saw the Olympics as an opportunity for much-needed community investment, others worried that the same dynamics from London and other former host cities would play out in their city.

Evans's first reaction was to voice these concerns through the normal channels. She encouraged NAACP members to attend town hall meetings about the bid and share their perspective. But after a few weeks, she noticed that her members were losing interest in the process. "They said,

'Look, we're doing all this work to attend meetings and make ourselves heard, but the city already knows what they want to do,'" Evans recalled. "It was obvious that the city was just going through the motions."

That's when she made a big decision: to opt out. Evans decided she wasn't going to participate in a system that didn't invite her participation. "We had tried to speak up and amplify our voices, but it was never enough," she said. "We had been playing on the terms of city leaders and economic developers for too long. We needed to try something new."

Evans called a moratorium on attending city meetings about the Olympics. And she decided to seek out a new model for economic development that would respect the lived experience of residents of color.

"Often, leaders in Boston believe that our communities have nothing to offer," Evans told us. "Our expertise is not recognized and not valued, so it's either not sought or it's dismissed or ignored. The processes that do exist feel like formalities; it doesn't feel like they're enacted with good faith. And we can't and we won't be satisfied with that."

So Evans teamed up with a local activist named Aaron Tanaka—one of the leading thinkers behind the Boston participatory budgeting project Youth Lead the Change—to build that new model. At the time, Tanaka was executive director of the Boston Workers Alliance, an advocacy group led by unemployed and underemployed workers. He also served on the peer funding panel for the Haymarket People's Fund, the participatory foundation created by George Pillsbury and still running strong in Boston forty years later. He was also in the early stages of creating an ecosystem to advance the Solidarity Economy Fund in Boston; that ecosystem would become the Boston Ujima Project. Evans and Tanaka combined their backgrounds in activism and participation to design something new for the project: a democratic investment fund.

Designing the Ujima Fund

The flyer posed a question: "How can we capture the economic power of our communities to generate community-controlled wealth?" Posted on coffee shop cork boards and community centers around the neighborhood, the flyer invited those reading it to attend a learning initiative called the Boston Community Finance Working Group.

This was the first step in building the Ujima Fund. As was the case for the Disability Rights Fund, the journey from inception to first funding decision was a long one: five years of community meetings and iteration, starting with the question, "Who decides who decides?" But the result was a deep foundation of trust within the community.

The group was convened by City Life/Vida Urbana as well as two "new economy" organizations, Aaron Tanaka's Center for Economic Democracy and the Boston Impact Initiative, led by tech executive-turned-activist Deborah Frieze. Coordinated by CED fellow Xau Ying Ly, it met several times over the course of 2014. More than fifty people attended regularly, among them Boston-area organizers, activists, developers, funders, academics, small business owners, college students and community residents.

Phuong Luong, a solidarity member, was there for this early stage. At the time, she was living in Cambridge and working as a financial advisor to low-income families. "It was unlike anything I've ever gone to in Boston," she told us. "They were intentionally lifting up the voices of the people attending, not just the leadership. It was class-integrated. There were people in wheelchairs; there were old-lady anarchists."

The group decided to create a fund controlled entirely by residents—both current and displaced. After crowdsourcing $20,000 from more than one hundred eighty people, the Ujima Fund launched in 2018 with the mission to "make patient, collaborative sources of financing available to Boston's black, Indigenous and other communities of color, while enabling members of these communities to build assets as investors in their own economy."

Everything at Ujima is community-driven, from setting priorities to vetting investments. At the start of an investment cycle, the fund hosts "planning assemblies"—public events with food, music and childcare. The purpose was to get residents to share their desires for the development of the neighborhood, and build a pipeline of locally-owned businesses seeking investment.

Next, member-led committees screen those businesses on a series of collectively determined values, like how the business treats their workers and the affordability of their services. They also find out what kind of assistance the businesses might need: capital, legal advice, marketing or bookkeeping.

Finally, the businesses in the pipeline go to a member-led investment committee for vetting. "Like other funds, we're evaluating their financial history and projections, their plans for growth, and how that growth might increase their social and environmental impact," the fund's former manager, Lucas Turner-Owens, explained to us. The due diligence is boiled down into an investment opportunity report that is presented to voting members for their feedback or questions.

Once voting members see the report, they have a two-week period to ask questions directly to the business owners through the Ujima Investment Commons online portal. Following the close of that community-led due diligence period, a final report is issued with the recommendations and advice of Ujima's staff-appointed investment committee, made up of members with experience in small business lending, consulting and finance. With these two reports in hand (the investment opportunity report and the investment committee recommendation report), Ujima members then vote up or down the investment in question.

In December 2019, Ujima members undertook their first formal investment vote. The single business up for consideration was CERO (which stands for Cooperative Energy, Recycling, and Organics), a small composting startup based in the Boston neighborhood of Dorchester. After Massachusetts passed a composting requirement in 2014, CERO was an early mover, helping local businesses and farms collect and compost commercial food waste, diverting waste from landfills in the process.

They had built a steady customer base and were raising money to grow the business by hiring a full-time driver and buying a new truck. Residents who recommended CERO liked its business model, and they believed it had a clear path to scale in compost-crazy Massachusetts. But they also liked the way that CERO owner Josefina Luna, an immigrant from the Dominican Republic, had structured the business. CERO was designed as a worker-owned co-op, by activists in Aaron Tanaka's Boston Workers Alliance. Ninety percent of the worker-owners were people of color. Ultimately, any success for CERO would translate into financial success for its workers.

The vote took place on a weekend. A quorum of fifty percent (plus one) of Ujima's voting members is required, and the project needs to receive a majority vote of support. In the end, one hundred sixteen voting members cast a ballot in the final vote, and they overwhelmingly chose to give CERO a $100,000 loan. CERO used that money to hire a new full-time sales employee and a full-time driver, as well as buy a new truck.

Evans argued that by surfacing more voices, the Ujima Fund is coming to better decisions. "Because our process is more democratic, we're getting access to subject matter expertise and due diligence data that we wouldn't otherwise get. We ask residents, 'What needs are not being met in this neighborhood?', which investors don't typically ask."

Turner-Owens calls it a new type of market validation. "We're assessing the size of the need," he said. "If we hear from four hundred folks that there's a need for community-owned internet, or an organic grocery store, we have to believe that those residents will become paying customers of that service if we can provide it."

The Ujima Fund, like the Disability Rights Fund, is in a kind of perpetual beta mode. Evans and her team are constantly revisiting their assumptions, checking their assumptions and biases. For instance, they have to balance true engagement with what Turner-Owens calls "decision fatigue."

"Our vote for CERO happened alongside a lot of other things we were asking from our members," he told us. "We ask them so many questions, down to 'Which banks should we put our money in?' and 'Which products should we use in those banks?'—that particular one was a thirty-slide online poll. By the time we got to the CERO vote, I worried we had depleted goodwill. It has to be a balance."

Again like the Disability Rights Fund, Ujima's leadership has had to keep revisiting their assumptions about how to authentically involve a representative spectrum of the community. On one hand, they need to set expectations for non-voting solidarity members, who are often used to being in positions of authority. Turner-Owens reflected to us about the challenge of communicating to these members, who are mostly white, about their role in the process.

"We have to help them understand how to show up in solidarity and not expect to be in a position of authority," he said. "If someone who's done marketing campaigns for Nike shows up and says they want to help small businesses, we welcome them, but we also remind them that they'll have to be part of a larger team. We tell them, 'You'll be on a committee with residents, but you won't lead it. You're not just going to speak, you're also going to listen. It should be OK to not always be at the head of the table.'"

But the most important thing Ujima can do to authentically engage the community is to recruit more community members to participate. We met one Ujima member, Jordan Tavares, in a coffee shop in Roxbury, on what turned out to be the last weekend before the beginning of the COVID-19 pandemic lockdown. Tavares grew up in nearby Mattapan but moved away when the rent became unaffordable. ("Once you get a Whole Foods," he told us, "Things change.") He works for a nonprofit and mentors younger people in the neighborhood, but he's always been interested in real estate—and frustrated by the fact that "I can't invest in the community where I grew up."

Not long before we met Tavares, he was chatting with an Uber driver about his dreams of investing, and the driver told him about Ujima. Tavaras attended a meeting and became hooked; when we spoke with him, he was getting ready for his formal onboarding session with Nia Evans and others on the team.

"People who invest in this city might think they're doing a good thing," Tavares said. "But they're investing in the real estate—they're not investing in the people. Are you here for the community, or are you here to make a dollar? We need to get to the point where the people in the community own what's in it."

The Ujima Fund is part of a larger network of community-centered loan funds called Seed Commons. Other funds in the Seed Commons network also have participatory models; we'll talk more about them later in the book.

But before we get there, let's take a deeper look at Village Capital, the nonprofit we introduced in Chapter 4 that created a new model for democratizing investment in early-stage, impact-driven tech startups. It's been more than a decade since Village Capital first ran its peer-selected investment process in New Orleans in the wake of Hurricane Katrina. How has it turned out? We can answer that question by flying from Boston to Lagos, Nigeria.

From Silicon Valley to Silicon Savannah

It's a warm April day in Lagos, Nigeria. Fifteen people are sitting in a circle in a conference room, for a ceremony called "the hot seat". In the center is a Nigerian woman in her late twenties, Odunayo Eweniyi, known to her friends as Odun. She is getting ready to answer tough, incisive questions about the investability and social impact of her fintech startup, PiggyVest—with tens of thousands of dollars on the line.

Eweniyi needed $150,000 for her startup, and fast. She had launched PiggyVest a few months earlier with her friends Somto Ifezue and Joshua Chibueze, and it was taking off more quickly than expected. It started as a thought experiment and a bit of practice coding; the idea was to build an app to help millennials like Eweniyi's friends build a nest egg by stashing away a few dollars every day or every week. They'd shared the beta version of the app with friends on Facebook. Within two days, they had three hundred sign-ups. Now they were pushing two thousand, mostly thanks to word of mouth.

Eweniyi and her friends were operating on a shoestring budget, with no employees and a tiny office. With their user count steadily growing, they needed a license from the government to operate as a microfinance business. The license would cost $150,000, twenty-five times the average annual income in Nigeria.

Eweniyi had reached out to some investors to get the money for the license. But as a Nigerian-born fintech founder, she faced a tough statistical reality. A 2017 study found that more than ninety percent of funding for East African fintech startups went to expat entrepreneurs. Other data showed that traditional investors in Africa were less likely to back female founders.

But right now, Eweniyi wasn't pitching to traditional investors. In this hot seat session, part of a Village Capital startup accelerator, she was pitching to a cohort of other African fintech founders. And by the logic of the peer-selected investment model, those entrepreneurs would have the final say over whether or not she received investment.

But before we get too far into that story, let's look at how unusual this peer-selected process is, particularly on a continent where foreign venture capital investors have started to show up with their money and their biases.

The Danger of Digital Recolonization

In April 2019, the leaders of Jumia, an e-commerce company, rang the bell on the New York Stock Exchange to mark Jumia's initial public offering. It was a major moment; Jumia was the first billion-dollar company to come out of Africa. The unicorn was dubbed the "Amazon of Africa" and was generating hundreds of millions of dollars Jeff Bezos-style, selling everything from phones to blue jeans on a continent with a young population and growing purchasing power.

Headlines called Jumia "the first African IPO." But for many leaders in Africa's tech scene, that distinction rang false. The company's African co-founders had exited the company years earlier, and the Jumia leadership that showed up at the New York Stock Exchange primarily hailed from outside Africa. Issam Chleuh, a tech leader and accelerator founder based in Mali, summarized the situation in a widely shared op-ed. He wrote that the so-called first African IPO was actually "registered in Germany [and] founded by French entrepreneurs, who chose to base their engineering team in Portugal after claiming that there was no tech talent in Africa."

Chleuh was one of the African tech leaders who had painted a worrisome vision of the future that contrasted with the celebratory one in the news: a future in which Africa's tech scene is dominated by investors and players from outside the continent at the expense of native-born entrepreneurs. In his op-ed, he dubbed it *extractivism*. Others have called it *digital recolonization*.

Colonization is an open wound in Africa. When the African Union wrote its "Agenda 2063" in 2013, the vision was for an "integrated, prosperous and peaceful Africa, *driven by its own citizens*." The union had a reason to be so specific: After centuries of extraction and oppression for the benefit of European colonizers, Africans wanted control over their own destiny. If foreign investors ended up owning the continent's entrepreneurship ecosystem, it would be one more example of a valuable African resource controlled by forces outside the continent at the expense of those in it.

Traditional colonialism sputtered out in the early 1990s in most of Africa, with the fall of apartheid and the end of military control. But that was quickly replaced by an economic control that proved to be just as forceful and paternalistic. It has come to be known as neocolonialism: the practice of using capitalism, globalization and cultural imperialism to influence a developing country in the image of the West. Much has been written about how Western countries plunder billions of dollars each year from Africa's natural resources like minerals and natural gas. In the eyes of many critics, neocolonialism also shows up through the influence of international aid organizations like the World Bank and the United Nations. Many of these agencies were initially staffed with former officers of colonial agencies and, as we've discussed, they tend to set their agendas from the top down.

Digital recolonization is a legitimate fear, a version of neocolonialism playing out through the lens of impact investing. Indeed, by the time of the Jumia IPO, many impact investment committees consisted largely of white investors from California or France who were either staying in highly guarded hotels or living in Africa as expats. Some spoke Swahili or several other of the dozens of languages that are spoken on the continent, but many more spoke only English. They brought their culture, their values and their priorities.

They also brought a certain level of implicit racial bias. For instance, there was the troubling trend of "whitefronting," or hiring a white CEO for an African-founded company to appeal to foreign investors. Abdul-Karim Mohamed, an investor who manages Acumen's East Africa portfolio, did some digging to try to put a number to the problem. In 2018, he dove into the Global Impact Investing Network's annual database and pulled out two hundred eighty-six total transactions that occurred in sub-Saharan Africa the previous year. He broke down the deals by the race of the founding team.

Mohamed found some astonishing results. Out of those two hundred eighty-six deals, more than half went to companies that had *only* white founders. Overall, he estimates that white founders in Africa received funding at a rate eighty-seven times higher than their Silicon Valley peers. "In an effort to create Silicon Savannah and Yabacon Valley," Mohamed wrote in his analysis, "impact investors are fueling a system fraught with inequality, onto a continent that's not in need of more external meddling."

Exporting a Broken Model

In September 2016, Mark Zuckerberg, five years removed from his philanthropy experiment in Newark, showed up in Nairobi to survey the scene and give a speech at local startup incubator iHub about tech and innovation. Later that day, dressed in his trademark blue hoodie, he traveled across town for dinner with Kenya's Secretary of Information and Communications. They ate tilapia and ugali, a traditional Kenyan cornmeal dish, and talked about their shared goal to connect everyone in Kenya to the internet.

For many American and European venture capital investors like Zuckerberg, sub-Saharan Africa was an impact investing gold mine in the waiting. Despite deep-seated poverty, the continent has the highest rate of entrepreneurship in the world, in part because of its young and digitally literate population and in part because African leaders have invested heavily in tech hubs like iHub in Nairobi. There are five hundred incubators (co-working spaces) and accelerators (business training programs) like it across the continent.

The technorati in California and London loved to talk about the meritocracy inherent in their work, that anyone with an idea and some moxie could start a business. Why couldn't the same phenomenon be replicated across Africa, addressing the continent's challenges around healthcare and poverty while building jobs and local wealth in the process? To the investing community—particularly the mega-philanthropists who had built their careers in tech and taken to impact investing—this was nothing a little capital couldn't fix.

The only flaw with this plan? The Silicon Valley model that these leaders were exporting wasn't all that meritocratic to begin with.

When Zuckerberg visited Nairobi in 2016, tech and venture capital were still enjoying the tail end of a moment of glory in the public's eye—a "brief, balmy season" (to use a term from earlier in the book) when even former President Barack Obama openly pondered launching a VC firm in his final months in office. But the Silicon Valley dream was about to face reality. Around the time of Zuckerberg's trip, data began revealing that the vast majority of venture capital in Silicon Valley and other hot spots in the United States and Europe was flowing overwhelmingly to founders who were white, male and living in a small number of major cities.

Like so many up-by-your-bootstraps narratives, the myth of Silicon Valley meritocracy was a bit far-fetched. True, Larry Page and Sergey Brin started Google out of a trailer, and Mark Zuckerberg wrote the code for Facebook in his dorm room. But those trailers and dorm rooms were on elite campuses in Palo Alto and Boston, respectively. And those entrepreneurs benefited from backgrounds that were similar to the investors at venture capital firms. Just under half of VC investors in the United States attended either Harvard or Stanford. Eighty percent are male.

This lack of investor diversity was problematic enough in the United States, with its long history of institutional racism. (In a country that has hundreds of billion-dollar valuations, only thirty-four Black female founders have ever raised a million dollars for their startup.) When applied to Africa, the stakes were even higher. The entrance of white investors risked recreating the colonial power dynamics of not so long ago.

Flipping the Power Dynamics

This was the context in which Odun Eweniyi sat in front of her peer entrepreneurs during Village Capital's accelerator in Lagos. Sitting in the hot seat on the final day of the program, she wasn't sure if she would get selected for investment in the peer review process. But she was glad to be part of a startup funding model that flipped the traditional power dynamics of neocolonialism.

Three months before the hot seat, Eweniyi had flown to Ghana for the first meeting of the accelerator program. Rather than pitching to potential foreign investors, she was pitching to people who were just like her: founders of early-stage fintech startups in Africa focused on improving access to financial services. While not direct competitors, they had enough in common to understand the basics of each others' technology and customer base.

Over the course of several marathon sessions in the winter of 2017, the founders in the cohort spent more than one hundred hours getting to know each other, debating business models and acquisition strategies and offering frank advice. In January, they met in Accra, Ghana, where they spent four days presenting their business models and growth strategies in a conference center. In February, they met for another stretch in Nairobi, where they helped each other set milestones for growth.

"The month-long break was important, because you were able to internalize the feedback you got from the previous round," Eweniyi remembered. "We were able to really see whether the other entrepreneurs made progress and whether they had responded to constructive criticism."

On that final day of the program in March, the group gathered behind closed doors for the hot seat, where each entrepreneur took a turn getting peppered with tough questions posed by their peers. After the final member of the cohort had their turn in the seat, Eweniyi and the other founders retired to their rooms to put on their "investor hat" and rank each of their peers according to several criteria (entrepreneurs are not able to vote for themselves). When the final ranking was tabulated, Eweniyi's company PiggyVest came out on top. Along with a Kenyan startup, Olivine Technology, Eweniyi was guaranteed an offer of investment from VilCap Investments, Village Capital's affiliated venture fund.

A few months after the program, Eweniyi raised $1.1 million in seed funding from venture capital investors. With this funding, she and her partners were able to obtain that government license and further develop their product. The company has helped their more than one hundred eighty-five thousand users save more than $14 million.

Rethinking Ownership

The leaders of the Ujima Fund and Village Capital have something in common: Each organization sees itself as more than just a participatory investor. Rather, they are aiming for a wholesale reinvention of impact investing.

That means that each of them is running more than one experiment at any given time. Lucas Turner-Owens, the former manager at Ujima, has called the organization "R&D for the innovation economy" and told us how Ujima constantly tests out multiple process innovations beyond the democratic voting model. Village Capital also has a mandate to "reinvent the system" for investing in early-stage startups. When speaking to the leaders of each organization, it's clear that there's one type of process innovation that excites them both. It has to do with addressing the underlying root of the problem: wealth inequality.

This question of ownership gets back to the *who* of impact investing.

Rodney Foxworth, the CEO of Common Future, has written about the limitations of an impact investing ecosystem that, no matter how well intentioned, is still managed and owned by people by investors who tend to be wealthy, Western and white. "Is it not perverse," he wrote, "that Ivy League-educated white men from predominantly white male-dominated institutions are able to accrue wealth by investing in African American women entrepreneurs, while the majority of African American women are excluded from building wealth through impact investment vehicles?"

Ujima's model of community ownership is an intentional reaction to this problem. The Boston residents who vote on potential investments are not just deciders; they are also co-owners in the Ujima Fund. This is critical. Their wisdom is not just being sought; it's also being rewarded. When CERO and other future borrowers turn a profit, these residents will see part of the upside.

Ujima even takes this one step further with a clever financial tool: an "inverted capital stack." Usually, when a fund has multiple classes of investors, the class that puts the most money in—and is therefore perceived to have taken the most financial risk—accrues profits first. Ujima turns this perception on its head.

"We're redefining risk not simply in terms of absolute dollar amount of investment but in proportion of disposable capital put at risk," Nia Evans explained. "One hundred dollars for a working-class individual is a riskier investment than a $50,000 investment for a wealthy investor." When CERO pays back its loan, the capital stack will instead be paid out in an inverted manner. The local residents who invested the $50 minimum will get paid back first.

Village Capital, meanwhile, is also focused on building local wealth and ownership, a more recent development and natural evolution of its mission. For the first few years, the Village Capital team focused on honing their peer-selected investment model. But as they grew, they realized they didn't want to go it alone.

We spoke about this with Allie Burns, CEO of Village Capital. Burns is one of the few people who has experience with both sides of participatory funding: grantmaking *and* investing. She worked for years as an executive at the Case Foundation, the organization that ran the early-internet-era participatory grantmaking project Make It Your Own. Burns helped oversee follow-up projects like America's Giving Challenge (a precursor to Giving Tuesday) before moving over to Village Capital in 2017.

As CEO, Burns has prioritized reframing the organization around systems-level change. That means running more iterations of the peer-selected investment model, but also working as an intermediary that supports other, locally led-incubators, accelerators and seed funds.

"If we really want to democratize entrepreneurship at scale, we can't do it alone—and we shouldn't do it alone," Burns said. "In every single accelerator we've run, whether we were in New Orleans or in Nairobi, we've found ourselves partnering with local incubators and accelerators," Burns noted. "They have always been our most helpful partners, connecting us to the right people and providing regional context; they also continued the work on the ground after we left."

But these local hubs are consistently underappreciated, under-supported and underfunded. That's because most of these startup supporters are essentially startups themselves. "For a few years after the financial crisis, we saw a lot of corporate, foundation and government funding going into locally led tech hubs," Burns said. "Then funders moved on to the next new thing. Now, a lot of those organizations have been left hanging out to dry. They're still doing vital work, but they're often struggling to keep their doors open."

Over the past few years, Village Capital has started directly supporting these locally led incubators and accelerators. They've licensed the peer-selected investment model for free to dozens of tech hubs around the world, including several in Africa. One of those hubs is Suguba, the West Africa startup accelerator run by Issam Chleuh, the vocal critic of digital recolonization. Village Capital has also started running capacity-development programs for accelerators like Suguba to help them tap into best practices from their peers and learn to speak the language of corporate and foundation donors.

In the United States, where venture capital continues to flow mostly to white entrepreneurs, Burns is focused on supporting incubators and accelerators that back entrepreneurs of color, as well as those based in regions outside the typical VC hotbeds of New York, Boston and Silicon Valley. During the pandemic, Village Capital partnered with the Travelers Foundation to provide unrestricted grants to several such hubs across the country—including WePower, an accelerator in St. Louis, Missouri, that supports Black and Latinx founders creating living-wage jobs.

From Boston to Nairobi and beyond, community-led models for investing are pioneering a new way to build wealth. Just like participatory grantmaking has done around the world, experiments that flip power dynamics or rewrite the rules of traditional finance are generating interest and excitement. They are also starting to show good results.

Will participatory funding scale? Even with the positive showing to date, the obstacles remain. It isn't fast. Coordinating with lots of people on equal footing is challenging. The mindset shift required will be easier for some people than for others. Can we imagine a world where participation is baked into foundation board rooms? Where impact investors shout each other down on panels with boasts about who cedes the most control? And if so, how? And what can readers of this book do? That's what we'll explore in the following chapters.

PART THREE

7

SCALING PARTICIPATORY GRANTMAKING

It was a cloudy but warm October evening in 2018 on a rooftop in Mexico City's Roma Norte neighborhood. The fifteen people gathered on the roof were some of participatory grantmaking's biggest advocates. They were there because they had seen firsthand that participatory grantmaking *worked*. And it was time to spread the gospel.

Diana Samarasan was on the roof to represent the Disability Rights Fund, which had just made its eightieth grant and was now operating in thirty-four countries, up from an original six. The fund had made significant progress on building their movement. When DRF launched, only a handful of countries had ratified the UN's disability rights treaty. But by 2018, more than one hundred and seventy countries had ratified it, and dozens of those victories tied directly back to activists funded by DRF.

Katy Love was there too, representing the Wikimedia Foundation. She had tested participatory grantmaking on a larger scale, running an entirely open-sourced model with an annual grantmaking budget of more than $7 million. By 2018, her grantmaking team supported the growth of knowledge content and communities through more than two hundred grants in eighty countries, working directly with hundreds of community leaders. Even at such a large scale, the participatory grantmaking model still worked.

Mutisya Leonard was there, representing UHAI EASHRI. The fund was a contemporary of the Disability Rights Fund that focused on the rights of sex workers and LGBTQ+ people in East African countries like Kenya and Rwanda. They had run more than a dozen rounds of their participatory grantmaking process and had already established a strong and interconnected movement for social justice in a particular part of the world.

The group was gathered in Mexico City to celebrate the release of a new guide, *Deciding Together: Shifting Power and Resources Through Participatory Grantmaking*. The guide was written by Cynthia Gibson, the mind behind the Case Foundation's Make It Your Own program and an earlier Ford Foundation-sponsored report on participatory grant-making, and edited by Jen Bokoff, a grant manager at a hub for grant-makers called Candid. *Deciding Together* was a treasure trove of information on the what, how and why of participatory grantmaking. It was going to be unveiled to the public the following day at the annual Human Rights Funders Network conference taking place down the street.

As speeches were delivered in between bites of churros and mole, it became clear that there was one thought on all the speakers' minds: *More people should be doing this*. More major foundations. More individual donors. More family offices. The idea needed to scale up and become mainstream, perhaps even to the level Edgar Villanueva envisioned in *Decolonizing Wealth*: a future where at least half of the people who make decisions about grantmaking have authentic knowledge of the issues and the communities involved. That would require a massive shift of power in the field of philanthropy.

The vision might have been ambitious, but it wasn't outlandish. Philanthropy is constantly evolving, swayed by industry trends and external forces. "Philanthropy is as much an *object* as an *agent* of historical change," writes historian Benjamin Soskis, "a product of the broader political, economic, and social context in which philanthropy operates."

Of course, many of the changes in the past two decades trended toward centralization and concentration. But by the time the advocates gathered in 2018, the pendulum was starting to swing in the other direction. Some of the pressure was external, stemming from rising awareness of racial inequality and loud critics like Villanueva and Anand Giridharadas. But there was plenty of motivation coming from inside philanthropy as well. A survey released around the same time as the Mexico City event found that only seventeen percent of foundation CEOs believed that philanthropy was "making a significant difference in society."

It might be instructive to look at the last time philanthropy was at a turning point. We shared the story of the Funding Exchange, the network of trust funders like George Pillsbury who launched participatory funds in the 1970s and '80s focused on social justice. The young pioneers of the Funding Exchange were initially ridiculed by the older philanthro-py establishment as "fat kittens" who would "soon grow bored." Pillsbury, who was mostly known for his family's baking business, was derided behind closed doors as a "flaky flour child." But by the mid-'70s, Pillsbury and his friends were advocating for their peers and parents to come around to their way of grantmaking. "It was important to make our voices heard," said Obie Benz, who founded one of the original FEX funds. "It was our responsibility to try to influence the larger, wealthier founda-tions."

That meant going to events outside their comfort zone—for instance, the annual meeting of the establishment Council on Foundations, which Benz recalled as "mostly men in suits." At the 1975 conference, one FEX leader sparked controversy when he asked the audience to rethink "how power is distributed in our society, how it is achieved and maintained, and for whose benefit it is used." Two years later, Pillsbury and other FEX leaders landed a spot on the "Phil Donahue Show" to promote their new guide for donors, *Robin Hood Was Right*. "Suddenly, we had more credibility," Pillsbury recalled.

What happened next? Recall that the FEX had a vision to change two things about philanthropy—*what* was funded, and *how* funding decisions were made. On the first pillar, FEX was remarkably successful. FEX leaders are widely credited with getting philanthropy to focus more on social justice. They played a role in the creation of the Ms. Foundation for Women, the National Committee for Responsive Philanthropy, the Tides Foundation and some of the first funders for LGBTQ+ rights. These organizations have had a lasting effect on philanthropy in the United States, bringing money and attention to organizers and activists.

On the second pillar, participatory grantmaking, FEX had more limited success. In the 1970s FEX leaders or allies launched a dozen new participatory funds in cities across the United States. But they had trouble convincing the old guard—the large, institutional foundations with a long history of doing things their own way. The idea of shifting power remained niche, never truly *transforming* philanthropy. There were a few experimental participatory programs by old guard foundations in the 1980s and '90s, but this momentum was wiped out as the cultural pendulum swung back toward market-based approaches.

Decades later, on the roof in Mexico City, the group was very aware of this potential fate. And they were determined to make sure that this time around, participatory grantmaking would stick. As FundAction's Rose Longhurst recalled, "There was a real sense that something was happening. This was the start of something."

The day after the rooftop party, Bokoff led a half-day workshop, called the "Institute on Participatory Grantmaking," for sixty-eight philanthropy practitioners from around the globe—a number that exceeded their expectations. Many of the attendees came from the very foundations that would need to be receptive of the idea of participatory grantmaking was going to scale.

Institutional Foundations

Ford. MacArthur. Open Society. These are the foundations with household-name recognition, even among non-philanthropists; those in the field usually have an opinion about them. The Bridgespan Group defines these institutions as "independent foundations where the original donor is no longer alive, or, if the donor is living, where there is substantial staff and other infrastructure to manage the giving."

Though institutional foundations represent a small corner of philanthropy, their influence extends well beyond their size. When the Ford Foundation does something interesting, the *New York Times* will cover it. This is true even as the field becomes more crowded with billionaire philanthropists. In 1993, the top ten foundations accounted for fifteen percent of foundation giving; by 2014, they accounted for only four percent. But they're still pacesetters for the larger field.

These foundations, often by design, are more bureaucratic and deliberative. They tend to have longer time horizons for their grantmaking visions, which means they're slower to respond to trends. Nancy Roob, CEO of the poverty-focused foundation Blue Meridian Partners, told researchers, "The fundamental structures and operating models of foundations haven't changed much over the last several decades. This is largely due to the combination of no outside force requiring them to change and few variations on the basic operating model to inspire innovation."

They can also be skeptical of major structural innovations, including participatory grantmaking. They demand hard data before changing the way they do things. In 2015, the Ford Foundation's Chris Cardona articulated this skepticism about participatory grantmaking, telling an Inside Philanthropy journalist, "I think it's a question for the field—how well it works, how applicable it is in larger national and international foundations. I don't think, from what I've heard from the field, we have a good sense of what the answer to that is. Some hypotheses, some hunches."

Part of the concern stems from failed attempts in the past. In the 1990s, the Open Society Institute, founded by George Soros and later renamed Open Society Foundations, tested out a participatory process that involved appointing a board of grassroots leaders in the southern United States to vet and approve grants. Gara LaMarche, who at the time served as vice president and director of US programs for the foundation, later wrote, "It quickly posed some difficult issues. Would those making the grant decisions be excluded from applying for funds, to avoid conflicts of interest? What influence would they have on Soros's thinking about how much money to spend, since the amount he was willing to experiment with was quite unequal to the scale of the change effort?" The program eventually closed down.

Gibson and Bokoff wrote the *Deciding Together* guide to address these concerns head on. They acknowledge up front that participatory grantmaking is difficult. "It's like any collaborative process," Gibson told us. "It's full of minefields, difficulties and challenges." But they go on to show that fifty years of experimentation have led to some clear best practices.

Regarding conflicts of interest, they quote Moukhtar Kocache from Rawa, who challenges the assumption that having a vested interest in a decision is a bad thing: "We've been so traumatized in philanthropy to develop artificial methods of transparency and accountability... But doesn't that castrate the personal and social capital that can be really important in making decisions?" On the topic of time and resources, they quote Mutisya Leonard, who speaks about his experience with UHAI EASHRI. "Yes, it can be expensive to consult with and involve people in decision-making," he says. "But... we've seen that our process builds more trust among peers. Where does that fit in the usual cost-benefit analysis?"

Still, advocates of participatory grantmaking know that the real roadblock to participatory grantmaking doesn't have to do with these solvable problems. It has to do with grantmakers' *mindsets*: the will to challenge their fundamental perceptions about what their jobs should be.

Hannah Paterson, a grantmaker who is one of the leading experts on participatory practices, has written extensively on this topic from a place of personal experience. "Participatory methods can feel like a threat to our professional expertise," she said. "What are funders here for if they aren't here to make decisions about funding or strategy? Is our role null and void? This self-preservation is an obvious and fair enough reaction—we want to cling on to our jobs."

This existential fear is real; and it's part of the reason it's so encouraging to see the major foundations that have begun experimenting with participatory funding.

Piloting Participation

In August 2019, the John D. and Catherine T. MacArthur Foundation relaunched its arts portfolio for the city of Chicago, changing both the program's name and its process for distributing grants.

With its $7 billion endowment, the MacArthur Foundation is one of the largest foundations in the world. Though the foundation gives grants globally, it has always had a strong focus on its home turf of Chicago, and the city's thriving arts scene. But for years, grants tended to go to symphonies and museums. In 2017, a map of the program's direct grantmaking portfolio showed that almost none of the grantees were based in the low-income or diverse neighborhoods that made up much of Chicago.

Cate A. Fox, a senior program officer at MacArthur, wrote in 2019 that the foundation knew they needed to change. Their grantmaking criteria "had the unintended consequence of excluding significant parts of the city's population and a variety of art forms and genres that contribute to the richness of the cultural sector," she said. "Moreover, our well-intentioned program may have helped to perpetuate the structural racism that exists in the arts sector and society as a whole."

Inspired by the *Deciding Together* guide, MacArthur designed and led a deliberative process to find a solution. The foundation eventually landed on a model involving a panel of five to twelve community stakeholders that recommends slates of grant recipients for consideration to the foundation's board. According to program officer Geoffrey Banks, the model ultimately changed the day-to-day role of staff. "As we expected from conversations with other funders, our role as program officers shifted to providing guidance, support and information to the panelists so they could make informed decisions," he noted. In early 2021, MacArthur president John Palfrey cited the success of the participatory arts program as the reason that the foundation was creating a community advisory board to guide a new $125 million fund.

Across the Atlantic Ocean, another major foundation was piloting participatory grantmaking: the London-based National Lottery Community Fund, which distributes money raised by the United Kingdom's lottery. It's one of the largest foundations in the United Kingdom, awarding about £600 million a year.

NCLF is chartered by the UK Parliament, so it has a long-standing commitment (and legal obligation) to public accountability. In 2015, as part of a new strategic framework called Putting People in the Lead, NCLF committed to pilot a small participatory fund called the Leaders with Lived Experience Programme, championed by Derek Bardowell, then the fund's UK portfolio lead, and run by participatory grantmaking leader Hannah Paterson.

Along with her NCLF colleague Conor Cross and Knowledge Equity Initiative founder Baljeet Sandhu, Paterson began with a series of public workshops in five working-class cities across the United Kingdom. Following a fund design retreat with lived experience leaders facilitated by activist Nusrat Faizullah, the group coalesced around a community advisory board model: local boards made up of people with lived experience and NLCF staff would decide on grants of £20,000 and £50,000. The first twenty grant recommendations were sent to the foundation's leadership to check for legal concerns tied to their quasi-public status, but they all ultimately received the green light.

After the pilot ended, Paterson brought the results to NCLF's new UK portfolio lead, who was supportive of a continued expansion because of the groundswell of excitement the pilot's grantees had generated. In August 2020, the foundation announced an expansion of their participatory grantmaking. They launched the Phoenix Fund, a £1.4 million grantmaking vehicle to support Black communities in the UK. The fund is a partnership with the Global Fund for Children as well as a national coalition of Black leaders in philanthropy, including Paterson's colleague Shane Ryan and Ubele initiative founder Yvonne Field.

Mama Cash: Going All In

Mama Cash is the oldest international women's fund in the world, and they've always paved their own unique path. They were founded in 1983 in the Netherlands by five feminist activists who saw that traditional grantmakers were failing to support women's issues. The fund's name is a riff on the alter ego of "Mama Cass" Elliot, a singer with the Mamas and the Papas.

The fund has become a powerhouse in feminist philanthropy, distributing nearly €60 million to more than six thousand women's, girls', trans and intersex nonprofits around the world. Name a successful advance for women's rights in the past three decades, and it's likely that Mama Cash was an early funder.

When the fund first began, there were no paid staff, so activists were the ones making funding decisions. But as the fund grew and professionalized, staff started making more decisions about grants, and the activists gradually transitioned into a more advisory role. Coco Jervis, Mama Cash's Grants Director, told us that this was largely a result of donor expectations and the restrictions and earmarks that came with them.

"There's not necessarily a huge pool of institutions and governments willing to fund feminist funds," she said. "So we've tried to be transparent about our grants, but we have not necessarily been participatory."

That started to change about a decade ago, in what Jervis called a "return to our roots." When the Red Umbrella Fund launched in 2012, Mama Cash incubated the small organization. Shortly after that, buoyed by their positive experience with participatory grantmaking, Mama Cash joined the donor collaborative With and For Girls Collective. In 2017, Mama Cash decided to pilot two small participatory funds of its own, including the Solidarity Fund, a meta-fund governed by the leaders of small women's funds around the world.

In 2019, Mama Cash's leaders had an internal discussion. The pilots had gone well. What was next? They made a decision to go all in—to transition Mama Cash's entire $4 million yearly grantmaking process to a participatory model.

Jervis knew this transition wouldn't happen overnight and needed to model a shift in power. "We wanted to ensure that the process wasn't completely extractive," she told us. Jervis and her team spoke with more than a dozen other participatory grantmakers, including their fellow members of the With and For Girls Collective and the Wikimedia Foundation's Katy Love. They also interviewed dozens of long-term grantees, and in an effort to be transparent, they shared those interviews with their full community. In total, the process to design the model took more than eighteen months.

They landed on a two-step model that synthesizes best practices from several different participatory grantmakers. Mama Cash staff will screen applicants to ensure that they are eligible but otherwise will take a hands-off approach. Instead, eligible grant applicants will provide input and guidance on which issues to prioritize in a given year, and also will lead the process of whittling down an average of 1,200 applicants a year to recommend one hundred to receive funding. Final funding decisions are made by a committee reflective of the community the grants intend to serve. In June 2020, Mama Cash began making this transition internally. By January 2021, all of its funds were set to be disbursed through participatory grantmaking.

For Jervis, the process has been as much a mindset shift as it was a shift in process. "The hardest thing we've had to do internally is to reorganize ourselves in order to learn how to share power," she said. "It's an evolving process."

Once the move is complete, Mama Cash will not only be the oldest international women's fund in the world. It will also be its largest fully participatory grantmaker.

Individual Donors

In July 2020, philanthropist MacKenzie Scott made a surprising announcement: She was giving away more than $1 billion dollars. What made her gift remarkable wasn't the dollar amount; Scott is part of the billionaire philanthropy class that includes Jeff Bezos, her ex-husband. Rather, her announcement made waves because of *how* she planned to give the money away.

Instead of staffing up a brand-name foundation, she chose to give the money away directly. She convened a group of nonprofit leaders "with key representation from historically marginalized race, gender and sexual identity groups" to identify organizations working on progressive causes. Among her first one hundred sixteen grantees was the International Trans Fund, where a peer panel of young trans people from places as far-flung as Russia, Singapore and Brazil will distribute her donation to trans rights activists around the world.

Individual donors are those who "give while they live" but choose not to set up a traditional foundation. This has become far more common in recent years. Remember that the Giving Pledge now has one hundred eighty signers, representing a total of $1 trillion in assets, and is still growing. That's already higher than the entire size ($890 billion) of the United States foundation market. If institutional foundations are deliberately bureaucratic, individual donors can pretty much do whatever they want with their money. The Bridgespan Group describes today's mega-donors as "willing to experiment" and bringing an "innovative orientation to their philanthropy."

When you look at examples of individual donors ceding control over grant decisions, it often takes the form of direct donations to participatory funds (like Scott's donation to the International Trans Fund). Another common tool is donor collaboratives. The Native Voices Rising fund, a grantmaking collaborative led by Common Counsel, includes more than forty individual donors, some contributing as little as $1,000. The fund gives decision-making power to a group of twenty-five Native leaders.

Over the past few years, numerous interesting vehicles have emerged to enable these donors to give up control. One vehicle is donor-advised funds, or DAFs, a hot-button issue in philanthropy. Think of a DAF as a one-person foundation. Donors set up a fund with a nonprofit sponsor, often a community foundation, with money that is treated by the IRS as one big tax-deductible charitable donation. Over time, a percentage is paid out as grants to wherever the donor "advises." The percentage of philanthropic dollars managed by DAFs has tripled in the past decade; there are now half a million individual DAFs in the US, representing $100 billion in assets.

Critics are quick to deride DAFs as tax shelters, and it's a fair point. Unlike foundations, DAFs don't have a required minimum five percent annual payout, so they can be used as a way to hoard money without paying taxes. But reformers see an opportunity to use DAFs as a tool to decentralize decision-making power.

RSF Social Finance is one of them. RSF, a nonprofit based in San Francisco, has been offering DAFs for thirty years. For the past decade, RSF has been practicing participatory grantmaking, using a closed collective model called shared gifting. It has also begun offering ways for donors to set up their DAFs in a more thoughtful way. For instance, their "flow funding" model, based on an idea originally created by Rockefeller descendant Marion Rockefeller Weber, lets a donor choose a cause close to their heart and invite leaders with lived experience to distribute funding around the issue.

Over the past few years, RSF's head of philanthropy, Kelley Buhles, noticed that donors, inspired by the shared gifting circles, wanted to take it even further—they wanted to relinquish complete control. "Our donors started asking us: How can we give communities ongoing control over funding decisions?" Buhles recalled.

In 2020, RSF Social Finance rolled out a new model for donors called "community-led funding." The model puts community leaders in the donor's interest area fully in charge. Donors provide ongoing financial support, and community leaders have sustained autonomy over how the funds are distributed.

"Ten years ago, the people talking about investing their DAF for impact were considered radical, and now that's getting normalized," said Buhles. "We could be on the same path with participatory grantmaking."

For individual donors, there's one more creative option for giving money away more authentically and effectively: participatory trust funds.

It's tempting to think of the history of LGBTQ+ activism in the United States as a steady wave of progress, but activists on the ground know it's more complicated than that.

Some of the highest-profile advocates in the fight for marriage equality, like the Washington, DC-based Human Rights Campaign (HRC), have been criticized over the years for advancing a narrow agenda that aligns with the priorities of their wealthy, often white and often cisgender donors. In 2011, the same year that Barack Obama announced he had "evolved" on marriage equality, a group of trans activists made the news when they publicly criticized HRC's $50 million budget and accused the organization of "eagerly [selling] trans people up the river."

Around this time, Karen Pittelman was working as a volunteer for the Sylvia Rivera Law Project in New York City, a small nonprofit that serves low-income or people of color who are transgender, intersex and/or gender nonconforming. She saw how hard it was for the organization to compete for fundraising with behemoths like HRC. "A lot of the funding was going to these larger LGBT organizations that might have one program for trans rights," she recalled.

Pittelman had recently come into a large inheritance that she was intent on giving away. She teamed up with Gabriel Foster, a transgender activist, to launch a new participatory fund: the Trans Justice Funding Project. They set out to build a legal structure that would allow them to directly fund activists easily and with as few strings attached as possible.

Ultimately, they incorporated the fund as a noncharitable trust. It was an uncommon choice, but it worked for their goals. Traditional foundations are often incapable of reaching many activist groups that might be operating without 501(c)(3) status—many small activist groups rely on nothing more formal than PayPal transfers from friends and family. Grants from noncharitable trusts have less onerous reporting requirements for both the donor and the grantee, making it an effective option for directly supporting smaller and unincorporated groups without raising red flags at the IRS.

Pittelman tells us that the noncharitable trust model also allows her to give in a way that is more authentic. She doesn't like that philanthropy puts activists in a position where, by taking money, they have to implicitly endorse an extractive capitalist system. Grassroots activists also have legitimate fears of being co-opted by large funders or being trotted out for "reputation laundering." The noncharitable trust model mitigates some of this risk by precluding donors from getting a tax deduction for their giving.

Though Pittelman rightly points out that "just because you are not getting a tax deduction for your donation doesn't mean you can't do lots of other messed-up stuff," it's also true that donors to TJFP get nothing from their donation except the knowledge that they are funding activists on the ground.

Convincing the Field

Let's go back to that roof in Mexico City. Over the next three years, the grantmakers on that roof took on a role that was usually held by people on the other side of the funding table: that of reformers and activists. They've been working with growing intensity, numbers and coordination to convince their peers in the field of philanthropy to shift power.

To start, they're making the case in venues that philanthropists frequent. That means speaking about participatory grantmaking at mainstream philanthropy conferences—surfacing hard conversations about structural change at a moment when foundation leaders are talking openly about diversity, equity and inclusion. (In 2020, the Rawa Fund's Moukhtar Kocache spoke on panels about power sharing at major global philanthropy conferences like WingsForum and the Salzburg Global Seminar.) It also means speaking to more progressive philanthropy audiences, like those at the Human Rights Funders Network or the EDGE Funders Alliance.

They are arguing their case in print. As the coronavirus pandemic spread across America, the influential *Chronicle of Philanthropy* published an op-ed encouraging grantmakers to loosen restrictions on funding. Diana Samarasan and Katy Love responded with a strongly worded letter to the editor challenging funders to "go further" and ask, "Who is sitting at funder decision-making tables?" The letter also included a challenge for funders to self-reflect: "Why does it take a crisis for funders… to reconsider how funding is done?"

Finally, they are investing in research to build their case—finding the data to convince the most skeptical funders. Chris Cardona, the program officer for philanthropy at the Ford Foundation, is responsible for giving grants to research and advocacy that will make philanthropy more equitable and effective. In 2019, Cardona signed off on a $300,000 grant to fund research projects that could "help make the case and build a body of evidence for participatory approaches." Cardona's goal is to provide an answer to the first question that any strategic philanthropist would ask: Does participatory grantmaking lead to better, stronger philanthropic outcomes?

The grants will cover a broad range of research topics, including case studies, toolkits and ecosystem maps. The Haymarket People's Fund and Disability Rights Fund both received grants to document what's worked—and what hasn't—over the past decade. The Women's Funding Network received a grant to map participatory practices among one hundred women's funds. Cardona was praised for creating a "steering committee" of advocates from outside the Ford Foundation to decide how to spend the $300,000, embedding some participation in the research itself.

From Fringe to Mainstream

Mainstreaming participatory grantmaking will be an uphill battle.

One challenge will be the splintered nature of modern philanthropy. Thirty years ago, when Funding Exchange leaders were advocating for participatory grantmaking, they were able to reach a solid chunk of the philanthropic community just by attending Council on Foundations meetings. But that's changed; there are now more than 250,000 foundations around the world. And they represent multiple subcultures. Inside Philanthropy's David Callahan has noted "We can no longer speak of a single philanthropy 'establishment'...who govern access and influence." Instead, philanthropy now has regional personalities: ecosystems centered on "legacy foundations" and the types of people who run them.

Each of these ecosystems will respond to different arguments about the value of participation. New York philanthropy is very influenced by the finance industry; the biggest givers are old school industrial titans or hedge fund managers. So they will likely respond best to data and research that shows that participatory funding is money well spent. Meanwhile, the Bay Area crowd is very tech-centric; they might respond best to the language of disruption and human-centered design. In London, the defining social justice issues that animate philanthropists are tied to ethnicity and class, and this framing has been used effectively for regional campaigns like #ShiftThePower.

Another concern is that participatory grantmaking will be framed only as a tool to make philanthropy more effective—rather than as an ethos that demands philanthropists let go of power. This is partly a question of messaging. On a recent call with participatory grantmaking activists, Moukhtar Kocache argued that "We need to anchor the work that we're doing away from technicalities and into larger concepts of political philosophy: colonialism, reparations, feminism. If we just focus on the nitty gritty stuff, and don't align our work with larger political frameworks, then we're constantly going to be defending the little things, and we'll only be given a perfunctory space."

Perhaps the biggest concern among the participatory grantmaking activists who gathered on that roof in Mexico City is that it will remain a fad. As Inside Philanthropy's Tate Williams wrote in a 2018 article, "There is a danger that the powerful concept underlying participatory grantmaking could get lost amid partial measures. That it will become a new buzzword that appears in strategic plans, but is rarely truly implemented."

The other possible outcome is the opposite: participatory grantmaking fundamentally changes philanthropy. "When we typically talk about mainstreaming, we talk about bringing practices on the fringe into the field. With participatory grantmaking, is that the goal?" Jen Bokoff asked us. "Or does mainstreaming mean that philanthropy starts shifting to inclusive practices like this—where the way that foundations operate now is considered fringe?"

8

THE IMPACT INVESTING RESET

Most years, the annual Social Capital Markets conference (SOCAP for short) is held in San Francisco, on a wharf in Golden Gate National Park overlooking Alcatraz Island.

It's a fitting location—adjacent to the city's venture capital scene, but somewhat off to the side. The investors who gather at SOCAP are interested in "increasing the flow of capital toward social good," and the conference organizers have done as much as anyone to build the brand of impact investing from a catchphrase in 2008 to a $500 billion industry today.

Conferences like SOCAP's are important because the field of impact investing is in a constant state of conversation with itself. The first few years of the conversation were about quantifying the *value* of impact investing, building the case that investors should shift their resources to businesses that offered both a social and financial return. The next few years were about measuring impact, determining the best way that value could be quantified.

Then came 2020. SOCAP's conference was held online for the first time ever, and every conversation inevitably circled back to the triple crises engulfing the world: the coronavirus pandemic, climate change and a global reckoning with racial inequality. The moment seemed to mark the beginning of a new cycle in the impact investing meta-conversation: a debate about power.

One of the virtual panels that addressed this topic head on was led by Jed Emerson, an icon of the impact investing old guard. Emerson coined the term "blended value" in 2000 and wrote the influential book *The Purpose of Capital: Elements of Impact, Financial Flows, and Natural Being.* The topic of the panel was appropriately meta ("The State of the State of Impact Investing"). Emerson was joined by investors of color, like Dr. Gillian Marcelle of Resilience Capital Ventures and Common Future's Rodney Foxworth, who made the case that the moment demanded a shift in who makes investment decisions.

Emerson agreed, but he wondered aloud what it would take to actually see these structural reforms. "If we are really serious about shifting who's in the room when decisions are made...these changes are not going to be comfortable," he said. "I'm not convinced that people [in the impact investing industry today] are really willing to do that."

This is the challenge facing advocates of participatory investing: Many investors have never heard of it, and those who have inevitably ask a lot of questions. Isn't it time-intensive and resource-intensive to set up a deliberative process? What about fiduciary duty—does offloading decisions to people without traditional financial expertise create a legal liability? And how do you actually go about designing a participatory fund or transitioning to a participatory process?

This question of *how* is probably the biggest thing holding back participatory investing. We spoke with one investor who launched a place-based impact fund in 2016 and generally supported the idea of ceding decision-making power. But he told us that when he launched the fund, he had heard of the concept of community boards but never considered building one out because he didn't know where to start. "I have a small team," he said. "It was more of an operational and structural challenge than a philosophical one."

Although there is not yet an impact investing equivalent to the *Decid-*

ing Together report—or the tight-knit group of grantmakers who met on the roof in Mexico City—there is a small but growing community of practice around participatory investing. One of the hubs for this community is Transform Finance, a nonprofit founded in 2013 by Morgan Simon and Andrea Armeni.

Simon is well-known in the social sector as a leading advocate for social justice investing; in addition to Transform Finance, she has also launched the Responsible Endowments Coalition, the Toniic network for impact investors, and Candide Group, which we'll discuss later in the chapter. Armeni, a former lawyer, calls Transform Finance a "translator" between activists and investors, an "on-ramp for organizers to people in positions of power." The organization's projects include a boot camp for social justice activists on strategies for influencing capital, as well as the Transform Finance Investor Network, a community of practice for asset owners and managers interested in non-extractive practices. The community now represents more than $2 billion in capital.

In 2019, Transform Finance launched the Capital and Equitable Communities Project, a first-of-its-kind initiative to create a formal taxonomy for participatory investing strategies. Led by an advisory board that includes leaders from RSF Social Finance, Boston Ujima Fund and others, its initial goal is to build a field guide for fund managers, sharing case studies and governance structures for participatory funds.

"We want to make the case for community-engaged processes around capital deployment," Armeni told us. "That means substantiating the hypothesis that such processes lead to positive outcomes by aligning the goals of both capital deployers and communities—all while creating agency, power and knowledge for the community stakeholders."

Scaling participatory investing will mean three things: growing the participatory funds that are already out there, designing new funds and encouraging old-guard investors and foundations to incorporate outside voices into their investing process. Let's look at a few recent examples of each.

Growing Ujima

One major challenge for place-based impact investing is that it tends to scale to the size of institutional finance, rather than the size of the community. That's not always for the best.

Lucas Turner-Owens, the former manager of the Ujima Fund, told us that he used to get asked all the time about scale. If Ujima was offered a $5 million investment, would the fund take it? His response was that they would have to turn it down. Growing too big, too fast would defeat the purpose of the community-driven model by diluting the percentage owned by community members. Though Ujima members are the only ones who can vote on investments, members own roughly half of the fund's shares; an injection of $5 million from a single investor would lower that stake to just eight percent and would limit participation from smaller investors.

This is a common conundrum for neighborhood-based loan funds. Most mainstream investors are looking to make that kind of sizable investment. Thanks to economic concentration, the average size of a first-time fund recently rose to a record high of $42 million. For the managers of these large funds, it simply makes mathematical sense to invest in a small number of large bets rather than in many smaller ones. That's because the cost to conduct due diligence for a $50,000 investment—the kind that Ujima would ask for—is roughly the same as the cost of due diligence for a $5 million project.

Seed Commons is working to address that problem with a creative solution called risk pooling. Recall that Seed Commons is a network of two dozen locally rooted loan funds across the United States. Each of the funds lends to a marginalized community and operates under the principles of non-extractive finance. The network includes several funds that engage in participatory investing in one way or another, from the

Ujima Fund to the Southern Reparations Loan Fund, which is led by and lends to Black and immigrant communities in Appalachia.

Seed Commons founder Brendan Martin told us that the nonprofit acts as a bridge between large investors and small community loan funds. Sure, Ujima cannot accept that hypothetical $5 million investment, but Seed Commons can, and they can divvy it up equitably among the Ujima Fund and its cousins around the country.

They do this through a vehicle that pools investments to several different locally rooted funds at once. As Martin told us, "When you go to market as a $1 million loan fund, you have to find the most sweet, benevolent impact investor who'll say, 'You guys are tiny, it's not even worth the transaction costs for me put money in, but I'll do it because I'm nice.' But if you go to market with one hundred of those $1 million funds, then it becomes a lot more reasonable."

Designing New Funds

Thousand Currents has always been grassroots-driven. The foundation was created in the 1980s by a group of returned Peace Corps volunteers who had seen the failure of the top-down model of international aid firsthand. They banded together to create a foundation that would partner with on-the-ground community leaders, including smallholder farmers and Indigenous leaders, to build economic self-sufficiency in the Global South.

In 2014, Thousand Currents' leaders realized that many of the organizations they partnered with needed loans to succeed, not just grants. But they also recognized that the traditional models that most impact investors used for lending to the Global South were extractive. They set out to create an investment fund from scratch that would challenge the power dynamics and norms of impact investing: a resource for grassroots groups working to create economic initiatives that challenge mainstream paradigms and that prioritize *buen vivir*, or wellbeing. That became the name of their new fund.

In building the Buen Vivir Fund, they used the same principles of co-design as the Disability Rights Fund, Ujima and so many others. It took a while: two thousand, nine hundred thirty-four hours to be exact, divided among eighty-one people from six countries over twelve months. Gaithiri Siva, who is now director of the Buen Vivir Fund, told us, "We knew that working together with our grassroots partners would enable us to co-create an alternative approach that didn't perpetuate systems of extraction and exploitation."

The end result was an innovative loan fund, rare for international investing, that employs a participatory governance model. The fund chooses loans and investments through a members assembly made up of eighteen voting members: ten grassroots lenders from Asia, Africa and Latin America, and eight institutional investors. The assembly has the same power as a traditional investment committee: It approves loans, prospective assembly members and the terms under which capital is loaned. The fund ran its initial investment cycle in 2018–20 with $1 million in committed capital. The fund then made investments in ten organizations in South America, South Asia and sub-Saharan Africa through a combination of grants and loans.

One of the investor-members of the Buen Vivir Fund is Morgan Simon, the Transform Finance leader who also co-founded the investment advisory Candide Group. The firm helps families, foundations and athletes direct their capital toward social justice and sustainability. In 2019, Candide announced the Olamina Fund, a $40 million participatory vehicle that funnels money to locally-led community funds run by women and people of color. Investment decisions are made in partnership with a "community advisory board" made up of racial and economic justice activists, all of whom are people of color.

Though Olamina's structure made it appropriate for any number of investment entities, Candide Group was interested in finding ways for

DAFs to have a greater impact. Remember that DAFs are essentially warehouses for money, and that money is expected to earn interest before it is given away. That means that in the meantime, the money is usually managed by mainstream financial institutions like Fidelity or Vanguard. These mainstream institutions tend to have basic screens for environmental and social impact but generally do not go deeper than that. Simon told us that investors are getting more impatient with the reactive nature of these screens. "There is a lot of money in donor- advised funds that is sitting around, not being leveraged proactively for justice," she told us. "That's often been a critique of these funds, at a time when there's so much need. Investors that I speak with want to know: 'How can I activate my assets more thoroughly?'"

The Olamina Fund isn't the only participatory vehicle receiving support from DAFs. The Kataly Foundation's $50 million environmental justice initiative, hosted on Impact Assets' DAF platform, recently convened nine grass-roots environmental justice organizers—all of whom are women of color—from across the United States and Puerto Rico to determine the best way to distribute their DAF capital through both grantmaking and investments. As National Black Food and Justice Alliance organizer Dara Cooper, one of the nine people who designed the new process, told *Impact Alpha*, "It's not charity, it's not paternalistic—it's doing the right thing."

The model, which is still a work in progress, had an unexpected trial run thanks to COVID-19; so far, they have disbursed $5 million in emergency pandemic response funding. Having a design team so close to the ground helped move things along quickly, according to Cooper, who noted, "We know what our folks are doing—we don't need them to jump through hoops to get funding."

The Buen Vivir Fund, the Olamina Fund and the Kataly Foundation are all new funds that were designed with participation in mind. Now, let's look at a foundation that has been investing its endowment in impact for years but which only recently started transitioning to a participatory model.

The Heron Foundation: Going All In

The F.B. Heron Foundation has always been a pioneer in using finance to advance its mission. Heron was created in 1992 as a traditional grant-maker but became an early adopter of program-related investments in 1996, with a commitment to align one hundred percent of its endowment with its mission—a remarkable commitment even today. Over the next twenty years, Heron invested progressively more of its endowment in impact-driven venture capital firms and community loan funds.

In 2016, Heron reached that goal ahead of schedule. It was a significant achievement: At $300 million, it's one of the largest endowments in the world to be invested fully in a mission-aligned portfolio. But for Dana Bezerra, who was Heron's vice president of capital markets at the time, hitting the goal felt like a letdown. "It felt like a boom-splat," Bezerra told impact investing news site Impact Alpha. "That felt like such a low bar."

When Bezerra became the foundation's president, she set a new "all in" vision for the foundation's endowment. Over the next decade, the foundation plans to transfer decision-making power over one hundred percent of the endowment to locally led investment committees around the United States. These committees will have full control over the endowment and will be able to commit Heron's assets without the need for signoff.

"We as a country have a long history of telling people what they need to do to advance, telling places what they should do about major issues (transit, education, etc.)," Bezerra says. "And we're trying to upend that and return to a place of really listening to wisdom in communities about what they think."

Heron is still building out the details of the new strategy, and Bezerra has written about how it is an ongoing process: "Given that we are a funder, and that necessarily means we come from a place of privilege, there's work to be done by us and others to restore power into the hands of the people who live in places. [That] takes trusted relationships. And relationships take time to build."

Bezerra has argued to anyone who will listen that this is a more authentic way for her foundation to serve the communities they all want to help: "Instead of extracting the wisdom from these communities in order to make deployment decisions, why don't we start a process of handing over the deployment?"

Reinventing Ownership

Back in Chapter 6, we wrote about the question of ownership: who ultimately profits from the investment decisions made by community-driven funds? At Jed Emerson's SOCAP panel, Rodney Foxworth pointed out the hypocrisy of investors who spoke about investing in communities of color in the midst of Black Lives Matter protests. Even if those investments are successful, he argued, the benefits will accrue to the mostly white and already-wealthy investors. "Wouldn't it be great if that return could actually go into the communities that have been excluded from building wealth and power?" he asked.

Some say the answer is to take traditional investors out of the equation entirely. Over the past few years, there's been a steady rise in equity crowdfunding platforms, which allow non-accredited investors to make small investments in early-stage companies and make a profit if they become successful. This is a boon for entrepreneurs who don't have the networks or wealthy family members to provide them with a "friends and family" round, but it also creates a new financial ecosystem outside big banks and investment firms.

Take the $10 billion (and growing) cannabis industry in the United States, which has been difficult for people of color to break into since states began legalizing marijuana. The drug is still illegal at the federal level, which means that legal cannabis businesses still can't get a loan from national financial i nstitutions. I n p ractice, t hat's a n e normous advantage for cannabis entrepreneurs who come from backgrounds or networks of wealth, and it locks out communities that have been most negatively affected by punitive drug laws. Just four percent of cannabis business owners are Black.

In 2016, a group of entrepreneurs launched Fundanna, an equity crowdfunding platform specifically for cannabis entrepreneurs and the people who want to invest in them. The minimum investment is $100, and much of the funding comes from non-accredited investors. One of the Black founders on the platform, Ari Zorn, raised $100,000 in his first nine months, including a surge in investors after he spoke at a Black Lives Matter protest. Once he receives his cannabis license, he will be the second Black cannabis entrepreneur operating legally in the state of Massachusetts.

Generation Titans, a Washington, DC-based nonprofit, takes a creative approach to equity crowdfunding. Founded by Raymar Hampshire and Max Skolnik, two alumni of Barack Obama's My Brother's Keeper initiative for men of color, Generation Titans has created entrepreneur "clusters" that support each other and collectively seek crowdfunding from their networks and communities. One of these clusters, Indigenous Futures, features four Indigenous-led startups based in Albuquerque, New Mexico. It includes the Wordcraft Circle of Native Writers and Storytellers, which runs an "Indigenous Comic Con," as well as Itality, which is focused on bringing Native-grown, healthy food to food deserts.

Skolnik told us that the purpose of these clusters is to move past the point where founders need to rely on far-away and hard-to-reach investors. "Founders of color shouldn't be in a position where they need to plead their case in a way that white people are comfortable with," he said.

"We need to present an assertive representation of community knowledge—where they go into the meeting with an investor as the experts." Hampshire adds: "It's not about getting a seat at the table. It's about creating a new table."

This question of building new tables is particularly relevant to tech and venture capital, where racial wealth disparities mean that white people are usually the ones with the capital. Arlan Hamilton has been a leader in this space. Hamilton is the exception to just about every unspoken rule in Silicon Valley: a queer Black woman without a college degree who launched her venture capital fund while living out of her car. She's made waves with her blunt and humorous style, appearing on the cover of *Fast Company* and speaking at major conferences; Mark Cuban has called her "the future of the business world."

In 2015, Hamilton launched Backstage Capital, which invests in women, people of color and founders who are LGBTQ+—groups that collectively receive less than ten percent of VC funding. She has loudly made the case for creating new institutions that act as a counterbalance to the thousands of venture funds led by white male investors. "If [traditional investors] don't make changes, I'm going to pay for the bricks and the stones to build a new house," she said in an interview. "The demand is: listen and believe us. Or else, we're going to take all of our wealth, talent, assets, information, and lived experience and build without you."

9

WHAT YOU CAN DO

When we first started writing this book, the world faced a lot of challenges—and then the COVID-19 pandemic made the need for solutions that much more urgent.

Anyone working in philanthropy or finance in any role—whether at a large or small institution, managing their own money or someone else's—can do something right now to start directly or indirectly shifting decision-making power to marginalized communities. Policymakers also have a part to play in creating the conditions for participatory decision-making to thrive. And even if you don't don't fall into one of those categories, there's still something you can do.

Remember that participatory decision-making is a journey, not a destination. It has several key principles: involve the people most affected by issues in decision-making about addressing them. Go beyond just *listening*, and make sure you engage, rather than inform. Be transparent. Remember that there is a role for experts and professionals, as partners and facilitators. And finally, remember that any participatory process should be in a constant state of iteration and self-reflection. The process is the point.

Participatory Grantmaking 101

Participatory grantmaking is possible for the vast majority of funders. In Chapter 7, we shared examples of foundations that explored participatory models, either by piloting a participatory process or seeding a new participatory fund. We expect that most grantmakers reading this will already have some sort of funding process in place. If that sounds like you, read on.

We like to talk about funding in the context of *design* because it's a good reminder that grantmaking is essentially problem-solving. The whole process is a flowchart: a series of decision points that aim to yield the best results. And despite a huge amount of variety from grantmaker to grantmaker, most funders design their processes around the three key decision points we outlined in Chapter 2. A good first step is to pull up the flowchart of your organization's grantmaking process, and interrogate how you make decisions at each of the following three points. At each point, you can move up the ladder of participation by intentionally and meaningfully bringing in stakeholders from the community you serve.

How am I building my theory of change?

A theory of change is a mini-manifesto that lays out what the grantmaker thinks is wrong with the world and how they want to go about solving it. It defines their values, priorities and vision for the future. Traditionally, this is set by the staff or board of trustees.

The participatory grantmakers we've profiled in this book have taken a variety of approaches to incorporating community voice at this stage. Some involve community stakeholders once at the beginning of a foundation's lifecycle; others bring them back in year after year to revisit and reassess priorities. However you do it, the important part is that you're not just passively asking for their input; the role you're asking them to play comes with a vote or other type of formal power.

How am I building a pipeline of ideas?

If you're expecting the best ideas to fall in your lap through an internet search, conferences or members of your network, you might be missing out on lower-profile but higher-potential applicants.

Many of the participatory grantmakers we've profiled tap into their network of former grantees—or simply ask members of affected communities—for recommendations on the activists and leaders they should know about. Several of them empower former grantees or peer reviewers to go out into the field and interview potential applicants or otherwise conduct landscape research to provide a sense of who's out there.

How am I vetting applicants and making final grant decisions?

This is the point at which decisions about funding are actually made: performing due diligence and making the final call about who to fund. There's some debate among participatory grantmakers about whether involving communities at this stage is the "purest" form of participatory grantmaking. Certainly, this is the stage at which power dynamics are most clearly at play.

There are numerous models for incorporating community voice in due diligence and final funding decisions. On one side of the spectrum are open collective models, like the Wikimedia Foundation, where just about anyone can weigh in through in-person or online voting. This approach makes sense for organizations like Wikimedia that already use elements of crowdsourcing. On the other side of the spectrum are closed collective models like DRF, which deputize a select but representative group of stakeholders to speak for the "community." This makes more sense for grantmakers that fund a specific demographic or issue area.

There are endless variations on both open and closed collectives; FRIDA, for example, has a voting process open to all applicants but not to the public writ large. You can read more about these models in the

Resources section. Just know that one model is not necessarily better than another; it's all about context.

Whatever you do, there are a few best practices that have started to emerge and are important to remember. Pay your stakeholders for their time and, if necessary, for their accommodations. As Jeremy Heimans and Henry Timms put it in their book *New Power: How Power Works in Our Hyperconnected World—and How to Make It Work for You,* "the crowd cannot be seen as an asset to be strip-mined."

Constantly interrogate your assumptions about what "representation" looks like. Cynthia Gibson, the civic engagement expert, told us that one of the most important success factors is to be proactive and intentional about involving people from all parts of a community or constituency, and "not just those who may be more inclined to participate or are automatically invited because of their titles, financial status, or social capital." Just putting out an open call for input, or inviting the few community members already in your network, does not guarantee true representation.

Finally, remember that every participatory grantmaking process is always in beta mode. It's iterative, messy and, just like life, never reaches perfection.

We know that change is hard. Even a pilot program can take years of approvals from boards and donors before it gets going. In many cases, the mindset challenges internally are just too strong for a quick change. If your organization is not ready to start a participatory pilot just yet, there are still several ways to experiment with participatory grantmaking without taking on what might be perceived as reputational or financial risk.

Many institutional funders who want to experiment with participation begin by "regranting" money to existing participatory funds to distribute as they see fit. Remember that most of the participatory funds we've talked about—the Disability Rights Fund, FRIDA and the others—are *public* foundations. They need to raise money just like the nonprofits they fund. Often, that money comes from larger foundations. For instance, the UK-based charity Comic Relief, famous around the world for its Red Nose Day campaign to end child poverty, is a major donor to FRIDA. The multibillion-dollar Open Society Foundations has put seed money behind the Red Umbrella Fund, Disability Rights Fund, Rawa and half a dozen others.

Julio Marcial, a former Ford Foundation grantmaker who now leads the Liberty Hill Foundation, told us that regranting was his entryway into participatory funding—a way for him to try it indirectly at a big institution. "I knew that I couldn't make my funding process participatory," he said. "But I could fund people who were already doing it. I was glad to find participatory funds out there that were addressing the same issues as I was."

There's a second way to experiment with participatory grantmaking with less skin in the game: donor collaboratives. Collaboratives like the With and For Girls Collective are essentially joint ventures between several foundations and individual donors. The structure often involves a pooled fund of grant money, and a small staff to do the work of building the participatory process and running grant cycles. The funders all serve in various advisory or oversight roles.

Advocates of participatory grantmaking endorse regranting and donor collaboratives as a way to expose institutional funders to participatory models. As University of Minnesota professor Jamie Bain elegantly put it, "Participatory grantmaking is like ballet: You can describe it as much as you want, but people don't get it till they see it." Still, the advocates see regranting and donor collaboratives as stepping stones to the next levels of commitment: running a pilot and eventually going all in.

It's worth noting that there are some situations where participatory grantmaking isn't recommended. One example is disaster response or other emergency funding. When people are standing on their roofs in a flooded town, for example, or facing an imminent drought, grantmakers may need to deploy capital as fast as possible. Another example is funding for scientific research or other projects that require specialized knowledge. Some grantmaking is indeed technical and needs to be led by PhDs—though in almost every case, there are questions around distribution and equity that should include communities, not just scientists.

For these cases—and any time that participatory funding doesn't make sense for a foundation for the time being—grantmakers can still practice principles of good human-centered design.

- **Avoid restricted grants.** In the first chapter, we wrote about the rise of restricted, strings-attached grants, which require grantees to spend money on a limited range of prescribed activities. These should be avoided. Restricted grants prevent grantees from adapting quickly to the situation on the ground and can prevent small organizations from making necessary investments in team or infrastructure. In the first few months of the coronavirus pandemic, mainstream philanthropy started to embrace non- restricted (or "general operating") grants in a historic way. Activists are urging them to continue that trend after the pandemic ends.

- **Make your application process more inclusive.** In the past two decades, there's been a dramatic rise in invite-only grantmaking policies. But limiting applicants to your direct network also limits the scope of good ideas. Even if you don't have an invite-only policy, consider ways to tap into new networks to source applications, particularly in marginalized communities—for instance, by sharing calls for applications with affinity groups.

- **Measure what matters.** Metrics are important, but reporting requirements can easily become overwhelming, especially for small nonprofits. Work with your grantees to identify what metrics matter most to people living in affected communities. There are resources out there to help with this, including the Equitable Evaluation Framework and the Social Investment Consultancy's blueprint for "user-centered evaluation design."

Change is not only hard; it can be lonely. We've heard time and again from grantmakers who are excited about reforming their funding process, but feel like they lack the resources and back-up inside their own institution. If that describes you, remember that there are several peer networks that are committed to helping grantmakers learn the principles of inclusive funding.

These networks range from large to small. That includes global communities like the Human Rights Funders Network and EDGE Funders Alliance that host conferences and forums for peer learning and collaboration. There are also smaller, membership-based resource networks that help equip individual donors or grantmakers with the latest knowledge and tactics. For instance, Justice Funders runs the Maestra Program, an executive-level program that trains foundation leaders how to "shift their practices away from extraction towards regeneration."

Finally, there is a growing community of practice specifically focused on building the field of participatory grantmaking. In Chapter 7, we talked about the group of peer grantmakers who gathered to celebrate the launch of the report *Deciding Together* in Mexico. That group has built out a formal network called the Participatory Grantmaking Community, a space for anyone interested in participatory grantmaking to connect, learn and share ideas. The group started small, with just a few dozen members in early 2020. As of early 2021, the community includes more than 300 people from several dozen countries, and they only continue to grow.

Participatory Investing 101

Making investments is inherently about managing risk. If the people weighing in on your investment decisions all look and think like you do, that creates its own risk; you are only hearing from a limited number of perspectives. That's why a growing number of investors are exploring models to engage outside stakeholders in decision-making. If that describes you, read on.

As we wrote in Chapter 2, impact investors use a funding process that is broadly similar to that of philanthropy: it can also be broken down into three decision points when a fund manager or investment committee reaches a conclusion that has financial consequences. First, investors *develop a theory of change* for their fund, signaling to the rest of the world the types of investments they want to make. Next, they build a *pipeline* of possible deals. Finally, they *vet* those deals, analyzing their ability to deliver financial and social returns.

If you want to build participatory principles into your investing, a good first step is to interrogate how you make decisions at each one of these decision points. Whether you're developing an investment thesis or conducting due diligence, you can move up the ladder of participation by intentionally and meaningfully bringing in stakeholders from the community you serve.

How am I building my investment thesis?

An investment thesis is often tied to a desired rate of return or social outcome, and setting an imperfect North Star can cause a fund to veer off course. Many investors revisit their investment thesis regularly; after all, markets are constantly changing.

The participatory investors we've profiled in this book have used a variety of mechanisms to involve outside stakeholders in thesis development. Some appoint community members to their investment committee. Others create an advisory panel of community stakeholders that can weigh in with wisdom from the ground—gathering intelligence like a journalist cultivating sources. As with philanthropy, what matters most is a meaningful role that comes with a vote or other type of concrete power.

These advisors don't need to have traditional finance expertise. Village Capital brings in community expertise through large advisory boards before each accelerator it runs. One recent advisory board for a program focused on "justice tech" startups included nonprofit leaders, criminal justice reform advocates, attorneys, foundation leaders, and people who had been involved with the criminal justice system.

How am I building deal flow?

Are you relying on pitch competitions and your immediate networks to find deal flow? Consider tapping into broader networks. Also, try to eschew flashy pitch events in favor of authentic conversations in which you can get to know a social entrepreneur.

Arlan Hamilton's firm, Backstage Capital, has a policy of responding to cold emails from entrepreneurs, which most other VC funds would ignore. True, you might end up speaking with founders who are too early stage or not the right fit; but you could also build a relationship that pays dividends down the road.

If you're serious about opening up your network, you'll have to be proactive about it. McKeever Conwell, managing director of RareBreed Ventures, has pointed out that "It's not enough [for investors] to say you have an open-door policy." Instead, to truly cultivate a more diverse pipeline, "Go to the places VCs and investors don't go. Know that when you walk into those rooms, those people may not trust you. But it's up to you to do that work, not on them to find you."

How am I conducting due diligence and making final investment decisions?

Bringing outside stakeholders into this stage is the most challenging change to make for many investors; it gets right at the heart of a fund manager or investment associate's job. But as Village Capital has demonstrated, funds that democratize decision-making can perform just as well as those that rely on traditional investors.

The most direct option is to add community representatives to your investment committee, like the Buen Vivir Fund does. Another option is to form a separate community advisory board that plays a formal role in performing diligence and recommending investments, like the Olamina Fund. Adasina Social Capital, which connects social justice movement demands with activist shareholders, released a "Due Diligence 2.0" commitment in 2020 outlining ways to engage communities of color in the process. If your limited partners have concerns about fiduciary duty, you can test out a participatory model with a so-called "shadow board" that weighs in on investment decisions informally. Either way, it's important to be clear about exactly what role the community's voice will play. Is it one vote? Approval of a result? Setting investment criteria?

Whatever you do, make sure you adhere to common best practices. Pay your stakeholders for their time, interrogate your assumptions about "true" representation, and keep iterating. Remember that the process is the point.

If you're not ready to start participatory investing just yet, remember that there are several ways to experiment without taking on perceived reputational or financial risk. You can support participatory investors like Village Capital, or add neighborhood loan funds like the Boston Ujima Fund or Southern Reparations Loan Fund to your portfolio through Seed Commons.

You can also make sure to practice general principles of good human-centered design as you make decisions.

- **Put a premium on lived experience.** In the past few years, Kapor Capital and Jump Canon—two venture capital firms that invest in impact-driven startups—have started to put actual weight on the value of lived experience by measuring an entrepreneur's "distance traveled" during the diligence process. According to Jump Canon's managing partners, "We start with three questions: What has the founder earned and built, beyond what they inherited? What challenges and circumstances have they overcome? What net value have they produced? The larger the distance traveled, the larger the grit, persistence, leadership, empathy, stress tolerance and resourcefulness [that can be expected]."

  Another way to value lived experience is to invest with a specific "lens." Gender lens investing is the colloquial term for deliberately choosing investments that benefit women. One way to practice gender lens investing is to ask your portfolio companies about their compensation and promotion opportunities for female employees. There are other lenses out there; the Refugee Investment Network developed an analogous "refugee lens" for investments by working with displaced migrants to understand not only their needs but also the skill sets and perspectives they can bring to a new venture.

- **Use founder-friendly capital.** Venture capital hypes up "unicorn" companies valued at more than $1 billion. The collective Zebras Unite, which sprang from the "Zebras fix what unicorns break" manifesto, now advocates for more alternatives to hypergrowth, one-size-fits-all VC. "We believe that developing alternative business models to the startup status quo has become a central moral challenge of our time," the founders wrote. "These alternative models will balance profit and purpose, champion democracy, and put a premium on sharing power and resources.

Companies that create a more just and responsible society will hear, help, and heal the customers and communities they serve."

- **Adopt equitable impact measurements.** There are so many options out there for impact measurement; whatever you choose, make sure that you're considering the perspectives of people with lived experience. The Impact Management Project is building a consensus taxonomy for defining and measuring impact for impact investments, including how lived experience can be included in universal standards.

Similar to grantmaking, there are a growing number of organizations and peer networks dedicated to helping investors explore inclusive decision-making practices. Transform Finance and Big Society Capital have both developed taxonomies of participatory investing, which you can find in the Resources section. Networks like Mission Investors Exchange and Impact Assets serve as platforms for foundation leaders, individual donors and seasoned investors to share best practices around deploying capital for social and environmental change.

There are also a growing number of wealth advisory and consulting firms that can help individual investors build new funds with an equity lens. For instance, the Sankofa Group, founded by former Ujima fund manager Lucas Turner-Owens, advises clients on things like fund design, alternative underwriting, impact metrics and how to raise capital. Sankofa recently helped the volunteer-led group Native Women Lead build an investment vehicle from scratch. The fund backs Indigenous women founders with a philosophy informed by the community's values: rootedness, deep relationships and rematriation.

The Role of Policymakers

Since we're Americans, we're going to focus this section on what policymakers in the United States need to do to create a more democratic economy in which participatory funding models can flourish. This includes direct reform around philanthropy and impact investing, but also broader structural change to end the era of billionaire altruism.

This isn't the first time that American policymakers have been challenged with outsized inequality. The First Gilded Age at the end of the nineteenth century had a lot of similarities to today: brand-new industries that the government didn't know how to regulate, a weak tax policy and a lack of labor regulations. That confluence led to the unfathomable wealth of barons like John D. Rockefeller and Andrew Carnegie, and created the conditions for top-down philanthropy and extractive finance today.

As the twentieth century began, the federal government woke up to this inequality. Frightened by labor strikes and rising populist anger that was starting to turn violent, they ushered in the reforms and regulations that defined the Progressive Era. Policymakers in the Progressive Era accomplished two goals that are relevant to this book: creating a regulatory structure around the social sector, and reducing economic inequality.

Here's what a second Progressive Era for philanthropy could look like.

Regulate the Social Sector

One of the landmark moments of the first Progressive Era was the Walsh Commission, a congressional panel that created the ground rules for what was then the burgeoning industry of philanthropy. Lawyer Frank P. Walsh, the commission's namesake, called the new Rockefeller and Carnegie foundations "a menace to the future political and economic welfare of the nation" because of their size and lack of public accountability. The result was a basic framework that placed limitations around how foundations could operate. One hundred years later, it's time to once again right-size the influence of these large and unelected institutions.

Congress has wide latitude over regulating foundations that it has never taken advantage of. Two reforms stand out as particularly effective. First, Congress could cap the size of foundations to help avoid the scenario in which a single foundation or funder has outsized influence. Second, it could incentivize everyday people to give to charity by creating a universal giving credit to broaden the base of small-dollar donors and tilt philanthropy away from the billionaire class.

A good place to start would be the creation of a federal "Office of Charitable Affairs," funded by foundation excise taxes. This idea, from *Just Giving* author Rob Reich, would add some accountability to philanthropy; for instance, it could encourage transparency by requiring board independence, banning compensation of family members and donor disclosures. It would also inevitably involve another high-profile congressional hearing in the style of the Walsh Commission, which couldn't hurt.

Policymakers also have a broad and underutilized ability to shape investment activity. Once again, it's about carrots and sticks. The first area where policymakers can focus is on clarifying rules around fiduciary duty. There are numerous interpretations of the responsibilities a fund manager has to their investors and shareholders. More than one investor we spoke with expressed concern about whether outsourcing decisions to non-accredited investors would be a violation of fiduciary duty and a potential legal risk. There has already been a push by impact investors to clarify that taking into account social returns is still consistent with fiduciary duty because it's a way of assessing an investment's risk in the *long term*. If the Biden administration further clarifies these rules, it should also consider a more explicit permission structure for including lived experience as part of due diligence.

The second priority for policymakers: easing restrictions on who can invest and what they can invest in. The Boston Ujima Fund is tenable because of a 2016 law pushed by the Obama administration that broad-ened the types of investments that could be made by non-accredited investors. That's why the Ujima Fund can accept

$50 investments from people who don't have the $300,000 required to be formally "accredited." Policymakers can continue to expand the definition of a non-accredited investor and reform the Depression-era laws originally designed to protect lower-income people from scams.

That brings us to our second solution: making the rich less rich and the poor less poor.

Reduce Economic Inequality

We all know it, but it bears repeating: Wealth is more concentrated at the top of the economic pyramid today than it has been at any other point in human history. Twenty-six billionaires around the world now own as much wealth as half the planet's population. This extreme concentration of wealth manifests itself in some very obvious and visual ways, like the gleaming new skyscrapers in New York City's Hudson Yards towering over bustling homeless encampments. But it also manifests in the way that the rich are using the social sector to remake society in their image.

There is a growing political will in the United States to reduce economic inequality, which will in turn reduce the power that the wealthy have over all of our lives. We think that three solutions are worth pointing out.

Tax the rich

In the first Progressive Era, Congress passed legislation to reduce the wealth gap that included estate taxes and the first-ever federal income tax. Today, calls for a wealth tax are louder than they have been in 100 years. And those calls are starting to come from the wealthy themselves.

In 2019, impact investors and philanthropists Liesel Pritzker Sim-mons and Ian Simmons coordinated an open letter to the 2020 presidential candidates co-signed with more than a dozen millionaires, titled "It's Time to Tax Us More." The signatories included other wealthy people who have been outspoken against massive wealth concentration like Abigail Disney, a grand-niece of Walt Disney. The letter explicitly called out the corrosive effects that come when a small number of people make decisions for the many: "Countries with high levels of economic inequality are more likely to concentrate political power and become plutocratic. The founders of America knew this, and feared that an economic elite might become ensconced as leaders and erode the effectiveness of the republic."

A wealth tax has the potential to be a truly bipartisan issue—in a 2019 poll, the *New York Times* found that two-thirds of Americans, including fifty-five percent of Republicans, would approve of a two percent wealth tax on people with wealth over $50 million. All that's needed is the political will.

Break up monopolies

It's not a surprise that some of the most ambitious Giving Pledgers, from Jeff Bezos to Mark Zuckerberg, are also the leaders of companies that have been frequently accused of monopolism.

For context: American industry has never seen such high levels of industry concentration. Virtually every sector in the US economy has been whittled down to a few mega-corporations. There are now four major airlines, three major drug stores, and two major toothpaste manufacturers. Big tech is at another level. Twenty years ago, columnists were fretting about big-box stores, but today, Amazon's market capitalization is larger than that of all publicly traded department stores in the United States *combined*.

Critics argue that these economic giants have been engaging in anti-competitive practices unchecked. They bully smaller competition—take Amazon's predatory price cuts designed to put Diapers.com out of business. Or they buy them outright like Facebook has done with Instagram and countless others, creating a "kill zone" because "it's easier to buy than compete." These criticisms are reflected in how these companies' CEOs, as philanthropists, throw their money around in a way that makes a mockery of the idea of a free market.

There is a solution: regulation. In the first Progressive Era, Congress passed legislation to reduce economic concentration by regulating monopoly power. Today, there is a similar anti-monopoly fight led in part by the American Economic Liberties Project.

Help low income people build wealth

This book has been about the power of locally driven solutions and the need to give people a voice in rebuilding their communities. A really simple way to do that is to help people build wealth. Economist Raj Chetty has found that people who receive technology patents in the United States are overwhelmingly white, male, and from wealthy families—he has written about a generation of "Lost Einsteins" who are prevented from contributing to society or to their communities.

One solution is to increase funding for community-development financial institutions (CDFIs) through the federal CDFI Fund, which grants out its annual appropriation to community development organizations and financial institutions that primarily lend to borrowers in marginalized communities. Advocates are now pushing for a $1 billion appropriation.

Another solution is direct cash transfers for marginalized groups. There's a lot of conversation around universal basic income, but many of the models out there are not specific enough in who they help. We like the idea of the "baby bonds" bill recently reintroduced by Senator Cory Booker and Representative Ayanna Pressley, which would give an investment account worth $1,000 to every newborn. Poorer families would receive additional cash for the duration of the child's lifetime. These bonds could easily grow to worth more than $40,000 by the time children reached age eighteen, all for less than two percent of the annual federal budget.

Your Money, Your Community

If you've made it this far in the book and you don't work directly in philanthropy, impact investing or policymaking, you're probably wondering what you can do on a personal level. The good news is that there are several paths available for anyone who wants to play their own part in decolonizing wealth.

The most direct thing you can do: Support some of the participatory funds that we've written about in this book. Philanthropic funds like the Disability Rights Fund and FRIDA take small-dollar donations through their websites; these donations are often put directly into the grant pools led by people with lived experience. Meanwhile, the Boston Ujima Fund and other Seed Commons funds are always looking for donations to support their operations and contribute to their funds.

There are also opportunities to make small-dollar investments in participatory models. Equity crowdfunding platforms like Fundanna, Republic and Wefunder accept investments as low as $100. SheEO, founded in Canada in 2015, pools gift capital from women who are mostly non-accredited investors to provide zero-interest loans to women and nonbinary social entrepreneurs. The minimum investment, made as a tax-deductible gift, is $1,100 per year. The donors, or "activators," get to vote on a finalist slate of entrepreneurs who then engage in a peer selection process similar to Village Capital's to decide how to divvy up the capital.

There's another option for those who want to support activists in their community even more directly: mutual aid. Mutual aid networks in the United States go back to communities of freed Black people during the Civil War and have been common in Black communities ever since, including the Black Panther Party's 1960s-era food programs to assuage hunger in inner-city neighborhoods. Mutual aid networks operate on a needs-based give-and-take; people in the network with money or items provide them to those in the network who need money or items.

Mutual aid drew increasing attention during the coronavirus pandemic, when neighborhood listservs and Facebook groups began to shift their primary functions from announcing yard sales or searching for lost pets to addressing immediate and essential needs. An immunocompromised woman needed someone to get her groceries; a "virtual tip jar" was announced for the now-unemployed servers and bartenders at a local pub; a group of people organizing their neighbors to protest threats of eviction asked for money to print flyers. As Rebecca Solnit wrote in May 2020: "A dozen years ago, the term 'mutual aid' was, as far as I can tell, used mostly by anarchists and scholars. Somehow it has migrated into general usage in recent years and now, in the midst of the pandemic, it is everywhere."

Mutual aid is about making things better in *your* community, directly and immediately. Aid networks can be led by anyone and can take money from anyone; they are a way for anyone to model participatory practices in the most localized way possible. Odds are that there are a dozen or more in your community right now. If not, you can go start one.

The Next Generation of Funders

In 2011, a group of millennials, many of them white, gathered at a nondescript row house in the Petworth neighborhood of Northwest Washington, DC, to talk about an important topic: their own privilege.

At the time, Petworth's demographics were shifting from mostly Black residents—the area neighbors Howard University, a well-known HBCU—to include more young white professionals, many of them recent liberal arts college drawn to the city by the optimism of the Obama era.

A number of these millennials came from inherited wealth and felt guilt about both their wealth and class privilege. The group had first met on the Save Our Safety Net campaign, a response to the DC mayor's proposed budget that would hamstring services for low-income residents without raising taxes on wealthier ones. Save Our Safety Net, which ultimately succeeded in raising taxes, connected the newer residents with others who shared their discomfort.

That was the initial purpose of these gatherings in Petworth: a chance for them to talk openly about their class privilege and how to use it to continue supporting DC residents. "We were all relieved to be able to speak frankly to one another about what our class privilege meant," said Cathy Meals, who participated in the early gatherings. "That was the first time we realized there were a lot of young people who had all this money and wanted to give it away but didn't feel comfortable with the power dynamics."

If Meals and her friends had been gathering in the 1970s, their search for other young people who wanted to give away their inheritance might have led them to discover the Funding Exchange. Instead, many of them joined an organization that could be considered the Funding Exchange's spiritual successor: Resource Generation.

Founded in the late 1990s, Resource Generation is a membership community of young people from backgrounds of wealth who are "committed to the equitable distribution of wealth, land, and power." Their several hundred members include Trans Justice Funding Project co-founder Karen Pittelman and several investors in the Boston Ujima Fund. The members are radically non-hierarchical and are committed to resourcing social justice movements. They also believe in participatory funding, a common topic at their annual conference, Making Money Make Change.

Resource Generation's first Washington, DC, chapter grew out of those gatherings in Petworth. Meals and her friends wanted to find a way to support efforts like Save Our Safety Net that were spearheaded by locals and longtime residents. They reached out to local activists and ended up creating a participatory fund, called the Diverse City Fund, where grant decisions are made entirely by activists and DC residents who have experienced gentrification first-hand. For example, the fund's criminal justice-related grants are decided by a local panel of returning citizens and their families.

Over the next thirty years, Baby Boomers are expected to pass down $68 trillion in assets to their millennial and Gen Z heirs. This will be the largest wealth transfer in human history, and it has the potential to reshape who is making decisions at the highest level of philanthropy and investing.

That's because there is reason to believe the rising generation of young givers and investors will do things differently. Anand Giridiharadas told the *Washington Post* that he routinely receives letters from "younger people who find themselves plutocrats, whether by inheritance or [because] they made money, who are in many cases very tortured and confused by the position in which they stand." Investor Gabe Kleinman wrote in a Medium post, "The new guard...have grown up in a time of radical transparency, lean business methodologies, and positive social change embedded in their everyday philosophies and actions. The idea of top-down, RFP-driven projects and siloed philanthropy simply don't make sense to them."

Indeed, Resource Generation is just one of several peer networks of young people from backgrounds of privilege who want to challenge the system that created their privilege. Nexus counts three thousand mostly-millennial donors across seventy countries. During the coronavirus pandemic, they've held numerous webinars about how to authentically resource the Black Lives Matter movement. The nonprofit 21/64, created with the Andrea & Charles Bronfman Philanthropies, provides multigenerational advising and training for young people coming into leadership of their family offices. Finally, Old Money New System, created in 2016 by a group of Resource Generation members, is creating a shared blueprint for non-extractive finance among the newly wealthy and the activists who share their values.

In addition to building new systems, young altruists are also changing things from within their own family foundations as they age into leadership. In Chicago, for instance, the Conant Family Foundation saw Resource Generation members Monica George and Sarah Frank age into leadership roles on the board of trustees. The young board members had read Edgar Villanueva's *Decolonizing Wealth* and were inspired to do things differently. According to a blog post, they asked themselves, "Could there be a more equitable process than three white people with wealth privilege deciding who should get the funding?"

The Conant staff worked with local Black-led organizations—including the Crossroads Fund, a Funding Exchange member—to create an external review team made up of Chicago residents who were offered a $1,000 stipend to participate. The first round of grants included seventeen recommendations, and the board committee unanimously accepted the list without change. In a follow-up survey, three-quarters of the residents involved said they "learned something new" about foundations or philanthropy.

This has even started to happen with descendants of the original modern philanthropist, John D. Rockefeller. In 2010, a new generation of Rockefellers aged onto the board of the David Rockefeller Fund, established in the '80s by John D. Rockefeller's grandson. The young board members pushed for the creation of the Canary Impact Fund, a participatory fund led by people with lived experience in the criminal justice system. A blog post on the fund's website describes the project as an "evolution of family philanthropy," and "a move away from top-down models of philanthropy and toward the kinds of partnerships that build power among disenfranchised communities rather than, however compassionately, acting for them."

Every young person who reaches the conclusion that their wealth is problematic has a different path to that realization, and many of those paths cross through Resource Generation. For Kate Poole, the path to

Resource Generation wound through Zuccotti Park. In December 2011, Poole, then a twenty-two-year-old Princeton graduate, traveled to New York City for the Occupy Wall Street protests. Just a few days before the protest, she had learned from her mother that she had two trust funds in her name worth several million dollars.

Poole has spent the past decade working with Resource Generation to push for participatory and non-extractive investment models. In 2018, she co-founded Chordata Capital, a wealth advisory firm that supports investors in moving money off of Wall Street and into community investments that focus on racial and economic justice. She's advised peers to invest in participatory funds like the Boston Ujima Fund and Seed Commons. And around the time that Buen Vivir Fund was launching, she co-created a funding collective, Regenerative Finance, that pooled together capital from investors—mostly wealthy millennials like her—to invest in the fund.

Poole, like so many other participatory funders, is constantly checking her own privilege at every step of her journey and experimenting with different ways to mitigate her own privilege. When she launched Chordata Capital with her friend Tiffany Brown, she realized there was an inherent power dynamic: Tiffany, a mixed-race Black woman who grew up working class, would need to quit her job to create this new venture, making her vulnerable if it failed in a way that Poole was not.

"We asked ourselves: What's this going to take?" she recalled. "What amount of commitment is it going to take to create a structure where we could actually share power across our differences? We decided to both write a love letter that was an expression of our beautiful commitment to each other. And then I gave her $120,000—unconditional, not as an employee—so that she had enough financial resources in case the project went south."

This unique business partnership—between someone who came from a background of privilege and someone who did not—might have been unthinkable just a decade ago. The rising generation of philanthropists and impact investors are ready to rewrite the rules. In a moment in history when money and power are more concentrated than ever, there's a new mantra echoing from stock exchanges to the Silicon Savannah: letting go.

AFTERWORD

"We will not let them silence your voices. We're not going to let it happen. I'm not going to let it happen."

Those words came in the middle of a rambling, angry speech that former President Donald Trump gave to thousands of supporters near the White House on the afternoon of January 6, 2021.

We were working on this book less than a mile away when Trump's supporters formed a violent mob and stormed the United States Capitol building with the goal of preventing Congress from certifying the results of the 2020 presidential election. Five people were killed as the mob stole classified information, ransacked the Senate, and terrorized members of Congress and their staff.

We've spent the past nine chapters writing about the urgent disconnect facing leaders in philanthropy and impact investing today. There are massive disparities in wealth, power and agency between those who decide what problems we will solve and those who live those problems every day. It's led to a crisis of faith in philanthropy and a crisis of legitimacy.

That same disconnect fueled the Big Lie that Trump and his enablers used to rally their supporters on January 6—and that they will continue to use for the foreseeable future. In democracies around the world, trust in government and democratic institutions is at an all-time low. From the United States to Brazil, France, Poland and countless other countries, this lack of trust has created an opening for demagogues to turn their supporters against "rigged" democratic institutions to which they no longer feel a connection.

So how do we repair that disconnect? How do we rebuild faith in democracy?

There is no single answer to this question. But in drawing on the themes of this book, we'd like to direct attention to one promising antidote to the crisis of democracy and the authoritarian impulse it creates. This antidote is not about winning any specific election or delivering a soaring speech. It's about a much more fundamental return to the principles of democracy: creating opportunities for citizens to practice democracy and proving that the system is not rigged beyond repair.

It's about making democracy a habit and exercising a civic muscle that has atrophied in America over the last half century.

Donald Trump won the 2016 presidential election for numerous reasons, but one reason doesn't get as much attention as it deserves: The majority of his primary voters had little or no connection to civic life.

In the 2016 primary campaign, Trump dramatically overperformed among a particular subset of Republican voters: those who had never participated in any civic or community activities, like neighborhood groups, parent-teacher associations, or even book clubs. In other words, he got the *Bowling Alone* vote.

Bowling Alone, of course, refers to Robert Putnam's landmark 2000 book about the accelerating decline of civic life in America at the end of the twentieth century. For two centuries, America was admired for its commitment to self-governance. In the 1830s, French philosopher Alexis de Tocqueville visited the United States and breathlessly wrote back home about America's countless voluntary associations. Another thinker at the time called America a "nation of presidents." Participation in the democratic process was a sort of shared civic religion.

That started to change in the latter half of the twentieth century, when enrollment in associations, clubs and religious services started to fall precipitously. Over the course of their lives, members of our grand-parents' generation were likely to be part of a junior league, social frater-nity, religious group or other type of leadership role in their community. By the turn of the century, those types of activities were outmoded. The 2010 census found that only one in ten Americans had served as an officer or committee member of a group or organization in the previous year. We live an atomized and fragmented culture.

Historian Yoni Appelbaum has made a compelling case that Trump was the natural end result of this long decline in civic culture. Ever since Putnam wrote *Bowling Alone*, he writes, Americans have only become more estranged from the "rituals" of democracy. "As participation in civic life has dwindled, so has public faith in the country's system of govern-ment," Appelbaum wrote in an article for the *Atlantic*. "A nation of pas-sive observers watching others make decisions is a nation that will succumb to anger and resentment."

Beyond Election Reform

The future of democracy should never rest on the results of a single elec-tion, but it felt a lot like it did during the first week of November 2020.

For four days in early November, the world was glued to the same television program—the rolling results of the US presidential election—in a way that we're not likely to see for a long time. Within seventy-two hours of polls closing, most of America, and most of the world, knew the names of many of Georgia's one hundred fifty-nine counties and all of Steve Kornacki's wardrobe choices.

Indeed, the stakes for an American election may never have been higher. When the networks called the race for Joe Biden in the late morn-ing of November 7—a gracefully warm Saturday in Washington, DC—the cathartic celebrations outside the White

House and in cities around the world had much more to do with the improved outlook for democracy than enthusiasm for Biden's candidacy.

Democracy won, if only barely. But the intense focus on that electoral victory—and the sense of finality about an election that could have turned out very differently, h ad s ixty thousand votes i n t hree s tates gone t he other way—fed into a narrow post-mortem understanding of what had gone wrong, and what we need to do to make sure it doesn't happen again. The 2020 election did nothing to diminish the disconnect that tens of millions of Americans feel from their government. Four in ten Americans say they feel lonelier than ever; a majority of American communities feel misunderstood by outsiders. Trust in government remains near an all-time low. As the January 6 insurrection made clear, the potential for demagogues to exploit this feeling of disconnect has not diminished.

This speaks to a broad misperception among the political class about what it will actually take to head off further attacks on liberal democracy. Elections are important. But there's an emerging network of pro-democracy activists and scholars who argue that backing pro-democracy candidates is only one part of the answer.

Meet the Democracy Beyond Elections project. The project is a coalition led by the Participatory Budgeting Project, the People's Action Institute and others who argue that we're thinking too small when it comes to solutions to our civic malaise. Josh Lerner, one of the project's creators, explained the name: "We're in a crisis of democracy, but our responses to this crisis have mostly been confined to sit within our dysfunctional political process." He advocates for a more expansive view of reform. "Yes, we should make voting more accessible and expand civic engagement. Yes, our elected officials should and must be responsive to us," he told us. "But no, this alone will not fix our democracy."

Lerner pointed out that in 2016, Americans spent more than six billion dollars in contributions to US presidential and congressional campaigns. That same year, foundations spent *one percent* of this amount—$74 million—on all non-electoral public participation programs combined. Such lopsided numbers point to the misguided belief that democracy is something that only happens on Election Day. Lerner and other advocates argue that to counter the disconnect in American politics, we need to invest in something called *participatory democracy*.

You'll notice that the phrase "participatory democracy" has the same genus as participatory philanthropy or participatory investing—and it shares many of the same principles. Advocates of participatory democracy argue that if we want to restore faith in government and stop the rise of illiberalism, we will need to take a more Athenian approach to the *how* of democracy: delegating decision-making authority directly to citizens (broadly defined), as opposed to an elite political and professional class. They argue that we need to *invest* in creating civic spaces and infrastructure for participation and deliberation on the local, state and federal levels.

There's a strong case to be made that such investments are a better use of funding in the long term than simply backing pro-democracy candidates for election. Why? Because these investments are not just a temporary salve for people's anger and distrust; they actually get at the root of the disconnect at the heart of our democracy.

Participatory democracy reformers want to exercise those atrophied democracy muscles by creating more opportunities for meaningful engagement—ones that directly address issues of equity and accountability, and have real significance beyond window dressing. Luckily, there are models around the world that are starting to make their way to the United States.

These democratic exercises can help reduce the disconnect that fuels authoritarianism by restoring to everyday people a sense of agency, a modicum of trust in their neighbors and a way to make themselves heard by telling their stories.

Agency

In 2014, political scientists Martin Gilens and Benjamin I. Page asked an important question: Just how much power does the average person have in setting federal policy? Their study's introduction put it more bluntly: "Who really rules?"

Their central finding echoed at least half a dozen other studies in the past decade: middle-class Americans have essentially no influence over what their government does. When a federal policy has strong support among the wealthy, the probability of that policy becoming law roughly doubles. But strong support among the middle class has virtually no effect. "In other words," Giles and Page wrote in a *Washington Post* op-ed, "the well-to-do get the policy outcomes they strongly prefer far more often than do average-income Americans."

People know when they're not being heard. Seventy percent of Americans today believe the political system is "rigged," a sentiment Donald Trump has regularly exploited. This messaging was effective because, in a sense, the criticism is true. Thanks to dark money, voter suppression and a general lack of transparency in the policymaking process, the rich and well-connected continue to have outsized influence over our collective future.

Advocates of participatory democracy have a straightforward solution to this problem: Give people real agency over how their government spends its budget.

We talked about participatory budgeting a lot in this book. To recap, budgets are essentially "moral documents," a statement of priorities that "tell us, mathematically, what areas, issues, things or people are most important to the creators of that budget, and which are least important." Participatory budgeting is a democratic process in which community members decide how to spend part of a public budget. It gives people real power over real money.

After its origins in Brazil in the late 1980s, participatory budgeting came to the United States in the wake of the Great Recession. The first experiments took place in Chicago in 2009, then in New York City two years later. It's since spread to dozens of cities across the country, funding everything from park improvements and street safety enhancements to technology and infrastructure upgrades for under-funded schools.

Participatory budgeting has many benefits, some of which we wrote about earlier. For instance, it was adopted as an anti-poverty measure in Porto Alegre, Brazil, and ultimately helped reduce child mortality by nearly twenty percent. For the sake of this Afterword, though, we simply want to show that participatory budgeting is a tool to restore a sense of agency for everyday Americans. It counters the notion that the system is rigged by giving people the chance to influence the system with real teeth behind their decisions.

The cause has recently been taken up by a broader set of activists. The Movement for Black Lives, the organizing group of Black Lives Matter, included in its policy platform a call for participatory budgeting at the local, state and federal level. This framing of participatory budgeting as a racial justice issue is a major step for a policy concept that can sometimes get bogged down in the technicalities of municipal budgeting.

This renewed activism is starting to see results. In 2020, as Seattle was consumed with protests against police brutality, activists issued a demand for a participatory budgeting process alongside their calls to defund the police. In December 2020, the Seattle City Council voted to cut the police budget by eighteen percent and simultaneously to allocate $30 million to a fund that will be distributed via participatory budgeting.

The process will be developed by a Black Lives Matter-affiliated activist group called the Black Brilliance Research Project, with support from the Participatory Budgeting Project. The group's initial "needs assessment" report hints at a set of priorities that involve cutting bloated police budgets and moving resources to needs like housing and mental health support for the formerly incarcerated and treatment for substance abuse.

It's a plan to "defund the police" that is more substance than slogan—and a way to return agency to communities that feel overpoliced and underrepresented.

Trust

Americans today fundamentally don't trust each other.

The level of partisanship in American politics has reached historic levels. This division is often personal. One recent study found that roughly half of Republicans say Democrats are "more immoral" than other Americans, while a similar number of Democrats say the same about Republicans. Another survey found that a third of Republicans and nearly half of Democrats would be "very unhappy" if their child married someone from the opposing party.

Social scientists have termed this "negative partisanship": disdain for the opposing political party now outweighs affection for one's own party.

To state the obvious, it's bad for democracy when people across the political spectrum harbor deep resentment toward those who do not share their views. It makes the daily grind of policy making nearly impossible, turning issues large and small into a life-or-death political cage match. More fundamentally, it fuels the notion that America has become ungovernable. Indeed, academics have found that "pernicious polarization"—when a society is split into mutually distrustful "Us vs. Them" camps—is a prelude to democratic collapse.

But as Ezra Klein and others have argued, these topline numbers on polarization can be misleading. When it comes to individual issues, Americans aren't nearly as polarized as they seem. The COVID-19 relief bill that passed in early 2021 barely squeaked through a divided Senate, but its provisions—relief for state and local governments, stimulus checks, and funds for expanded testing—were supported by more than seventy percent of Americans, regardless of party affiliation. There's similar majority support around other hot-button policy questions, from expanding gun control to increasing border security.

Still, it's hard to understand this beyond an intellectual level, because- for the most part, we never talk to each other. We live in self-imposed political bubbles, based on where we live, how we get our news and what we see on social media. In one recent study, the most isolated Democrats say they expect that ninety-three of their encounters will be with other Democrats; Republicans provided a similar response.

Advocates of participatory democracy see one potential solution to this problem of broken trust and divided allegiance: policy juries.

Policy juries are independent commissions that convene a represent- ative sample of citizens to weigh in on a public policy issue. Like trial juries, they emphasize deliberation and cooperation. Members of the jury hear from experts and spend hours or sometimes months discussing and debating with people who were recently strangers.

Policy juries are a relatively new invention, but they already have a remarkable record of lowering the temperature in intense political envi- ronments. For a recent example, we can look to the Republic of Ireland, where citizens came together to find a solution to one of the most polar- izing issues in the world.

Abortion is a politically sensitive topic in Ireland, to say the least. More than seventy-five percent of the country population identifies as Catholic, and many of the country's laws reflect the church's influence, including a nineteenth-century ban on abortion in the country's Consti- tution.

In 2016, the Irish government partnered with Atlantic Philanthro- pies to run a "Citizens' Assembly" on the topic of abortion, as part of their "We the Citizens" project. They selected a random sample of nine-ty-nine Irish citizens. (Their selection method? Hiring a market research firm to knock on doors and ask people if they wanted to participate.) The gathered citizens were posed with the question of whether or not to effectively legalize abortion by amending the constitution.

The process was intensely deliberative. Over the course of one year, the ninety-nine Irish citizens attended weekend-long sessions, where they listened to presentations from legal and ethics experts, activists and people with lived experience around abortion. Each presentation was followed by small-group discussions led by trained facilitators. The idea was to get the participants not just to parse what they heard but also to connect with one another. After weeks of deliberation, the Citizens' Assembly recommended repealing the abortion ban. The outcome triggered a national referendum vote in 2018, and after historic turnout, the Irish electorate surprised the world by voting in favor of the amendment's repeal, legalizing abortion in one of the most Catholic countries in the world.

This process succeeded where elite decision-makers had failed. But the larger point is that it got people talking to each other.

Policy juries have recently started to take hold in the United States. Oregon, Massachusetts and California have run small citizens' assemblies with the help of the nonprofit Healthy Democracy. Th e b ng- est-running example is the Citizens' Initiative Review in Oregon, which formally launched in 2010 and convenes a random, demographically representative group of citizens to evaluate ballot initiatives for local and state elections.

The 2018 review process focused on affordable housing: in particular, a Portland-area ballot initiative to fund affordable housing. The jury listened to testimony on the initiative's likely effects on reducing homelessness, the cost to taxpayers, and the various oversight mechanisms available to administer it. In the end, they produced a "Citizen's State ment" outlining pertinent information for voters, including the fact that more than half of Portland renters paid more than thirty percent of their income in rent.

Beyond voting, jury duty is one of the last remaining ways that people tangibly and constructively interact with government. Policy juries double down on what already works. They are designed to make policy debates constructive rather than divisive; to keep the temperature lower than in electoral bodies like the US Senate; and to blunt the natural incentives for partisanship. In an era of "alternative facts," tasking citizens with identifying what matters most takes the conversation out of a hyper-partisan frame and brings it into a community-centered one.

Storytelling

In 2014, the New York City Council passed a historic bill to curb the invasive practice of stop-and-frisk policing, which disproportionately criminalized New Yorkers of color. During the roll call, one council member dedicated his vote to a trans woman of color named Giselle, whom he had seen share a piece of performance art in which she reenacted a frightening encounter with a police officer who accused her of soliciting sex work.

"Giselle had a real, concrete effect on me," the council member told a reporter. "[Her performance] really helped me solidify my thinking on that issue."

We've talked so far about rather wonky formats for discussing policy debates: budget referenda and jury deliberations. In this final section we'll talk about one more type of participatory democracy that is a bit different: legislative theater. What began as an experiment among Brazil-ian artists has since morphed into a global model for immersive storytelling for social change. It's a model that provides a platform for marginalized people who might otherwise feel that the system is "rigged" against them.

Like participatory budgeting, legislative theater has its roots in Brazil. Augusto Boal was a theater director and community organizer who organized low-wage workers in his free time. In 1971 he was kidnapped off the street by the military regime and exiled to Argentina, where he stayed for five years. During that time he studied the work of Paulo

Freire, the author of *Pedagogy of the Oppressed*. Inspired by Freiere and by his theater background, Boal created a new format of political engagement called Theatre of the Oppressed.

The military regime fell in the early 1980's, and Boal returned to Brazil. He rented a theater and started putting on shows that featured oppressed people sharing their personal stories in front of an audience of "spect-actors" who shared their opinions and experiences as part of the performance.

Boal was nominated for a Nobel Peace Prize for Theatre of the Oppressed, and since then the idea has spread to more than seventy countries, including the United States. One example is Theater of the Oppressed NYC, co-founded by one of Boal's proteges, Katy Rubin, and the venue for Giselle's performance. The program is run by a small staff and volunteers out of an auditorium in Hell's Kitchen. In a typical show, the actors present an original play "chronicling an unresolved problem resulting from systemic oppression." The audience is invited to break the fourth wall, stepping onto the stage and sharing or acting out possible ways to address that problem. Later on, these performances are re-created for an audience of policymakers to generate discussion on solutions and even inform draft legislation.

"We want to take back the storytelling process and demand change-from the people who are actually facing the problem," said Rubin. "The philosophy is that everyone is an actor, both the audience member and the performer."

Legislative theater can have real policy impacts, but it can also engage new kinds of people in the policy process: think theater kids rather than Model UN kids. It's a creative way to restore the civic religion of democracy by activating people's imaginations—and a promising idea to provide a potentially more welcoming entryway into the democratic process.

A Rebellion Against History

"Democracy is a rebellion against all of history," writes journalist Stephen Kinzer. "To sustain democracy requires constant effort because it's a very unnatural form of government. And when you start to take it for granted, it tends to collapse."

Liberal democracy is in a precarious state. We cannot take it for granted, nor can we take for granted that winning elections alone will preserve this unnatural form of government. As we pointed out above, Americans spend one hundred times more money on electing candidates to office than they do on supporting organizations that build the infrastructure for participatory democracy. There is a real danger that pro-democracy funders–foundations, individual donors and political advocacy groups–will continue to lose sight of the bigger picture as they engage in a never-ending campaign finance arms race with backers of illiberal candidates.

Now is the time to *invest* in democracy beyond elections. So what does that look like? Any funders who are concerned about the state of liberal democracy should learn more about a number of growing organizations that are advancing participatory democracy:

- The Participatory Budgeting Project is a nonprofit that promotes participatory budgeting, primarily in the United States and Canada. Since 2009, it has supported dozens of governments, public institutions, and organizations in launching and deepening participatory budgeting processes. This support ranges from technical assistance to implementing full processes. The Participatory Budgeting Project also runs the Democracy Beyond Elections project. The project maintains a running list of communities that engage in participatory budgeting and invites contributors to get engaged at the local level and with the project itself.

- Healthy Democracy is a nonpartisan organization based in Oregon that designs and coordinates policy juries and other deliberative democracy programs. This organization has pioneered the Citizens' Initiative Review process that we wrote about above, which brings together randomly selected and demographically representative members of a particular region to debate and produce a report on ballot measures. Healthy Democracy also designed a replicable model for citizens' juries on the municipal level that go one step further: These policy juries provide city councils with detailed policy recommendations on the topic at hand.

- Theater of the Oppressed NYC is only one of several local legislative theater organizations, whose groups are invariably small, community-led productions that need financial support. In Washington, DC, Sojourn Theatre runs a semi-annual production, The Race, that promotes inquiry into the civic process. Their most recent production, just days before the 2020 presidential election, invited audience members to answer questions like "Why would you follow someone?" and "Is diplomacy a sign of weakness in a leader?" In Manchester, England, local officials have started turning to legislative theater to inform their homelessness prevention strategy, leading to policy proposals that include sharing data across health and social services, as well as training peer advocates with lived experience.

- Finally, there's People Powered, a project of the Global Hub for Participatory Democracy led by Josh Lerner. It's a connector, training ground and advocacy organization that serves as a central resource hub for all of the above ideas that likens itself to a "global union for participatory democracy workers." This organization practices what it preaches. In 2020, People Powered convened participatory democracy leaders from twenty-eight countries to engage in a planning process to build out the hub's strategic plan in a fully participatory process.

Restoring democracy is a bigger project than reorienting philanthropy and impact investing. But it rests on the same principles: equity, accountability, and space for new voices. It relies on the assumption that when people feel that they have agency over their future, they will bring their best selves to the process of building a better world.

We're going to need that motivation as we re-engage with the world after more than a year of isolation. We're going to want to get out of our homes and connect with people again, and we're going to want to do it in a more intentional way than we did before. Rebuilding democracy will be a process, but just like with participatory funding, the process is indeed the point.

RESOURCES

There is a wealth of information available on participatory funding—on the Internet, in reports, in academic literature.

This book has been more about the *why* than the *how* of participatory grantmaking and investing. For those who want to dig deeper, and learn from the successes and missteps of the past, we compiled a list of resources to get you started. Though by no means exhaustive, we believe these resources to be especially comprehensive and useful:

This report is the top resource on best practices in participatory grantmaking: *Deciding Together: Shifting Power and Resources Through Participatory Grantmaking* by Cynthia Gibson and Jen Bokoff: https://www. issuelab.org/resources/32988/32988.pdf

Candid has a deep repository of participatory grantmaking information:https://grantcraft.org/content/takeaways/participatory-grant-making- additional-resources/

Participatory grantmaking expert Hannah Paterson curates advice and events on her website https://hannahpaterson.com/ and Medium page: https://hannah-paterson.medium.com/

The National Community Capital Coalition offers a practical guide to community investment funds that take a participatory approach: *Community Investment Funds: A How-To Guide for*

Building   Local   Wealth,   Equity,   and   Justice: https://comcapcoalition.org/wp-content/uploads/   2020/03/Community-Investment-Funds-Final.pdf

Transform Finance leads a working group called Capital and Equitable Communities that is building a taxonomy for community-led investing-models:http://transformfinance.org/capital-and-equitable-communities

"The Financial Activist Playbook for Supporting Black Lives," from Candide Group's Jasmine Rashid, is a good starting point for understanding how power dynamics can play out in personal finances: https://medium.com/candide-group/the-financial-activist-playbook-for-supporting-black-lives-fb9616470c4

Big Society Capital and the Young Foundation's *Nothing About Us Without Us: Bringing Lived Experience Insight into Social Investment* includes a number of social enterprise case studies: https://bigsocietycapital.com/latest/nothing-about-us-without-us-lived-experience-insight-social-investment/

USERS: Putting Users' Vices at the Heart of Evaluation from The Social Investment Consultancy is a guide for bringing community voice into impact measurement practices: https://www.tsiconsultancy.com/wp-content/uploads/2019/05/TSIC_USERS-1.pdf

The Centre for Knowledge Equity is a good jumping-off point for learning more about how to value lived experience in decision-making: https://knowledgeequity.org/

ACKNOWLEDGMENTS

Participatory to the end, this book would not have been possible without a whole community of people behind it.

We spoke to more than one hundred people for this book, on six continents—mostly during the intensity and uncertainty of a global pandemic. Not all of these people are quoted or featured in these pages, but their collective generosity with their time and knowledge profoundly shaped *Letting Go*. Thank you for trusting us with your stories and your wisdom.

Aaron Tanaka, Abdul Karim-Mohamed, Allen Frimpong, Allie Burns, Andrea Armeni, Andrea McGrath, Ann Lewis, Astrid Scholz, Aunnie Patton Power, Ayla Schlosser, Baljeet Sandhu, Barry Lynn, Ben Jealous, Benjamin Soskis, Bill Schambra, Bob Lehrman, Bob Pattillo, Bonnie Chiu, Brandolon Barnett, Brendan Martin, Bryce Roberts, Cathy Meals, Chris Cardona, Cindy Gibson, Coco Jervis, Curt Lyon, Dana Bezerra, David Plotz, Diana Samarasan, Dwi Ariyani, Edgar Villanueva, Erika Seth Davies, Florian Schalliol, Gaithiri Siva, Gemma Bull, George Pillsbury, Grace Lyn Higdon, Hannah Paterson, Issam Chleuh, Jamaa Bickley-King, Jane Leu, Jasmine Sudarkasa, Jed Emerson, Jen Bokoff, Joe Waters, Jonny Price, Jordan Tavares, Josh Lerner, Jovana Djordjevic, Julio Marcial, Karen Pittelman, Kate Poole, Katy Love, Kelley Buhles, Kristian Nammack, Lady Lawrence Carter, Laura Tomasko, Leanne Pittsford, Leila Hessini, Leisel Pritzker Simmons, Lucas Turner-Owens, Magda Pochec, Maggie Dugan, Manprit Vig, Marjorie Kelly, Marnie Thompson, Max Skolnik, McKenzie Smith, Michael Scott, Mike Rogers, Morgan Simon, Moukhtar Kocache, Natasha Friend, Nate Wong, Nia Evans, Nkechi Feaster, Odun Eweniyi, Paul-Gilbert Colletaz, Perry Nunes, Peter Goldmark, Peter O'Flynn, Phuong Luong, Raymar Hampshire, Rehana Nathoo, Rose Longhurst, Ross Baird, Rubie Coles, Ruby Johnson, Rodney Foxworth, Sarah Miller, Sarah Jacqz, Sarina Dayal, Shari Davis, Sherrell Dorsey, Swatee Deepak, Tara Sabre Collier, and Vicki Saunders.

Thank you to Edgar Villanueva, whose book *Decolonizing Wealth* was a major inspiration for this project. We're honored to be able to continue the conversation you brought to so many people's attention.

Thank you to the extraordinary team that helped us to research, edit, design, lay out, and print *Letting Go*. We are deeply grateful to our editor, Lisa Kaufman, who helped us turn a very rough draft into a true manuscript with a coherent and consistent argument. Thank you also to Brian Bies, Iram Allam, Jemiscoe Chambers-Black, Kathleen Murray, Laura Adeniyi, Melanie Cohen, Natasha Peterson, Renee Shuey, Sarah Coleman, Tom Scanlan, and Tricia Levesque. A special thank you to Allie Burns, who (unknowingly) set this entire project into motion when she introduced us.

We also want to thank our friends, family, and colleagues who weighed in on drafts, helped us brainstorm, offered advice, connected us to fascinating people who made the book better, and generally made the whole experience more rewarding.

Thank you to our dogs, Jack and Zora, for the noisy entertainment they so eagerly provided while we were trying to write.

Lastly, thank you to all of the people out there who have done the hard work of trying a different kind of giving and investing. You are the inspiration for this book, and we're here to bolster your fight.

From Meg:

My maternal grandmother once said that "you don't live *in* a community, but *for* a community" – words that kept coming to mind as this book unfolded. In writing these acknowledgments, I saw that this is not just true of the people in *Letting Go*. It's also true of me.

I am so lucky to have two parents who endlessly encourage, support, and love me. Thank you, Mom and Dad, for everything.

Just like when we sat through each other's ski races and basketball games, my brothers Jeff and Chris are unfailingly supportive. Along with my amazing sisters-in-law Courtney and Chloe, they gave advice, edits, and empathy (yes, even you, Jeff). Thank you to the rest of my wonderfully supportive extended family, and to my late grandparents, who I hope I've made proud.

Piper, Keenan, Bowen, and Haven: I can't wait to share this book with you as you seek out ways to change the world with your own special gifts. In the meantime, we'll stick to picture books!

Thank you to Jen Udden for explaining publishing to me (repeatedly!); to Emily Crockett and Dante Atkins for coming up with "letting go" as a possible title; to Katie Minetti for graciously hosting me during our Before Times reporting trips; to Allison Haley, who provided the necessary virtual breaks for British television and gin (and, of course, veterinary advice); and to Amelia Shister, Hayden Mulligan, and Sarah Wysocki for being my first phone calls whenever I needed a reminder that I can do hard things.

Professionally, I am where I am today because other women lifted me up along the way. In fact, each major step I took toward *Letting Go* can be traced to another woman listening, advising, and pointing me toward exactly what I needed to do next.

As a high school student, Patricia Gray took me seriously when I told her I wanted to be a writer and shared the practical wisdom I'd need to make it happen. In her seminar at Mount Holyoke College, Priscilla Painton pushed me to write and report more sharply, and then gave me the opportunity and encouragement to keep going; she remains a mentor and inspiration. As a graduate student at Georgetown, Lynn Ross recommended me for an internship at the White House Office of Management and Budget because "they need people who can write," which led me straight to the office of Kathy Stack. She and Mary Ellen Wiggins were not just extraordinary bosses. They are the ones who introduced me to what would become my professional home: impact investing, the social sector, and the idea that money can and must do good.

Thank you, all of you. I hope that one day I can do for another motivated young woman what each of you did for me.

Many other colleagues, clients, teachers, and mentors have offered me important counsel, opportunities, constructive feedback, levity breaks, and a deeper understanding of why this work matters. Thank you for what you do and the generous spirit in which you do it:

Amy Stillman, Anjali Deshmukh, Annie Donovan, Caitlin Offinger, Corrine Demas, Dan Czitrom, David Bank, Dennis Price, Deven Comen, Dmitriy Ioselevich, Elizabeth MacBride, Emily Gustafsson-Wright, Eric McDowell, Erika Poethig, Francesca Spoerry, Fran Seegull, Gary Glickman, Georgie Benardete, Glenn Gamboa, Hallie Easley, Jennifer Stoff Sood, Jonathan Greenblatt, Justin Milner, Karam Hinduja, Kelly Walsh, Krisztina Tora, Loretta Chao, Nate Wong, Neanda Salvaterra, Noemie Levy, Oliver Wagg, Rayanne Hawkins, Rebecca Fries, Rehana Nathoo, Sir Ronald Cohen, Ron Day, Sigrid Senamaud, Scarlett Kuang, Sonal Shah, Sukanya Narain, Suzanne Biegel, and Tim West.

Last but certainly not least, thank you to my extraordinary community of sounding boards, subject-matter experts, strategists, champions, cover art critiquers, inspiration, and (crucially) gif/meme providers: you made this book better and me more joyful while writing it:

Abigail Collazo, Adrienne Wong, Allison Alt, Allison Rague, Amanda Valerio (power hen!), Ava Bagley, Bethany Quinn, BJ McDuffie, Charlotte Clymer, Daina Agee, Dan Hess, Emily Usher Shrair, Gavin Baker, Heather Rodgers, Jillian Rubino, Julianna Pieknik, Julia Cohen, Mallory Cohn, Marie-Ellen Ehounou, Molly Neel, (Lady) Molly Smith, Nicole Varma, Rachel Colyer, Sally Brzozowski, Sandi Fox, Sandi Giver, Sarah Hart, Simmy Singh, Spencer Northey, Shelley Thompson, and Vashti Joseph.

From Ben:

There were so many people who helped shape this book.

Thank you to my family who spent two years listening to me talk about this idea as it evolved: Mom and Dad, who gave the earliest feedback; Adam, who somehow turned into the book's editor, graphic designer, web developer and accountant; Josh, who helped me articulate the concept of "letting go" of power early on; Janna, Nick and Aunt Ivy, who weighed in on language and the cover, cousin Dani, who lent me books on writing; Aunt Doryce and Uncle Allen, who lent me books on history and democracy; and cousin Jeff, who offered room and board over a long weekend in Woodstock that marked the moment when this project transitioned from a rough idea into a real book.

Thank you to all of the friends who were a part of the creative process for *Letting Go* from the very beginning, way back in April 2019: Aaron Thaul, who provided feedback and moral support all along; Alex Berger, who gave me the chance to teach a session on storytelling; Andrea Durham Cambron, who made sure I was up to date on Twitter hot takes; Andy Kroll, who shared tips on how to conduct interviews over burgers and fries; Carolyn Davis, who helped me envision the actual process of creating a long piece of writing; Chelsea Geyer, who managed to match my long brainstorm emails with an even *longer* email; Dan Brooks, who sparked my interest in urban development and the power of the hyperlocal; Dan Fleishaker, who gave me pro bono advice on storytelling; David Gray, who helped inform the idea early on; Donna Byrd, who has always encouraged me to write in my own voice.

Thank you also to Eric Wingerter, who taught me an invaluable skill, how to brainstorm; Hallie Ryan, who long ago got me thinking about the need to challenge my own privilege; Herbie Ziskend, who encouraged me to write under my own name about topics that inspired me; Isaac Fradin, who read more early drafts than anyone else and always had critical but constructive feedback; Francella Chi de Chinchilla, who made some early introductions that helped open many doors, Jess Goldstein, who introduced me to a top-notch writing spot on the roof of the Kennedy Center; Joe Kapp, who shared some real talk about the project early on; Kai Agajani, who read an early draft and provided regular feedback; Layla Zaidane, who weighed in with first-person wisdom about the grind of nonprofit fundraising; Lisa Allen, who I plan to hire as my next graphic design consultant once she's done photographing Mars.

Thanks to Lucas Turner-Owens, who was the book's very first interview and connected us to an incredible ecosystem in Boston; Malcom Glenn, who inspired ideas around topics from Baby Bonds to inclusive economic development; Mazin Melegy, who helped sketch out the book's thesis in a patented Refrigerator Session; Mike Seid, who introduced me to the world's greatest productivity tool, LoFi Hip Hop Girl on Youtube; Nora Lessersohn, who kindly listened to me ramble when the book was very half-baked; Rebecca Snow, who served as a sounding board early on; Rob Coleman and Becca Gross, who were gracious hosts at a time in the process that I needed a change in scenery; Rob Griffin, who regularly helps me make (some) sense out of the state of our democracy Owen Schochet, who listened to the book's idea evolve over dozens of runs and games of 1-1; Serene Habayeb, who has served as a moral compass and meditation buddy; and Scott Jones, who went through the process of writing a book alongside me and Meg (buy his book, The Free Agent Mindset).

Thank you finally to the many other friends who made introductions, passed along tips or weighed in on the design of the cover: Aaron Coleman, Andy Newbold, Annette Konoskofe-Graf, Anuraag Dalal, Audrey del Rosario, Barbara Rosen, Beth Foster, Bexy Scarpelli, Bill Fegan, Bradley Baird, Brian Austin, Brian Scarpelli, Carl Bellin, Carolyn Zelikow, Danny Solow, David Michaelson, Emily Stephenson, Gabe Wittenburg, Jake Erlich, Jamal Hagler, Jeffrey Gregor, Jess Girard, Julia Alpaio, Kate McElligott, Lindsay Tiell, Lisa Cuesta, Mark Fleming, Marli Keeley, Max Sinsheimer, Meghna Rao, Melaura Hoffman, Miranda Peterson, Miriam Warren, Nicky Vogt, Rachel Rubinstein, Rose Jackson, Sam Novey, Sarah Schultz, Scott Tiell, Rishi Malhotra, Quentin James, and Stephanie Brown-James.

Letting Go started out as a project for Village Capital called *Rabble Rousers*, and it never would have gotten off the ground if not for the vision and example of the incredible team that has made letting go of power a career choice. Thanks to all the VilCappers past and present who weighed in on the development of this book: Adedana Ashebir, Alex Fife, Amanda Jacobson, Allie Burns, Andrew Hobbs, Annie Wood, Branden Houser, Brenda Wangari, Dahlia Joseph, Dahler Battle, Daniel Cossío, Donna Byrd, Dustin Shay, Emily Edwards, Heather Matranga, Inder Takhar, Jamie Mims, Lewam Kefela, Mai Le, Marcia Chong Rosado, Matt Zieger, Rachel Crawford, Rob Tashima, Ross Baird, Rustin Finkler, Sofía Cándano, Stephen Wemple, and Tina Nyamache. (I'm sure I'm forgetting many others!)

Writing a book takes a lot of mental energy, and it's easy to put off a deadline. With that in mind, thank you to the friends near and far who keep me inspired with your persistent levels of creativity and creative output: Adielenah Perez, Ashley Littles, Cassidy Ginivan, Courtney Sexton, Harish Chatrathi, Jazerai Allen-Lord, Jesse Thaul, Jonathan Kincaide, Justin Snyder, Kyle Gildea, Ray Azucena, Shaquille Pariag, Simmie Terell and Zalina Zangieva.

ENDNOTES

INTRODUCTION

"Activist Courtney Martin has called it": Martin, Courtney. "The Reductive Seduction Of Other People's Problems." Medium. BRIGHT Magazine, June 27, 2019. https://brightthemag.com/the-reductive-seduction-of-other-people-s-problems-3c07b307732d.

"half a trillion dollars worth of capital": Mudaliar, Abhilash, and Hannah Dithrich. Rep. Sizing the Impact Investing Market, 2019.

"Black Lives Matter presented": Zahniser, David, and Dakota Smith. "Black Lives Matter Leaders Meet with L.A. Politicians, Saying 'Defund the Police." Los Angeles Times, June 5, 2020.

"Participatory budgeting is now used": "What Is PB?" Participatory Budgeting Project, July 17, 2020. https://www.participatorybudgeting.org/what-is-pb/.

"named most-promising sector reform effort": IP Staff. "Philanthropy Awards, 2018." Inside Philanthropy, 2018.

"In 2011, Kristi Kimball and Malka Kopell": Kimball, Kristi, and Malka Kopell. 2011. "Letting Go (SSIR)". Ssir.Org. https://ssir.org/articles/entry/letting_go.

"In the words of Roxanne Nazir": Nazir, Roxanne. 2019. "Are You Ready To Become An Activist Philanthropist?". Grantcraft. https://grantcraft.org/content/blog/are-you-ready-to-become-an-activist-philanthropist/.

CHAPTER 1

"To appear on the Oprah Winfrey show": Strauss, Valerie. "The Real Story: Why Mark Zuckerberg's $100 Million Gift To Newark Schools Was Announced On Oprah's Show". The Washington Post, September 24, 2015.

"this was not some sort of… publicity stunt": Zax, David. "Mark Zuckerberg Announces Details of $100 Million Grant to Newark Schools." Fast Company, September 24, 2010. https://www.fastcompany.com/1691042/mark-zuckerberg-announces-details-100-million-grant-newark-schools

"with a high school graduation rate that hovered": Stetser, Marie, and Robert Stillwell. 2014. "Public High School Four-Year Ontime Graduation Rates And Event Dropout Rates: School Years 2010–11 And 2011–12". U.S. Department of Education.

"The Prize, a book-length postmortem": Russakoff, Dale. 2015. The Prize. Mariner Books.

"Booker tried to make up for that": Russakoff, Dale. 2014. "Schooled". The New Yorker, 2014.

"It wasn't real community engagement—it was public relations": Russakoff, The Prize.

"You can't just cobble up a bunch of money": Garfield, Leanna. "Mark Zuckerberg once made a $100 million investment in a major US city to help fix its schools — now the mayor says the effort 'parachuted' in and failed." Business Insider, May 12, 2018. https://www.businessinsider.com/mark-zuckerberg- schools-education-newark-mayor-ras-baraka-cory-booker-2018-5

"private sector consultants" Russakoff, Dale. 2014. "Schooled". The New Yorker, 2014.

"My mom, she would've been fit to be tied": Garfield, Leanna. "Mark Zuckerberg". Business Insider.

In His Judgment

"Rockefeller's net worth was $400 billion": Eschner, Kat. 2017. "John D. Rockefeller Was The Richest Person To Ever Live. Period". Smithsonian Magazine. https://www.smithsonianmag.com/smart-news/john-d-rockefeller-richest-person-ever-live-period-180961705/.

"In 1889, Andrew Carnegie wrote": Carnegie, Andrew. "The Gospel Of Wealth | Carnegie Corporation Of New York". Carnegie Corporation Of New York. Accessed February 28, 2021. https://www.carnegie.org/about/our-history/gospelofwealth/.

"Members of Congress called Rockefeller's new foundation": Neklason, Annika. 2019. "Philanthropy Serves The Status Quo". The Atlantic. https://www.theatlantic.com/politics/archive/2019/07/philanthropy-serves-status-quo/593089/.

Billionaire Philanthropy

"The point of the dinner..." "Loomis, Carol. 2010. "The $600 Billion Challenge". Fortune. https://fortune.com/2010/06/16/the-600-billion-challenge/.

"A study on the winners and losers in philanthropy": Lindsay, Drew. 2018. "Who's Raising The Most: The 100 Charities That Are America's Favorites". The Chronicle Of Philanthropy. https://www.philanthropy.com/article/whos-raising-the-most-the-100-charities-that-are-americas-favorites/?cid2=gen_login_refresh&cid=gen_sign_in.

"This trend inspired Vox's Dylan Matthews": Matthews, Dylan. 2015. "For The Love Of God, Rich People, Stop Giving Ivy League Colleges Money".

Vox. https://www.vox.com/2015/5/12/8590639/stephen-schwarzman-yale-donation.

The Moneyball Playbook

"Michael Porter, an economist" "Porter, Michael E., and Mark R. Kramer. "Philanthropy's New Agenda: Creating Value." Harvard Business Review, November 1999.

"When he coined the term 'moneyball philanthropy'": Meiksins, Rob. "Moneyball Philanthropy – Is the Work of the Nonprofit Sector Like Baseball?" Nonprofit Quarterly, June 30, 2014. https://nonprofitquarterly.org/moneyball-philanthropy-is-the-work-of-the-nonprofit-sector-like-baseball/.

"Benjamin Soskis, a historian of philanthropy": Soskis, Benjamin, and Stanley N. Katz. Rep. 50 Years of U.S. Philanthropy. William and Flora Hewlett Foundation, 2016.

"Only six percent of large foundations had an invite-only policy in place" Soskis, 50 Years.

"only eight percent of grant funding goes to nonprofits with a Black leader": Rendon, Jim. "Nonprofits Led by People of Color Win Less Grant Money With More Strings (Study)." The Chronicle of Philanthropy, May 7, 2020. https://www.philanthropy.com/article/nonprofits-led-by-people-of-color-win-less-grant-money-with-more-strings-study/?cid2=gen_login_refresh&cid=gen_sign_in.

Out of Touch

"Outside, a Nigerian man turn to the camera": Africa for Norway - New Video! Radi-Aid - Warmth for Xmas. Youtube, 2012. https://www.youtube.com/watch?v=pkOUCvzqb9o&ab_channel=SAIHNorway.

"One famous example is the Global Alliance for Clean Cookstoves": Morrison, Sara. "Undercooked: An Expensive Push to Save Lives and

Protect the Planet Falls Short." ProPublica, July 12, 2018. https://www.propublica.org/article/cookstoves-push-to-protect-the-planet-falls-short.

"The New Yorker called the project": Ibid.

"ProPublica interviewed a woman": Ibid.

"only one failed big-dollar campaign": Matthews, Dylan. "Billionaires Are Spending Their Fortunes Reshaping America's Schools. It Isn't Working." Vox, October 30, 2018. https://www.vox.com/future-perfect/2018/10/30/17862050/education-policy-charity.

"The Gates Foundation, for instance": Mitchell, Katharyne. "The Billionaire Curse." Aeon, July 27, 2020. https://aeon.co/essays/the-enterprise-of-philanthropy-does-well-out-of-doing-good.

"Inside Philanthropy founder David Callahan": Callahan, David. Twitter Post. February 17, 2020. 9:46 PM. https://twitter.com/DavidCallahanIP/status/1229598073963171840

Teddy Shleifer, a writer for Recode": Shleifer, Teddy. Twitter Post. February 18, 2020. 12:10 AM. https://twitter.com/teddyschleifer/status/12296342- 17874579457

The Rise of Impact Investing

"Flew to Santa Barbara": The Economist, May 19, 2012.

"Warren Buffett was skeptical": Ibid.

"The Ford Foundation recently": "Ford Foundation Commits $1 Billion from Endowment to Mission-Related Investments." Ford Foundation, April 5, 2017. https://www.fordfoundation.org/the-latest/news/ford-foundation-commits-1-billion-from-endowment-to-mission-related-investments/.

"Jeff Bezos joined Bill Gates": Dillow, Clay. "Here's Why Bill Gates, Jeff Bezos, Jack Ma and Other Investors Are Pouring Billions into Clean-tech Ventures." CNBC. March 28, 2019. Accessed March 14, 2021. https://

www.cnbc.com/2019/03/28/gates-bezos-and-other-investors-are-pouring-billions-into-clean-tech.html.

"In the words of Jacqueline Novogratz": "Manifesto -." Acumen. February 19, 2021. https://acumen.org/manifesto/.

"The United Nations estimates": "Citing $2.5 Trillion Annual Financing Gap during SDG Business Forum Event, Deputy Secretary-General Says Poverty Falling Too Slowly | Meetings Coverage and Press Releases." *United Nations*, United Nations, 25 Sept. 2019, www.un.org/press/en/2019/dsgsm1340.doc.htm.

"One frequently-cited example is the Playpump": "Steller, Daniel, "The PlayPump: What Went Wrong?" *State of the Planet*, 1 July 2010, blogs.ei.columbia.edu/2010/07/01/the-playpump-what-went-wrong/.

"promised to hack healthy eating": Juicero. "A Note from Juicero's New CEO." Medium. April 21, 2017. Accessed March 15, 2021. https://medium.com/@Juicero/a-note-from-juiceros-new-ceo-cb23a1462b03.

"Nearly eight in ten employees": Burns, Danielle, et al. *Racial Disparities in the Workforces of Sustainable, Responsible, and Impact (SRI) Investing Mutual Funds*. 22 Jan. 2019, www.responsible-investor.com/storage/images/uploads/reports/Racial%2BDisparities%2Bin%2BSRI%2BFunds%2C%2B-Published%2BJanuary%2B22%2C%2B2019.pdf.

"In the United Kingdom": Chiu, Bonnie. "Still White, Still Male: New Report Quantifies Impact Investing's Diversity Problem." *NextBillion*, 21 Oct. 2019, nextbillion.net/impact-investing-diversity-problem/.

The Never-Ending Pledge

"Anand Giridharadas calculated": "Giridharadas, Anand. "Billionaires Won Corona." *The.Ink*, The.Ink, 9 Sept. 2020, the.ink/p/billion-aire-wealth-just- got-wealthier.

"several major foundations took out bonds": Daniels, Alex. "Foundations Turn to Bond Market in Response to Rising Need." *AP NEWS*, Associated

Press, 19 Feb. 2021, apnews.com/article/business-endowments-coronavirus-pandemic-philanthropy-california-58b9c13fada392117d-636cae2054fc90.

"A new $500 million impact fund": Tembo, Dorothy, and Jean-Philipe De Schrevel. "A New Fund to Kickstart Sustainable Investment." World Economic Forum. January 19, 2020. Accessed March 14, 2021. https://www.weforum.org/agenda/2020/01/sdg500-the-fund-kickstarting-sustainable-development-goals-investment/.

CHAPTER 2

"In his book": Walker, Darren. "Ignorance Is the Enemy Within: On the Power of Our Privilege, and the Privilege of Our Power." Ford Foundation. September 12, 2016. Accessed March 14, 2021.

"Ford grants supported": "Ford Foundation Commits $1 Billion from Endowment to Mission-related Investments." Ford Foundation. April 05, 2017. Accessed March 14, 2021. https://www.fordfoundation.org/the-latest/news/ford-foundation-commits-1-billion-from-endowment-to-mission-related-investments/.

"When Walker was named": Gelles, David. "How Being a 13-Year-Old Busboy Prepared Darren Walker to Lead the Ford Foundation." The New York Times. September 26, 2019. Accessed March 14, 2021. https://www.nytimes.com/2019/09/26/business/darren-walker-ford-foundation-corner-office.html

"In 2015, he held a press conference": Walker, Darren. "Listening for Change: Why Foundations Need to Pay Attention to What Grantees Are Saying." Ford Foundation. December 05, 2016. Accessed March 14, 2021. https://www.fordfoundation.org/just-matters/just-matters/posts/listening-for-change-why-foundations-need-to-pay-attention-to-what-grantees-are-saying/.

"Philanthropy can no longer grapple": Walker, Darren. "Why Giving Back

Isn't Enough." The New York Times. December 17, 2015. Accessed March 14, 2021. https://www.nytimes.com/2015/12/18/opinion/why-giving-back-isnt-enough.html.

"About fifteen percent of the world's population": "Disability Inclusion Overview." World Bank. October 1, 2020. Accessed March 14, 2021. https://www.worldbank.org/en/topic/disability

Nothing About Us Without Us

"More than seventy percent of people with disabilities": Ibid.

"In the 2012 US presidential election": Vasilogambros, Matt. "How Voters With Disabilities Are Blocked From the Ballot Box." The Pew Charitable Trusts. February 1, 2018. Accessed March 14, 2021. https://www.pewtrusts.org/en/research-and-analysis/blogs/stateline/2018/02/01/how-voters-with-disabilities-are-blocked-from-the-ballot-box.

"In Indonesia… only three percent of disabled people voted": Cameron, Lisa, and Diana Contreras Suarez. "Disability in Indonesia: What Can We Learn from the Data?" Accessed 2021. https://www.monash.edu/__data/assets/pdf_file/0003/1107138/Disability-in-Indonesia.pdf.

"One study from 2008 found": Dickson, Jim. "Philanthropy's Blind Spot: Supporting People with Disabilities." National Committee For Responsive Philanthropy. May 6, 2011. Accessed March 14, 2021. https://www.ncrp.org/publication/responsive-philanthropy-spring-2011/philanthro-pys-blind-spot-supporting-people-with-disabilities#_edn2.

"A more recent study found": Walton, Dan. "Disability-inclusive ODA: Aid Data on Donors, Channels, Recipients." Development Initiatives. July 3, 2020. Accessed March 14, 2021. https://devinit.org/resources/disability-inclusive-oda-aid-data-donors-channels-recipients/.

"The majority of grants for disabled people": "Key Facts On U.S. Foundations." Index of /gainknowledge/research/keyfacts2014. 2014. Accessed March 14,2021.http://foundationcenter.org/gainknowledge/research/keyfacts2014/.

"as one disability rights activist put it": Dickson, Jim. "Philanthropy's Blind Spot: Supporting People with Disabilities." National Committee For Responsive Philanthropy. May 6, 2011. Accessed March 14, 2021. https://www.ncrp.org/publication/responsive-philanthropy-spring-2011/philanthropys-blind-spot-supporting-people-with-disabilities#_edn2.

"Back then, it was a rallying cry": Golding, Frank. "Nothing About Us Without Us." SOCIAL JUSTICE FOR CARE LEAVERS. August 10, 2015. Accessed March 14, 2021. https://frankgolding.com/nothing-about-us-without-us/.

"How could I have overlooked?": Walker, Darren. "Ignorance Is the Enemy Within: On the Power of Our Privilege, and the Privilege of Our Power." Ford Foundation. September 12, 2016. Accessed March 14, 2021. https://www.fordfoundation.org/just-matters/just-matters/posts/ignorance-is-the-enemy-within-on-the-power-of-our-privilege-and-the-privilege-of-our-power/.

"Those who courageously": Ibid.

From Diversity to Accountability

"Every one of the top": Wang, Jennifer. "Americas Top Givers: The 50 Philanthropists That Gave the Most in 2018." Forbes. November 20, 2019. Accessed March 14, 2021. https://www.forbes.com/top-givers/#7e1a49c766ff.

"seventy-two percent of board members are white": Fottrell, Quentin. "The Boards of Americas Most Powerful Foundations Are Filled with Wealthy, Privately-educated White Men." MarketWatch. May 06, 2017. Accessed March 14,2021.https://www.marketwatch.com/story/the-boards-of-americas-most-powerful-foundations-are-dominated-by-wealthy-white-men-2017-05-03.

"Black people represent": Rendon, Jim. "Nonprofits Led by People of Color Win Less Grant Money With More Strings (Study)." Philanthropy.com.

May 7, 2020. Accessed March 14, 2021. https://www.philanthropy.com/article/nonprofits-led-by-people-of-color-win-less-grant-money-with-more-strings-study/.

"Transgender people represent": Francisco Maulbeck, Ben, and Lyle Matthew Kan. "The Philanthropic Closet: LGBTQ People in Philanthropy." Funders for LGBT Issues. October 15, 2018. Accessed March 14, 2021. https://lgbtfunders.org/research-item/the-philanthropic-closet-lgbtq-people-in-philanthropy/.

"There are similar… numbers for the Native American community": "Our Goals." Global Philanthropy Project RSS2. Accessed March 14, 2021. https://globalphilanthropyproject.org/.

"fewer than forty Native people…serve in key leadership roles": Barron, Jessica, Eileen Egan, and Raymond Foxworth. "Starting with Hiring: How to Welcome Native Leaders to the Philanthropic Sector." Non Profit News | Nonprofit Quarterly. December 03, 2020. Accessed March 14, 2021. https://nonprofitquarterly.org/starting-with-hiring-how-to-welcome-native-leaders-to-the-philanthropic-sector/.

"Fewer than a quarter": "Disability in Philanthropy and Nonprofits." April 2019. https://www.respectability.org/wp-content/uploads/2019/04/Disability-in-Philanthropy-and-Nonprofits-RespectAbility-FINAL.pdf.

"For example, women represent": Spruill, Vicky. "Gender Gap, Lack of Diversity in Foundation Staff Persist, Study Finds." Philanthropy News Digest (PND). February 05, 2018. Accessed March 14, 2021. https://philanthropynewsdigest.org/news/gender-gap-lack-of-diversity-in-foundation-staff-persist-study-finds.

The Ladder of Participation

"Authentic knowledge, he writes": Villanueva, Edgar. *Decolonizing Wealth: Indigenous Wisdom to Heal Divides and Restore Balance.* Berrett-Koehler, 2018.

"This experience led Arnstein to publish": Arnstein, Sherry R. "A Ladder of Citizen Participation," JAIP, Vol. 35, No. 4, July 1969, pp. 216-224 https://lithgow-schmidt.dk/sherry-arnstein/ladder-of-citizen-participation_en.pdf

"There are nearly 150 oversight boards in the United States": Ajilore, Olugbenga. "How Civilian Review Boards Can Further Police Accountability and Improve Community Relations." Scholars Strategy Network. June 25, 2018. Accessed March 14, 2021. https://scholars.org/brief/how-civilian-review-boards-can-further-police-accountability-and-improve-community-relations.

The Funding Process

"There is a critical difference": Arnstein, "A Ladder of Citizen Participation"

"There has only ever been one woman": Zillman, Claire. "How Jane Fraser Broke Banking's Highest Glass Ceiling." Fortune. October 19, 2020. Accessed March 14, 2021. https://fortune.com/longform/citi-ceo-jane-fraser-first-woman-wall-street-bank-citigroup-glass-ceiling/.

Participation in Impact Investing

"multiple studies show that investors": https://www.nber.org/system/files/working_papers/w18141/w18141.pdf

"Jeff Bezos's impact fund": Dillow, Clay. "Here's Why Bill Gates, Jeff Bezos, Jack Ma and Other Investors Are Pouring Billions into Clean-tech Ventures." CNBC. March 28, 2019. Accessed March 14, 2021. https://www.cnbc.com/2019/03/28/gates-bezos-and-other-investors-are-pouring-billions-into-clean-tech.html.

"One study of social networks": Beauchamp, Zack. "The Unbearable Whiteness of Social networks." Vox. August 22, 2014. Accessed March 14, 2021. https://www.vox.com/xpress/2014/8/22/6056835/white-black-social-networks-ferguson.

"Wharton professor Laura Huang found": "Who's the Most Attractive Investment Opportunity of All? Good-looking Men" Knowledge@ Wharton, May 26, 2015, accessed March 14, 2021. https://knowledge. wharton.upenn.edu/article/whos-the-most-attractive-investment-opportunity-of-all-good-looking-men

"The average venture capital firm reviews": O'Dell, J. "Here's a Look inside a Typical VC's Pipeline (a Must-read for Entrepreneurs)." VentureBeat. April 19, 2014. Accessed March 15, 2021. https://venturebeat. com/2014/04/19/heres-a-look-inside-a-typical-vcs-pipeline-a-must-read-for-entrepreneurs/.

What Does Structural Reform Look Like?

"As activist Audre Lorde famously said": "Meaning of 'The Master's Tools Will Never Dismantle the Master's House." - Audre Lorde." Activist School. Accessed March 15, 2021. https://www.activistgraduateschool.org/on-the-masters-tools.

"After Darren Walker heard from activists": Laszlo Mizrahi, Jennifer. "How Foundations Can Ensure Diversity Efforts Include People With Disabilities." Philanthropy.com. December 20, 2016. Accessed March 14, 2021. https://www.philanthropy.com/article/how-foundations-can-en-sure-diversity-efforts-include-people-with-disabilities/?cid2=gen_login_refresh&cid=gen_sign_in.

"The following summer, Walker's chief of staff": Winig, Laura, and Susan Crawford. "Noorain Khan and Disability Inclusion at the Ford Foundation." Harvard Law School The Case Studies. December 2018. Accessed March 14, 2021. https://casestudies.law.harvard.edu/noorain-khan-and-disability-inclusion-at-the-ford-foundation/.

"Following a yearlong audit": Ibid.

"In 2018, they hosted the Disability Rights": Ibid.

"since their permanent headquarters was being refitted": "Accessibility."

Ford Foundation. Accessed March 14, 2021. https://www.fordfoundation. org/about/the-ford-foundation-center-for-social-justice/accessibility/.

"In 2019, Walker teamed up with fifteen": "Amidst COVID-19 Crisis, Disability Inclusion Fund Launches Rapid Response Fund." Ford Foundation. April 22, 2020. Accessed March 15, 2021. https://www. fordfoundation.org/the-latest/news/amidst-covid-19-crisis-disability-inclusion-fund-launches-rapid-response-fund/.

"Decisions about funding": Ibid.

"A few weeks after the COVID-19 pandemic": Ibid.

CHAPTER 3

"Every year, more than a thousand people travel": Patton, Anna. "Skoll World Forum Audience Urged to Face Uncomfortable Truths." The Social Enterprise Magazine - Pioneers Post. April 09, 2019. Accessed March 15, 2021. https://www.pioneerspost.com/news-views/20190409/skoll-world-forum-audience-urged-face-uncomfortable-truths.

"He grew up poor": Villanueva, Edgar. *Decolonizing Wealth: Indigenous Wisdom to Heal Divides and Restore Balance.* Berrett-Koehler, 2018.

"Can be traced back to a history of exploitation": Ibid.

"Philanthropy, Villanueva told the crowd": "Edgar Villanueva: Decolonizing Wealth: 2019 Skoll World Forum." Facebook Watch. May 03, 2019. Accessed March 15, 2021. https://www.facebook.com/SkollFoundation/videos/593742151112432.

"*Forbes* described it as a celebration": Dolan, Kerry A. "Questioning Big Philanthropy At The Skoll World Forum: Is It Too Powerful And Out Of Touch?" Forbes. April 17, 2019. Accessed March 15, 2021. https://www. forbes.com/sites/kerryadolan/2019/04/16/questioning-big-philanthropy-at-the-skoll-world-forum-is-it-too-powerful-and-out-of-touch/#1f-b628a66253.

"Shortly after his keynote": Ibid.

"students at the university were petitioning": Mohdin, Aamna. "Protesters Rally in Oxford for Removal of Cecil Rhodes Statue." The Guardian. June 09, 2020. Accessed March 15, 2021. https://www.theguardian.com/world/2020/jun/09/protesters-rally-in-oxford-for-removal-of-cecil-rhodes-statue.

"They were initially met with resistance": Ibid.

"Femi Nylander, one of the student activists": Ibid.

Philanthropy's "Brief, Balmy Season"

"What philanthropy historian Benjamin Soskis calls": Soskis, Benjamin. "The Importance of Criticizing Philanthropy." The Atlantic. May 12, 2014. Accessed March 15, 2021. https://www.theatlantic.com/business/archive/2014/05/the-case-for-philanthropy-criticism/361951/.

"Soskis wrote that": Ibid.

"The Obama White House launched": "Office of Social Innovation and Civic Participation." National Archives and Records Administration. Accessed March 15, 2021. https://obamawhitehouse.archives.gov/administration/eop/sicp.

"Gara LaMarche, president of the powerful donor collective": LaMarche, Gara. "Big Philanthropy Faces a Reckoning, Too." The Nation. May 02, 2020. Accessed March 15, 2021. https://www.thenation.com/article/politics/philanthropy-politics-billionaires/.

"The Edelman Trust Barometer": "2020 Edelman Trust Barometer." Edelman. January 19, 2020. Accessed March 15, 2021. https://www.edelman.com/trust/2020-trust-barometer.

"a number of books came out": LaMarche, Gara. "Big Philanthropy Faces a Reckoning, Too." The Nation. May 02, 2020. Accessed March 15, 2021. https://www.thenation.com/article/politics/philanthropy-politics-billionaires/.

"sociology professor Linsey McGoey published": McGoey, Linsey.

"No Such Thing as a Free Gift: The Gates Foundation and the Price of Philanthropy." Amazon. October 4, 2016. Accessed March 15, 2021. https://www.amazon.com/Such-Thing-Free-Gift-Philanthropy/dp/1784786233.

"In 2015, Giridharadas landed a fellowship": Tabor, Nick. "How Well-Meaning Liberals Paved the Way for Trump." Intelligencer. August 27, 2018. Accessed March 15, 2021. https://nymag.com/intelligencer/2018/08/anand-giridharadas-on-winners-take-all.html.

"*Winners Take All: The Elite Charade of Changing the World*": Giridharadas, Anand. "Winners Take All: The Elite Charade of Changing the World." Amazon. August 28, 2018. Accessed March 15, 2021. https://www.amazon.com/Winners-Take-All-Charade-Changing/dp/0451493249.

"including his very own folk": Mann, Jonathan. YouTube. February 08, 2019. Accessed March 15, 2021. https://www.youtube.com/watch?v=Vb-V4GA3iWtQ&ab_channel=JonathanMann.

"*Just Giving: Why Philanthropy Is Failing Democracy and How It Can Do Better*": Reich, Rob. "Just Giving: Why Philanthropy Is failing Democracy and How It Can Do Better." Amazon. November 20, 2018. Accessed March 15, 2021. https://www.amazon.com/Just-Giving-Philanthropy-Failing-Democracy/dp/069118349X.

Impact Investing in the Spotlight

"Giridharadas has tweeted": Nuzzolillo, Gino. "Eat the Rich before They Eat Us." The Chronicle. January 28, 2020. Accessed March 15, 2021. https://www.dukechronicle.com/article/2020/01/eat-the-rich-before-they-eat-us-inequality-student-life

"Edgar Villanueva has argued": Villanueva, *Decolonizing Wealth*.

"On Valentine's Day 2016, Scholz" Jennifer, Mara. "Sex & Startups." Medium. February 16, 2016. Accessed March 15, 2021. https://medium.com/zebras-unite/sex-startups-53f2f63ded49

"A follow-up manifesto in 2017 announced": Jennifer, Mara. "Zebras Fix What Unicorns Break." Medium. March 8, 2017. Accessed March 15, 2021. https://medium.com/zebras-unite/zebrasfix-c467e55f9d96.

"Foxworth grew up in a working-class Baltimore neighborhood": Foxworth, Rodney. "Do Good by Giving Up More: A Vision of Restorative Investing." Medium. November 26, 2018. Accessed March 15, 2021. https://medium.com/commonfuture/do-good-by-giving-up-more-a-vision-of-restorative-investing-ae987cf5750d.

"Foxworth found himself sitting on countless panels": Ibid.

"On stage at Skoll, Foxworth argued": Dolan, "Questioning Big Philanthropy At The Skoll World Forum: Is It Too Powerful And Out Of Touch?"

"Foxworth argues that impact investing needs": Audette, Melanie, Global Endowment Management, and Matt Onek. "Impact Investing Can Fight Racism and Wealth Gaps - If Conducted in New Ways." Mission Investors Exchange. August 20, 2018. Accessed March 15, 2021. https://missioninvestors.org/resources/impact-investing-can-fight-racism-and-wealth-gaps-if-conducted-new-ways.

"Bill Gates wrote a blurb for *Winners Take All*": Giridharadas, "Winners Take All: The Elite Charade of Changing the World."

"Darren Walker wrote in his 2019 autobiography": "From Generosity to Justice." Ford Foundation. Accessed March 15, 2021. https://www.fordfoundation.org/just-matters/ford-forum/the-future-of-philanthropy/from-generosity-to-justice/

Can the World Be Deprogrammed?

"The rollout of the Paycheck Protection Program": Cerullo, Megan. "Up to 90% of Minority and Women Owners Shut out of Paycheck Protection Program, Experts Fear." CBS News. April 22, 2020. Accessed March 15, 2021. https://www.cbsnews.com/news/women-minority-business-owners-paycheck-protection-program-loans/.

"Canada began giving its residents $2,000 per month": Boyer, Emily. "Canada Already Paying Unemployed Citizens $2,000 per Month for Coronavirus Relief." WJXT. April 17, 2020. Accessed March 15, 2021. https://www.news4jax.com/news/local/2020/04/17/canada-is-already-paying-its-unemployed-citizens-2000-per-month-for-coronavirus-relief/.

"Over the summer of 2020, more than seven hundred fifty foundations": "A Call to Action: Philanthropy's Commitment During COVID-19." Council on Foundations. March 12, 2021. Accessed March 15, 2021. https://www.cof.org/news/call-action-philanthropys-commitment-during-covid-19.

"Six out of ten foundations reported": Emily Finchum-Mason, Kelly Husted. "Philanthropic Foundation Responses to COVID-19 - Emily Finchum-Mason, Kelly Husted, David Suárez, 2020." SAGE Journals. Accessed March 15, 2021. https://journals.sagepub.com/doi/full/10.1177/0899764020966047.

"A number of foundations... began to delay interest payments": Kharas, Alexandra LaForge and Cyrus. "How Impact Investors Can Respond to COVID-19." Arabella Advisors. August 18, 2020. Accessed March 15, 2021. https://www.arabellaadvisors.com/blog/how-impact-investors-can-respond-to-covid-19/.

"The Kresge Foundation suspended interest payments": "Kresge Suspends $1 Million in Interest Payments for 6 Months in Response to Pandemic." Kresge Foundation. August 13, 2020. Accessed March 15, 2021. https://kresge.org/news-views/kresge-suspends-1-million-in-interest-payments-for-6-months-in-response-to-pandemic/.

"the John D. and Catherine T. MacArthur Foundation announced": "$25 Million Toward an Equitable Recovery - MacArthur Foundation." RSS. Accessed March 15, 2021. https://www.macfound.org/press/press-releases/25-million-toward-equitable-recovery.

"...philanthropy's 'matrix moment'": Kawaoka-Chen, Dana. "Philanthropy, This Is Our "Matrix" Moment . . . What Will You Choose?" Medium. April

01, 2020. Accessed March 15, 2021. https://medium.com/justice-funders/philanthropy-this-is-our-matrix-moment-what-will-you-choose-283cd-ff53056.

"On stage at Oxford that day, he didn't excoriate": "Edgar Villanueva: Decolonizing Wealth: 2019 Skoll World Forum."

"Villanueva lays out seven principles": Villanueva, *Decolonizing Wealth*.

CHAPTER 4

"a Yale student named George Pillsbury": Lurie, Theodora. "Change, Not Charity: The Story of the Funding Exchange." May 2017. https://funding-exchangehistory.files.wordpress.com/2017/05/funding_exchange_history_spring_2017.pdf.

"a new ad campaign featuring a "dough boy": "Pillsbury Doughboy." Wikipedia. March 05, 2021. Accessed March 15, 2021. https://en.wikipedia.org/wiki/Pillsbury_Doughboy.

"private schools and debutante parties.": Lurie, "Change, Not Charity"

"communal giving practices woven through... inidigenous cultures": Tardi, Carla. "What You Should Know About Tontines." Investopedia. August 28, 2020. Accessed March 15, 2021. https://www.investopedia.com/terms/t/tontine.asp.

"mutual aid societies in freedman communities": Fernando, Christine. "Mutual Aid Networks Find Roots in Communities of Color." AP NEWS. January 21, 2021. Accessed March 15, 2021. https://apnews.com/article/immigration-coronavirus-pandemic-7b1d14f25ab717c2a29ceafd40364b6e.

"only a few small private foundations at the time": Lurie, "Change, Not Charity"

"Pillsbury moved to Boston after graduation": Ibid.

"Pillsbury and his friends pooled together some money": Ibid.

"'Our parents give to the symphony'": Ibid.

"'Reluctantly wealthy, they fund radical groups": "Reluctantly Wealthy, They Fund Radical Groups." The New York Times. March 04, 1977. Accessed March 15, 2021. https://www.nytimes.com/1977/03/04/archives/reluctantly-wealthy-they-fund-radical-groups.html.

"the fund would have a participatory grantmaking model": Lurie, "Change, Not Charity"

"According to a 1977 *New York Times* article": "Reluctantly Wealthy, They Fund Radical Groups."

"The fund helped organize": Sullivan, James. "When Bob Marley Came to Allston - The Boston Globe." BostonGlobe.com. July 18, 2019. Accessed March 15, 2021. https://www.bostonglobe.com/arts/music/2019/07/18/when-bob-marley-came-allston/gNl1m7sG4QbqJraEaPFxbO/story.html.

"Haymarket became a blueprint": Lurie, "Change, Not Charity"

Open-Sourced Altruism

"Jimmy Wales founded Wikipedia in 2001": "History of Wikipedia." Wikipedia. February 25, 2021. Accessed March 15, 2021. https://en.wikipedia.org/wiki/History_of_Wikipedia.

"Wikipedia volunteers were adding": "Size of Wikipedia." Wikipedia. March 10, 2021. Accessed March 15, 2021. https://en.wikipedia.org/wiki/Wikipedia:Size_of_Wikipedia:

"Wales and his team noticed a major flaw in their editing community": Projects, Contributors To Wikimedia. "Funding Free Knowledge the Wiki Way - Wikimedia Foundation Participatory Grantmaking." Wikisource, the Free Online Library. July 24, 2017. Accessed March 15, 2021. https://en.wikisource.org/wiki/Funding_Free_Knowledge_the_Wiki_Way_-_Wikimedia_Foundation_Participatory_Grantmaking.

"They built an open-source grantmaking practice": Ibid.

"Jean Case was Director of Marketing at AOL": "Jean Case." Case Foundation. August 16, 2019. Accessed March 15, 2021. https://casefoundation.org/profile/jean-case/.

"Dubbed Make It Your Own": Gibson, Cynthia M. "Citizen-Centered Solutions." September 2010. https://casefoundation.org/wp-content/uploads/2010/09/Citizen-Centered-Solutions-Report.pdf.

"Several 'citizen-centered phases'": Gibson, "Citizen-Centered Solutions."

"The Financial Times likened it to 'open source' software": "Networking for the Benefit of Others." Financial Times. November 02, 2007. Accessed March 15, 2021. https://www.ft.com/content/b94c9c48-896c-11dc-b52e-0000779fd2ac.

"the 'closed circuit' of traditional grantmaking": Strom, Stephanie. "Foundation Lets Public Help Award Money." The New York Times. June 26, 2007. Accessed March 15, 2021. https://www.nytimes.com/2007/06/26/us/26charity.html.

Democratizing Finance

"born out of the grisly factories of Great Britain": Laville, Jean-Louis. "The Solidarity Economy: An International Movement." RCCS Annual Review. A Selection from the Portuguese Journal Revista Crítica De Ciências Sociais. October 01, 2010. Accessed March 15, 2021. https://journals.openedition.org/rccsar/202.

"In the aftermath of a brutal military dictatorship": "Solidarity Economy in Brazil." Solidarity Economy in Brazil - P2P Foundation. Accessed March 15, 2021. https://wiki.p2pfoundation.net/Solidarity_Economy_in_Brazil.

"economists from thirty countries gathered in Peru": "History and International Meetings." RIPESS. Accessed March 15, 2021. http://www.ripess.org/who-are-we/history/?lang=en.

"Take the Southern Reparations Loan Fund": "About." Southern Reparations Loan Fund. Accessed March 15, 2021. https://southernreparations.

org/about/.

"There are now more than 500 "unicorn" companies" "The Complete List Of Unicorn Companies." Accessed March 15, 2021. https://www.cbin-sights.com/research-unicorn-companies.

"what investor Ross Baird calls "blind spots"": Baird, Ross. "The Innovation Blind Spot: Why We Back the Wrong Ideas-and What to Do about It." Amazon. 2018. Accessed March 15, 2021. https://www.amazon.com/Innovation-Blind-Spot-Wrong-Ideas_and/dp/1944648615.

"Female entrepreneurs receive less than 15 percent": "About Us ◆ Village Capital." Village Capital. Accessed March 15, 2021. https://vilcap.com/about-us.

"In September 2009": Capital, Village. "Village Capital's 10 Year Impact Report." News & Views ◆ Village Capital. Accessed March 15, 2021. https://newsandviews.vilcap.com/reports/ten-year-impact-report.

"They ran their first test in New Orleans": Ibid.

"Over the next decade, Village Capital ran": Schleifer, Theodore. "A New and Intriguing Idea to Increase Investment in Women-led Startups." Vox. February 04, 2019. Accessed March 15, 2021. https://www.vox.com/2019/2/4/ 18202842/startups-venture-capitalists-diversity-women-village-capital.

"slightly *better* at picking": Ibid.

The Inside Argument: Tapping into the Value of Lived Experience

"When the *New York Times* wrote": Strom, "Foundation Lets Public Help Award Money."

"Participatory budgeting, which goes back to ancient Greece": Gelman, Valeria Lvovna, and Daniely Votto. "What If Citizens Set City Budgets? An Experiment That Captivated the World-Participatory Budgeting-Might Be

Abandoned in Its Birthplace." World Resources Institute. November 02, 2018. Accessed March 15, 2021. https://www.wri.org/blog/2018/06/what-if-citizens-set-city-budgets-experiment-captivated-world-participatory-budgeting.

"In 1990, the *vilas* residents organized…": Ibid.

"according to one article": Ibid.

"According of data from the World Bank": Bank, World. "Brazil : Toward a More Inclusive and Effective Participatory Budget in Porto Alegre, Volume 1. Main Report." Open Knowledge Repository. January 01, 2008. Accessed March 15, 2021. https://openknowledge.worldbank.org/handle/10986/8042.

"more than seven thousand governments": Yves Cabannes, Zhuang Ming. "Participatory Budgeting at Scale and Bridging the Rural—urban Divide in Chengdu - Yves Cabannes, Zhuang Ming, 2014." SAGE Journals. Accessed March 15, 2021. https://journals.sagepub.com/doi/full/10.1177/095624781-3509146.

"Fourteen countries use participatory budgeting on the national level": Josh Lerner, Steve Dubb, Martin Levine, Anne Eigeman, and Eileen Cunniffe. "From Defunding to Reinvestment: Why We Need to Scale Participatory Budgeting." Non Profit News | Nonprofit Quarterly. June 26, 2020. Accessed March 15, 2021. https://nonprofitquarterly.org/from-defunding-to-reinvestment-why-we-need-to-scale- participatory-budgeting/.

"Youth Lead the Change": Grillos, Tara. "Youth Lead the Change: The City of Boston's Youth-Focused Participatory Budgeting Process." August 2014. https://scholar.harvard.edu/files/grillos/files/pb_boston_year_1_eval_0.pdf.

"'Vote Fest' events": "Vote Fest." Accessed March 14, 2021. https://www.boston.gov/calendar/vote-fest.

"One paper tied Brazil's": PBPadmin. "Lessons from 30 Years of a Global

Experiment in Democracy." Participatory Budgeting Project. April 24, 2020. Accessed March 15, 2021. https://www.participatorybudgeting.org/lessons-from-30-years-of-pb/.

"A Harvard study of Youth Lead the Change": Grillos, "Youth Lead the Change: The City of Boston's Youth-Focused Participatory Budgeting Process."

"One reader at the Baring Foundation": Hutton, Ceri. "Monitoring and Evaluating Participatory Grantmaking." January 2016. https://baringfoundation.org.uk/wp-content/uploads/2016/06/Discussion-Paper-ME-for-Participatory-Grantmaking.pdf.

The Outside Argument: Decolonizing Wealth

"Vu Le, editor of the website Nonprofit AF": Justice Funders. "Finding Power in Practice: How Trust Can Liberate Philanthropy from Played Out Narratives." Medium. May 14, 2018. Accessed March 15, 2021. https://medium.com/justice-funders/finding-power-in-practice-how-trust-can-liberate-philanthropy-from-played-out-narratives-f1dcf0cc8294.

CHAPTER 5

"An earthquake measuring 6.2 on the Richter scale": "Magnitude 6.3 Quake in Central Java." NASA. Accessed March 14, 2021. https://earthobservatory.nasa.gov/images/16767/magnitude-63-quake-in-central-java.

"Yogyakarta, home to": "2006 Yogyakarta Earthquake." Wikipedia. February 22, 2021. Accessed March 14, 2021. https://en.wikipedia.org/wiki/2006_Yogyakarta_earthquake.

"Including the launch of a children's center": "Dwi Ariyani." Disability Rights Advocacy Fund. November 26, 2020. Accessed March 14, 2021. https://drafund.org/about/staff/dwi-ariyani/.

"Most grantmakers were centralized": UN Partnership to Promote the

Rights of Persons with Disabilities Multi-Donor Trust Fund. March 01, 2016. Accessed March 14, 2021. https://www.ilo.org/jakarta/whatwedo/projects/WCMS_211048/lang--en/index.htm.

The Disability Rights Fund

"In December 2006": "Convention on the Rights of Persons with Disabilities (CRPD) Enable." United Nations. Accessed March 14, 2021. https://www.un.org/development/desa/disabilities/convention-on-the-rights-of-persons-with-disabilities.html.

"The UN made the historic move": "The United Nations Convention on the Rights of People with Disabilities." Disability Justice. August 31, 2020. Accessed March 14, 2021. https://disabilityjustice.org/the-united-nations-convention-on-the-rights-of-people-with-disabilities.

"More robust protections for disabled people": Kanter, Arlene S. "Let's Try Again: Why the United States Should Ratify the United Nations Convention on the Rights of People with Disabilities." SSRN. May 14, 2019. Accessed March 14, 2021. https://papers.ssrn.com/sol3/papers.cfm?abstract_id= 3373259.

"This often leads to forced detention": "The final treaty read": Series, Lucy. "Article 12 CRPD: Equal Recognition before the Law." The UN Convention on the Rights of Persons with Disabilities: A Commentary. January 01, 1970. Accessed March 14, 2021. https://www.ncbi.nlm.nih.gov/books/NBK539188/.

"Diana Samarasan, the disability rights activist": "Diana Samarasan." Disability Rights Advocacy Fund. November 26, 2020. Accessed March 14, 2021. https://drafund.org/about/staff/diana-samarasan/.

Who decides who decides?

"There are a range of models": Evans, Lani. "Participatory Philanthropy." September 2015. https://philanthropy.org.nz/wp-content/uploads/2016/09/Participatory-Philanthropy-Churchill.pdf.

"The group chose a representative participation model": Love, Katy. "Deciding for All or All Deciding? Exploring Participatory Grantmaking." Disability Rights Fund. July 25, 2019. Accessed March 14, 2021. https://disabilityrightsfund.org/deciding-for-all-or-all-deciding-exploring-participatory-grantmaking-2/.

"Distributed more than $37 million in grants": "Financials." Disability Rights Fund. November 30, 2020. Accessed March 14, 2021. https://disabilityrightsfund.org/about/financials/.

Gender and justice

"The original Giving Pledge list": "The Giving Pledge – What about the Women?" TPI. September 17, 2010. Accessed March 14, 2021. https://www.tpi.org/blog/the-giving-pledge-what-about-the-women.

"Women may make up seventy-six percent of...": "The David and Lucile Packard Foundation Commitment to Diversity." December 31, 2018. https://www.packard.org/wp-content/uploads/2019/04/Commitment_to_Respect_and_Diversity_as_of_123118.pdf.

"Only five percent": Chiu, Bonnie. "Philanthropy Needs To Address The Funding And Equity Gaps For Women And Girls." Forbes. December 22, 2020. Accessed March 14, 2021. https://www.forbes.com/sites/bonniechiu/2020/12/21/philanthropy-needs-to-address-the-funding-and-equity-gaps-for-women-and-girls/?sh=20afee342e2f.

"Just one percent": https://www.awid.org/sites/default/files/atoms/files/awid_funding_ecosystem_2019_final_eng.pdf

"One study found": "She Pioneers." She Pioneers - Mama Cash History. Accessed March 14, 2021. http://history.mamacash.org/jewel/she-gives-core-funding/.

"Many of the earliest funds were bankrolled": "Accelerating Change for Women and Girls: The Role of Women's Funds." http://www.womensfundingnetwork.org/wp-content/uploads/2014/03/TheRoleofWomensFunds.pdf.

"More than one hundred forty-five women's funds": "Women's Foundations and Funds: A Landscape Study." Lilly Family School of Philanthropy. Accessed March 15, 2021. https://philanthropy.iupui.edu/institutes/womens-philanthropy-institute/research/foundations-funds.html.

"In 2018 the Women's Funding Network found…": Marek, Author Kiersten. "Womens Funds Show Philanthropy the Way to Transparency, Diversity ~ Philanthropy Women." Philanthropy Women. March 29, 2018. Accessed March 14, 2021. https://philanthropywomen.org/womens-funds/womens-funds-show-philanthropy-way-transparency-diversity/.

"FRIDA was dreamed up in 2009": "FRIDA Oficial Website - FRIDA: Young Feminist Fund." FRIDA | Young Feminist Fund. August 17, 2020. Accessed March 14, 2021. https://youngfeministfund.org/about-us/.

"'The movement to end gender-based violence'…": "Myths and Realities of #MeToo: Young Feminists in the Global South Speak out." OpenGlobalRights. Accessed March 14, 2021. https://www.openglobalrights.org/myths-and-realities-of-metoo-young-feminists-in-the-global-south-speak-out/.

"'The hashtag #donttellmehowtodress'": Apichatsakol, Mika. "#DontTellMeHowToDress." Tatler Thailand. June 26, 2018. Accessed March 14, 2021. https://www.thailandtatler.com/society/donttellmehowtodress.

"FRIDA has awarded around $7 million": Mohammed, Ro-Ann. "10 Journeys in 10 Years of FRIDA - FRIDA: Young Feminist Fund." FRIDA | Young Feminist Fund. December 02, 2020. Accessed March 14, 2021. https://youngfeministfund.org/10-journeys-in-10-years-of-frida/.

"she and her father created": Leber, Jessica. "How Teenage Activist Malala Yousafzai Is Turning Her Fame Into A Movement." Fast Company. September 01, 2015. Accessed March 14, 2021. https://www.fastcompany.com/3050372/how-teenage-activist-malala-yousafzai-is-turning-her-fame-into-a-movement.

"promoting traditional gender roles and banning gender studies in

schools": Mudde, Cas. "Why the Far Right Is Obsessed with "gender Ideology"." Why the Far Right Is Obsessed with "gender Ideology". September 20, 2019. Accessed March 14, 2021. https://www.newstatesman.com/world/europe/2019/09/why-far-right-obsessed-gender-ideology.

"The Abortion Dream Team": Anna Louie Sussman Anna Louie Sussman Is a New York-based Journalist with over a Decade of Experience Writing on Gender. "Meet Poland's Abortion Dream Team." Harper's BAZAAR. November 04, 2019. Accessed March 14, 2021. https://www.harpersbazaar.com/culture/features/a28690537/abortion-dream-team-poland/.

From rescue to rights

"As the most-visited city…": "Topic: Tourism in Venice." Statista. Accessed March 15, 2021. https://www.statista.com/topics/5979/tourism-in-venice/

"Tadej Pogačar, a forty-one-year-old Slovenian": "Tadej Pogačar & P.A.R.A.S.I.T.E. Museum of Contemporary Art." ♦ MGML. Accessed March 15, 2021. https://mgml.si/en/city-art-gallery/exhibitions/254/tadej-pogacar-parasite-museum-of-contemporary-art/.

"The museum's website explains that…": About… Accessed March 15, 2021. http://www.parasite-pogacar.si/about.htm.

"Thousands of sex workers carrying red umbrellas": "Under the Red Umbrella." Under the Red Umbrella | Sex Work Europe. Accessed March 15, 2021. http://www.sexworkeurope.org/campaigns/red-umbrella-campaigns.

"There are an estimated forty million sex workers in the world": "Forced Labour, Modern Slavery and Human Trafficking (Forced Labour, Modern Slavery and Human Trafficking)." Forced Labour, Modern Slavery and Human Trafficking (Forced Labour, Modern Slavery and Human Trafficking). Accessed March 15, 2021. https://www.ilo.org/global/topics/forced-labour/lang--en/index.htm.

"One recent study published by the National Institutes of Health":

Sawicki, Danielle A., Brienna N. Meffert, Kate Read, and Adrienne J. Heinz. "Culturally Competent Health Care for Sex Workers: An Examination of Myths That Stigmatize Sex-Work and Hinder Access to Care." Sexual and Relationship Therapy : Journal of the British Association for Sexual and Relationship Therapy. 2019. Accessed March 15, 2021. https://www.ncbi. nlm.nih.gov/pmc/articles/PMC6424363/.

"Project Lantern, an anti-trafficking initiative": "International Justice Mission Receives $5 Million Grant to Fight Sex Trafficking." The Bill & Melinda Gates Foundation. January 01, 0001. Accessed March 15, 2021. https://www.gatesfoundation.org/Media-Center/Press-Releases/2006/03/ International-Justice-Mission-Receives-Grant.

"As one woman involved in the peer review process said": Cash, Mama, and Mamacash. "Mama Cash Annual Report 2013." Issuu. Accessed March 15, 2021. https://issuu.com/mamacash/docs/mamacash_annual_ report_2013.

"Mobilized their network to oppose it": "Movements for Sex Workers Rights Unite to Halt an Anti-trafficking Bill in India." MamaCash. Accessed March 15, 2021. https://www.mamacash.org/en/movements-for-sex-work-ers-rights-unite-to-halt-an-anti-trafficking-bill-in-india.

"By July 2018, the Indian government": Ibid.

Community Builders

"Place-based strategies now account for $5 billion": "Global Impact." Community Foundation Atlas. Accessed March 15, 2021. https://commu-nityfoundationatlas.org/facts/.

"According to the Milken Institute": "Going Local: The Power of Place-Based Philanthropy." Milken Institute. Accessed March 15, 2021. https:// milkeninstitute.org/articles/going-local-power-place-based-philanthropy.

"Fewer than six paid employees": "Global Impact." Community Founda-tion Atlas.

"The sixteen original Funding Exchange funds": "Funding Exchange History." Funding Exchange History. Accessed March 15, 2021. https://fex. org/.

Rawa: Creative Palestinian Communities Fund

"In 1993, Palestinians became": History.com Editors. "Oslo Accords." History.com. February 16, 2018. Accessed March 15, 2021. https://www. history.com/topics/middle-east/oslo-accords.

"convene a meeting of philanthropy and development professionals": "Pocantino Convening Summary Report." http://rawafund.org/sites/ default/files/2015 CPCF REPORT w anex.pdf.

"Held its first community forum": "Participatory Grantmaking in Palestine: Taking the Time to Make It Just - GFCF : GFCF." Global Fund for Community Foundations. Accessed March 15, 2021. https:// globalfundcommunityfoundations.org/news/taking-the-time-to-make-it-just-so-communities-can-lead-five-lessons-from-a-new-participatory-community-led-initiative/.

Brooklyn Community Foundation

"one of the most historically diverse neighborhoods in one of the most diverse cities": "Crown Heights/Prospect Heights Neighborhood Profile." NYU Furman Center. Accessed March 15, 2021. https://furmancenter.org/ neighborhoods/view/crown-heights-prospect-heights.

"lost between ten and fourteen percent percent of its Black population": Anderson, K., C. et al, ""What's Happened to the People?" Gentrification and Racial Segregation in Brooklyn." Journal of African American Studies. January 01, 1970. Accessed March 15, 2021. https://link.springer.com/ article/10.1007/s12111-020-09499-y.

"'A tale of two cities'": Walker, Hunter. "Bill De Blasio Tells A Tale of Two Cities at His Mayoral Campaign Kickoff." Observer. January 27, 2013.

Accessed March 15, 2021. https://observer.com/2013/01/bill-de-blasio-tells-a-tale-of-two-cities-at-his-mayoral-campaign-kickoff/.

"She told a local paper": "How to Be Charitable, from Brooklyns Guru of Giving." The Bridge. December 22, 2017. Accessed March 15, 2021. https://thebridgebk.com/how-to-be-charitable-from-brooklyns-guru-of-giving/.

"As Clarke told a board member two weeks into her tenure": Remaley, Michael Hamill. "Listening and Evolving: How a Community Foundation Put Racial Equity at the Center of Its Work." Inside Philanthropy. April 10, 2019. Accessed March 15, 2021. https://www.insidephilanthropy.com/home/2019/4/2/listening-and-evolving-how-a-community-foundation-put-racial-equity-at-the-center-of-its-work.

"In 2015, the foundation launched": "What Happens When A Foundation Puts Residents In Charge of Local Grantmaking." Neighborhood Strength. Accessed March 15, 2021. https://neighborhoods.brooklyncommunityfoundation.org/.

"One video of a council meeting": Foundation, Brooklyn Community. "Neighborhood Strength Council Meeting." Vimeo. March 13, 2021. Accessed March 15, 2021. https://vimeo.com/224898828.

"In 2017, the board approved a grant": "Community Fund Grants." Brooklyn Community Foundation. January 01, 1970. Accessed March 15, 2021. https://www.brooklyncommunityfoundation.org/grants/brooklyn-college-foundation-inc?tid=178&tid_1=All&field_year_value[value][year]=2017.

CHAPTER 6

"One in three renters in the state": Facebook. Accessed March 15, 2021. https://d3n8a8pro7vhmx.cloudfront.net/clvu/pages/2727/attachments/original/1596574636/August_eviction_estimates_report.pdf?1596574636.

"A little alien in the belly of capitalism": PDF | The Emergence of the

Boston Ujima Project | ID: 3f462j43p | Tufts Digital Library. Accessed March 15, 2021. https://dl.tufts.edu/concern/pdfs/3f462j43p.

Opting out

"the Boston 2024 Partnership": Press, Associated. "Boston Bidders Hope Time Is Right for Frugal Games - The Boston Globe." BostonGlobe.com. November 23, 2014. Accessed March 15, 2021. https://web.archive.org/web/20170614032806/http://www.bostonglobe.com/metro/2014/11/22/boston-bidders-hope-time-right-for-frugal-games/Gg72bgH4vHrvQ7d-j4G6COO/story.html.

"Developers razed an East London… neighborhood": "Displaced by London's Olympics." The Guardian. June 02, 2008. Accessed March 15, 2021. https://www.theguardian.com/uk/2008/jun/02/olympics2012.

"A blown-up map from the 1930s": Larson, Sandra. "In Boston, interactive exhibit brings redlining impact home." Next City, October 2, 2019. Accessed March 15, 2021. https://nextcity.org/daily/entry/in-boston-interactive-exhibit-brings-redlining-impact-home

"Ta-Nehisi Coates": Coates, Ta-Nehisi. "The Case for Reparations." The Atlantic. March 05, 2021. Accessed March 15, 2021. https://www.theatlantic.com/magazine/archive/2014/06/the-case-for-reparations/361631/.

From Silicon Valley to Silicon Savannah

"Eweniyi and her friends were operating": Wrobel, Ben. "Flipping The Power Dynamics: Can Entrepreneurs Make Successful Investment Decisions?" News & Views ♦ Village Capital. Accessed March 15, 2021. https://newsandviews.vilcap.com/reports/flipping-the-power-dynamics-can-entrepreneurs-make-successful-investment-decisions

"A 2017 study found": Kariuki, Harriet. "Silicon Savannah or Silicon Valley? 90% of Funding in East Africa Goes to Foreign Startup Founders." Medium. August 30, 2018. Accessed March 15, 2021. https://medium.

com/@harriet436/silicon-savannah-or-silicon-valley-90-of-funding-in-east-africa-goes-to-foreign-startup-founders-c8cd894236c8.

The danger of digital recolonization

"In April 2019": Bright, Jake. "African E-commerce Startup Jumia's Shares Open at $14.50 in NYSE IPO." TechCrunch. April 12, 2019. Accessed March 15, 2021. https://techcrunch.com/2019/04/12/african-e-commerce-startup-jumias-shares-open-at-14-50-in-nyse-ipo/.

"Amazon of Africa": Kazeem, Yomi. "The "Amazon of Africa" Is Trying to Enable Third-party E-commerce Rather than Sell More Stuff." Quartz. Accessed March 15, 2021. https://qz.com/africa/1938532/jumia-can-be-africas-amazon-by-enabling-third-party-e-commerce/

"Digital recolonization": Smit, Norman. "Africa's Wicked Problems and Emotionally Flawed Leaders." African Leadership Institute. March 19, 2020. Accessed March 15, 2021. https://alinstitute.org/59-reading-library/880-africa-s-wicked-problems-and-emotionally-flawed-leaders.

"Western countries plunder": "World Is Plundering Africa's Wealth of 'billions of Dollars a Year.'" The Guardian. May 24, 2017. Accessed March 15, 2021. https://www.theguardian.com/global-development/2017/may/24/world-is-plundering-africa-wealth-billions-of-dollars-a-year.

"Initially staffed with former officials": "From Colonialism to Development: Reflections of Former Colonial Officers." Taylor & Francis. Accessed March 15, 2021. https://www.tandfonline.com/doi/abs/10.1080/14662040600624502.

"Mohamed wrote in his analysis": "Impact Investing Has Replicated Silicon Valley's Racial Funding Gap: White Founders Receive the Majority of African Impact Investing Dollars." LinkedIn. Accessed March 15, 2021. https://www.linkedin.com/pulse/impact-investing-has-replicated-silicon-valleys-racial-mohamed.

Exporting a broken model

"They ate tilapia and ugali": "Facebook Billionaire Founder Mark Zucker-berg Samples Ugali and Tilapia in Nairobi." Nairobi News. September 01, 2016. Accessed March 15, 2021. https://nairobinews.nation.co.ke/news/ facebook-billionaire-founder-mark-zuckerberg-samples-ugali-and-tilapia-in-nairobi.

"Tech hubs like iHub in Nairobi": Field, Anne. "Village Capital Helps Fledgling Accelerators, Incubators In Africa Up Their Game." Forbes. September 01, 2020. Accessed March 15, 2021. https://www.forbes.com/ sites/annefield/2020/08/29/village-capital-helps-fledgling-accelerators-incubators-in-africa-up-their-game/?sh=675956833fc2.

"Eighty percent are male": Harris, Ainsley. "Bros Dominate VC, Where 91% of Decision-makers Are Male." Fast Company. March 07, 2018. Accessed March 15, 2021. https://www.fastcompany.com/40540948/91-of-decision-makers-at-u-s-venture-capital-firms-are-men.

"Only thirty-four Black female founders have ever raised": Hinchliffe, Emma. "The Number of Black Female Founders Who Have Raised More than $1 Million Has Nearly Tripled since 2018." Fortune. December 02, 2020. Accessed March 15, 2021. https://fortune.com/2020/12/02/ black-women-female-founders-venture-capital-funding-vc-2020-project-diane/.

Rethinking ownership

"'Is it not perverse,' he wrote,": Foxworth, Rodney. "Wealth Inequality and the Fallacies of Impact Investing." Medium. October 04, 2019. Accessed March 15, 2021. https://medium.com/commonfuture/wealth-inequali-ty-and-the-fallacies-of-impact-investing-eea902924309.

"started… supporting locally led incubators and accelerators": Spiller, Sam, et al "Village Capital Taps 15 African Tech Hubs for VilCap Commu-nities Africa Initiative." Ventureburn. August 24, 2018. Accessed March 15, 2021. https://ventureburn.com/2018/08/vilcap-communities-africa/.

CHAPTER 7

"The fifteen people gathered on the roof": Bokoff, Jen. "This Week Two Years Ago, We Held a Participatory Grantmaking Institute in Mexico City for 68 Human Rights Funders. It Was-without a Doubt-a Highlight of My Career to Collaborate on That Project with Brilliant Leaders from around the World. @CandidDotOrg @hrfunders #ShiftThePower Pic.twitter.com/KR8Ekl9ley." Twitter. October 14, 2020. Accessed March 15, 2021. https://twitter.com/jenbo1/status/1316400652499722240.

"Annual grantmaking budget of more than $7 million": Projects, Contributors To Wikimedia. "Funding Free Knowledge the Wiki Way - Wikimedia Foundation Participatory Grantmaking." Wikisource, the Free Online Library. July 24, 2017. Accessed March 15, 2021. https://en.wikisource.org/wiki/Funding_Free_Knowledge_the_Wiki_Way_-_Wikimedia_Foundation_Participatory_Grantmaking#cite_note-5.

"Writes historian Benjamin Soskis": Benjamin Soskis and Stanley N. Katz. May 1, 2017. "Looking Back at 50 Years of U.S. Philanthropy." Hewlett Foundation. January 17, 2018. Accessed March 15, 2021. https://hewlett.org/library/looking-back-50-years-u-s-philanthropy/.

"Only seventeen percent of foundation CEOs": Powell, Alison, and Alison Powell Is Senior Director of the Philanthropy Practice at The Bridgespan Group. Willa Seldon Is a Partner in Bridgespan's San Francisco Office and Co-leads Its Children. "Reimagining Institutional Philanthropy (SSIR)." Stanford Social Innovation Review: Informing and Inspiring Leaders of Social Change. Accessed March 15, 2021. https://ssir.org/articles/entry/reimagining_institutional_philanthropy.

"Fat kittens": Teltsch, Kathleen. "NETWORK OF 'ALTERNATIVE' PHILANTHROPIES IS FORMING." The New York Times. July 05, 1983. Accessed March 15, 2021. https://www.nytimes.com/1983/07/05/us/network-of-alternative-philanthropies-is-forming.html.

"Obie Benz": Lurie, "Change Not Charity: The Story of the Funding Exchange."

"FEX leaders are widely credited": "The Funding Exchange Model of Grantmaking." National Committee For Responsive Philanthropy. May 11, 2017. Accessed March 15, 2021. https://www.ncrp.org/publication/responsive-philanthropy-winter-2011-12/funding-exchange-model-grant-making.

Institutional philanthropy

"Bridgespan Group defines": Powell, Alison, and Willa Seldon. "Reimagining Institutional Philanthropy (SSIR)." Stanford Social Innovation Review: Informing and Inspiring Leaders of Social Change. Accessed March 15, 2021. https://ssir.org/articles/entry/reimagining_institutional_philanthropy.

"In 1993, the top ten foundations accounted": Ibid.

"Nancy Roob": Ibid.

"telling an Inside Philanthropy journalist": Williams, Tate. "Power in Letting Go: How Participatory Grantmakers Are Democratizing Philanthropy." Inside Philanthropy. September 26, 2019. Accessed March 15, 2021. https://www.insidephilanthropy.com/home/2018/11/9/power-in-letting-go-how-participatory-grantmakers-are-democratizing-philanthropy.

"Gara LaMarche": LaMarche, Gara. "Big Philanthropy Faces a Reckoning, Too." The Nation. May 02, 2020. Accessed March 15, 2021. https://www.thenation.com/article/politics/philanthropy-politics-billionaires/.

"Hannah Paterson…has written extensively on this topic": Paterson, Hannah. "Staff, Skills and Operationalisation-Putting Participatory Grant Making (PGM) into Practice." Medium. February 09, 2020. Accessed March 15, 2021. https://hannah-paterson.medium.com/staff-skills-and-operationalisation-putting-participatory-grant-making-pgm-into-practice-340b566f500a.

Piloting participation

"Cate A. Fox": "Culture, Equity, and the Arts: Accepting the Invitation to Change - MacArthur Foundation." RSS. Accessed March 15, 2021. https://www.macfound.org/press/perspectives/accepting-invitation-change/.

"The foundation eventually landed on a model": "A Work in Progress: Participatory Grantmaking in the Arts - MacArthur Foundation." RSS. Accessed March 15, 2021. https://www.macfound.org/press/perspectives/work-progress-participatory-grantmaking-arts/.

"MacArthur president John Palfrey cited": Palfrey, John, and John Palfrey Is the President of the John D. and Catherine T. MacArthur Foundation. He Was Previously Professor of Law and Vice Dean for Library and Information Resources at Harvard Law School. "The Case for Foundations to Do More in Times of Crisis (SSIR)." Stanford Social Innovation Review: Informing and Inspiring Leaders of Social Change. Accessed March 15, 2021. https://ssir.org/articles/entry/the_case_for_foundations_to_do_more_in_times_of_crisis.

"In August 2020, the foundation announced": "The National Lottery Community Fund Commits £1.4 Million to a New Partnership with Global Fund for Children: The National Lottery Community Fund." The National Lottery Community Fund Commits £1.4 Million to a New Partnership with Global Fund for Children | The National Lottery Community Fund. Accessed March 15, 2021. https://www.tnlcommunityfund.org.uk/news/press-releases/2020-08-04/the-national-lottery-community-fund-commits-1-4-million-to-a-new-partnership-with-global-fund-for-children.

"NLCF is chartered by the UK parliament": "About The National Lottery Community Fund: The National Lottery Community Fund." About The National Lottery Community Fund | The National Lottery Community Fund. Accessed March 15, 2021. https://www.tnlcommunityfund.org.uk/about.

Mama Cash: Going All In

"The fund has become a powerhouse in feminist philanthropy": "Welcome to Our 35 Years of History." Mama Cash History Welcome to Our 35 Years of History Comments. Accessed March 15, 2021. http://www.history.mamacash.nl/.

"In 2017, Mama Cash decided to pilot": "The Solidarity Fund." MamaCash. Accessed March 15, 2021. https://www.mamacash.org/en/solidarity-fund-announcement.

"They landed on a two-step model": "Sharing Power." MamaCash. Accessed March 15, 2021. https://www.mamacash.org/en/sharing-power.

Individual donors

"In July 2020, Mackenzie Scott": Scott, MacKenzie. "116 Organizations Driving Change." Medium. July 28, 2020. Accessed March 15, 2021. https://mackenzie-scott.medium.com/116-organizations-driving-change-67354c6d733d.

"The Bridgespan group describes today's mega-donors": Powell, Alison, and Willa Seldon. "Reimagining Institutional Philanthropy (SSIR)." Stanford Social Innovation Review: Informing and Inspiring Leaders of Social Change. Accessed March 15, 2021. https://ssir.org/articles/entry/reimagining_institutional_philanthropy.

"The percentage of philanthropic dollars": "Donor Advised Funds Were Up Almost 300 Percent This Decade. Why?" Worth. December 30, 2019. Accessed March 15, 2021. https://www.worth.com/donor-advised-funds-were-up-almost-300-percent-this-decade-why/.

"In 2011, the same year that": "HRC Store Vandalized; Radical Queer Group Claims Responsibility." Washington Blade: Gay News, Politics, LGBT Rights. June 30, 2011. Accessed March 15, 2021. https://www.washingtonblade.com/2011/06/29/hrc-store-vandalized-radical-queer-group-claims-responsibility/.

Convincing the field

"In 2020, the Rawa Fund's Moukhtar Kocache": InfoWINGSWEB. "Power and the Role of Philanthropy - #WINGSForum2020 Virtual Summit." YouTube. November 30, 2020. Accessed March 15, 2021. https://www.youtube.com/watch?v=AsvQM0tW2_o&feature=youtu.be&ab_channel=WINGSontheAir

"Salzburg Global Seminar": "Looking Forward to Dec 9 Panel @Salzburg-Global on Participatory Grant-making Particularly in times of Crisis. Check out the Great Line up of Speakers including Our Own @MoukhtarK #ShiftThePower Pic.twitter.com/KG4BEN0vGk." Twitter. December 08, 2020. Accessed March 15, 2021. https://twitter.com/RawaFund/status/1336258156087881728.

"Chronicle of Philanthropy published an op-ed": Philanthropy.com. Accessed March 15, 2021. https://www.philanthropy.com/article/how-this-crisis-may-upend-grant-making-for-good/.

"Diana Samarsan and Katy Love responded": Philanthropy.com. Accessed March 15, 2021. https://www.philanthropy.com/article/flexibility-for-grantees-is-not-enough-let-them-decide-where-the-money-goes-letter-to-the-editor/.

"In 2019, Cardona signed off": "Participatory Grantmaking Matters Now More than Ever." Ford Foundation. Accessed March 15, 2021. https://www.fordfoundation.org/work/learning/learning-reflections/participatory-grant-making-matters-now-more-than-ever/.

"Inside Philanthropy's David Callahan has noted": Benjamin Soskis and Stanley N. Katz."Looking Back at 50 Years of U.S. Philanthropy." Hewlett Foundation. January 17, 2018. Accessed March 15, 2021. https://hewlett.org/library/looking-back-50-years-u-s-philanthropy/.

"there are now more than 250,000 foundations around the world": "The Global Philanthropy Report: Perspectives on the Global Foundation Sector." Center for Public Leadership - Harvard Kennedy School. Accessed

March 15, 2021.https://cpl.hks.harvard.edu/global-philanthropy-report-perspectives- global-financial-sector.

"regional campaigns like #ShiftThePower": Jenny Hodgson Barry Knight, Jenny Hodgson, and Barry Knight. "#ShiftThePower: From Hashtag to Reality." OpenDemocracy. Accessed March 15, 2021. https://www.opendemocracy.net/en/transformation/shiftthepower-hashtag-reality/.

"As Inside Philanthropy's Tate Williams wrote": Williams, Tate. "Power in Letting Go: How Participatory Grantmakers Are Democratizing Philanthropy." Inside Philanthropy. https://www.insidephilanthropy.com/home/2018/11/9/power-in-letting-go-how-participatory-grantmakers-are-democratizing-philanthropy.

CHAPTER 8

"One of the virtual panels": "Taking Stock: Are Impact Investors Really Ready to Take on the World's 'intersecting Crises'?" The Social Enterprise Magazine - Pioneers Post. October 23, 2020. Accessed March 15, 2021. https://www.pioneerspost.com/news-views/20201023/taking-stock-are-impact-investors-really-ready-take-on-the-worlds-intersecting.

Growing Ujima

"represents more than $2 billion in capital": "Investor Network." Transform Finance. Accessed March 15, 2021. http://transformfinance.org/investor-network.

"In 2019, Transform Finance launched": "Capital and Equitable Communities." Transform Finance. Accessed March 15, 2021. http://transformfinance.org/capital-and-equitable-communities.

"average size of a first-time fund": "First-Time Fund Managers." Spotlight. https://docs.preqin.com/newsletters/pe/Preqin-PESL-Feb-17-First-Time-Fund-Managers.pdf.

Designing new funds

"The end result was an innovative loan fund": Thorpe, Jodie, and John Gaventa. "Democratising Economic Power: The Potential for Meaningful Participation in Economic Governance and Decision-Making." March 2020. https://opendocs.ids.ac.uk/opendocs/bitstream/handle/20.500.12413/15193/Wp535_online.pdf?sequence=5&isAllowed=y.

"In 2019, Candide announced the Olamina Fund": "Candide Group Raises $40 Million Fund for Community Lenders Advancing Racial Justice." Impact Alpha. January 15, 2021. Accessed March 15, 2021. https://impactalpha.com/candide-group-raises-40-million-fund-for-community-lenders-advancing-racial-justice/.

"The Kataly Foundation's $50 million environmental justice initiative": Foundation, The Kataly. "In Solidarity: Introducing the Kataly Foundation." Medium. October 06, 2020. Accessed March 15, 2021. https://kataly.medium.com/in-solidarity-introducing-the-kataly-foundation-d080d-30886d6.

"told Impact Alpha": "How Impact Investors Are Using Donor-advised Funds to Shift Power to the People – and Communities." Impact Alpha. October 28, 2020. Accessed March 15, 2021. https://impactalpha.com/investors-are-beginning-to-use-donor-advised-funds-to-shift-power-to-the-people/.

The Heron Foundation: Going All In

"'It felt like a boom-splat'": "Dana Bezerra, Heron Foundation." Impact Alpha. May 15, 2020. Accessed March 15, 2021. https://impactalpha.com/agent-of-impact-dana-bezerra-heron-foundation/.

"'We as a country have a long history'": "Heron Presidential Podcast Ep. 2." Heron Foundation. July 01, 2020. Accessed March 15, 2021. https://www.heron.org/heron-presidential-podcast-ep-2/.

"Heron is still building out the details": Ibid.

Reinventing Ownership

"Take the $10 billion (and growing) cannabis industry": DSouza, Deborah. "The Future of the Marijuana Industry in America." Investopedia. January 28, 2021. Accessed March 15, 2021. https://www.investopedia. com/articles/investing/111015/future-marijuana-industry-america.asp.

"One of the Black founders on the platform": Massey, Meg, "Can Cannabis Entrepreneurs Advance Racial Equity?" Karma. August 25, 2020. Accessed March 15, 2021. https://karmaimpact.com/can-cannabis-entrepreneurs-advance-racial-equity/.

"'If [traditional investors] don't make changes'": Us, Future For. "Let Success Be Your Activism: A Chat With Arlan Hamilton." Medium. June 22, 2020. Accessed March 15, 2021. https://medium.com/@futureforus/let-success-be-your-activism-a-chat-with-arlan-hamilton-631904ed855e.

CHAPTER 9

Participatory Grantmaking 101

"As Jeremy Heimans and Henry Timms": Heimans, Jeremy and Henry Timmes. New Power: *How Power Works in Our Hyperconnected World - and How to Make It Work for You.* Place of Publication Not Identified: ANCHOR, 2019.

"Justice Funders runs the Maestra program": "Maestra Program." Justice Funders. Accessed March 15, 2021. http://justicefunders.org/maestra/.

Participatory Investing 101

"McKeever Conwell has pointed out": Massey, Meg, "Black Business Leaders on America in the Wake of George Floyd's Death." Karma. June 17, 2020. Accessed March 15, 2021. https://karmaimpact.com/what-next-black-business-leaders-share-thoughts-on-america-in-wake-of-floyd-death/.

"Due Diligence 2.0": "Due Diligence 2.0 Commitment." Due Diligence 2.0

Commitment. Accessed March 15, 2021. https://www.duediligencecommitment.com/.

"According to Jump Canon's managing partners": Canon, Partners @ Jump. "Distance-Traveled: A New Diligence Framework for Entrepreneurs and Their Phenomenal Capacity." Medium. November 06, 2018. Accessed March 15, 2021. https://medium.com/jumpcanon/introducing-distance-traveled-a-new-diligence-framework-to-evaluate-entrepreneurs-and-their-7b8570570184.

"Gender-lens investing": "GenderSmart." GenderSmart. Accessed March 15, 2021. http://www.gendersmartinvesting.com/.

"Refugee lens": "Refugee Lens." Refugee Investment Network. June 27, 2019. Accessed March 15, 2021. https://refugeeinvestments.org/resources/refugee-lens/.

"the founders wrote": Jennifer, Mara. "Zebras Fix What Unicorns Break." Medium. March 8, 2017. Accessed March 15, 2021. https://medium.com/zebras-unite/zebrasfix-c467e55f9d96.

"There has already been a push by investors": Mares, Lisa Woll and Judy. "The Department of Labor Is Attacking Sustainable Investments - And Harming Plan Participants." Institutional Investor. August 25, 2020. Accessed March 15, 2021. https://www.institutionalinvestor.com/article/b1n2lp9y127bwk/The-Department-of-Labor-Is-Attacking-Sustainable-Investments-And-Harming-Plan-Participants.

The Role of Policymakers

"The Walsh Commission": LaMarche, Gara. "Is Philanthropy Bad for Democracy?" The Atlantic. October 30, 2014. Accessed March 15, 2021. https://www.theatlantic.com/politics/archive/2014/10/is-philanthropy-good-for-democracy/381996/.

"It's Time to Tax Us More": Pay It Forward: Letter for a Wealth Tax. "An Open Letter to the 2020 Presidential Candidates: It's Time to Tax Us More." Medium. September 21, 2019. Accessed March 15, 2021. https://

medium.com/@letterforawealthtax/an-open-letter-to-the-2020-presidential-candidates-its-time-to-tax-us-more-6eb3a548b2fe.

"In a 2019 poll": Casselman, Ben, and Jim Tankersley. "Warren Wealth Tax Has Wide Support, Except Among One Group." The New York Times. November 29, 2019. Accessed March 15, 2021. https://www.nytimes.com/2019/11/29/business/economy/economy-politics-survey.html.

"Amazon's market capitalization": Desjardins, Jeff. "Amazon Is Now Bigger than Most Brick and Mortar Retailers Put Together." Business Insider. January 03, 2017. Accessed March 15, 2021. https://www.businessinsider.com/the-extraordinary-size-of-amazon-in-one-chart-2017-1.

"Amazon's predatory price cuts": Timothy B. Lee - Jul 30, 2020 6:42 Pm UTC. "Emails Detail Amazon's Plan to Crush a Startup Rival with Price Cuts." Ars Technica. July 30, 2020. Accessed March 15, 2021. https://arstechnica.com/tech-policy/2020/07/emails-detail-amazons-plan-to-crush-a-startup-rival-with-price-cuts/.

"creating a 'kill zone'": "American Tech Giants Are Making Life Tough for Startups." The Economist. Accessed March 15, 2021. https://www.economist.com/business/2018/06/02/american-tech-giants-are-making-life-tough-for-startups.

"Advocates are now pushing for a $1 billion appropriation": Mary Scott Hardwick / April 22. "CDFIs Call for $1 Billion in New CDFI Fund Grants as PPP Misses the Mark." Opportunity Finance Network. April 30, 2020. Accessed March 15, 2021. https://ofn.org/articles/cdfis-call-1-billion-new-cdfi-fund-grants-ppp-misses-mark.

"'baby bonds bill' recently reintroduced'": Landergan, Katherine. "Booker Reintroduces 'baby Bonds' Bill to Give All Newborns a $1K Savings Account." Politico PRO. February 04, 2021. Accessed March 15, 2021. https://www.politico.com/states/new-jersey/story/2021/02/04/booker-reintroduces-baby-bonds-bill-to-give-all-newborns-a-1k-savings-account-9425345.

"As Rebecca Solnit wrote in May 2020": "'The Way We Get through This Is Together': Mutual Aid under Coronavirus | Rebecca Solnit." The Guardian. May 14, 2020. Accessed March 15, 2021. https://www.theguardian.com/world/2020/may/14/mutual-aid-coronavirus-pandemic-rebecca-solnit.

Your Money, Your Community

"Save Our Safety Net": Facebook. Accessed March 15, 2021. https://www.facebook.com/SaveOurSafetyNet/.

"This will be the largest wealth transfer in human history": Schmitt, Jennifer Xia and Patrick Schmitt. "Philanthropy's Missing Trillions (SSIR)." Stanford Social Innovation Review: Informing and Inspiring Leaders of Social Change. Accessed March 15, 2021. https://ssir.org/articles/entry/philanthropys_missing_trillions.

"Anand Giridharadas told the Washington Post": Altman, Anna. "Their Families Built Fortunes. These Millennials Are Trying to Figure out How to Undo Their Class Privilege." The Washington Post. March 02, 2020. Accessed March 15, 2021. https://www.washingtonpost.com/magazine/2020/03/02/their-families-built-fortunes-these-millennials-are-trying-figure-out-how-undo-their-class-privilege/?arc404=true.

"Investor Gabe Kleinman wrote in a Medium post": Kleinman, Gabe. "The End of Big Philanthropy." Medium. August 08, 2017. Accessed March 15, 2021. https://medium.com/@gabekleinman/the-end-of-big-philanthropy-2f44c796fa09.

"Resource Generation members Monica George and Sarah Frank": "Millennials Are Ruining Trust Funds." In These Times. Accessed March 15, 2021. https://inthesetimes.com/article/millennials-trust-funds-resource-generation-money.

"The young board members had read": Bill Pitkin, Guest Contributor. "Moving the Rooms of Power: Participatory Philanthropy Is Gaining More

Traction." Inside Philanthropy. July 01, 2020. Accessed March 15, 2021. https://www.insidephilanthropy.com/home/2020/6/24/moving-the-rooms-of-power-participatory-philanthropy-is-gaining-more-traction

"According to a blog post, they asked themselves": "Shifting Power." Conant Foundation. Accessed March 15, 2021. https://www.conantfamily-foundation.org/reviewteamprocess

"A blog post on the fund's website": "The Evolution of Family Philanthropy: The David Rockefeller Fund." NCFP. Accessed March 15, 2021. https://www.ncfp.org/2020/08/04/the-evolution-of-family-philanthropy-the-david-rockefeller-fund/

AFTERWORD

"'We will not let them silence your voices'": "Transcript of Trumps Speech at Rally Before US Capitol Riot." U.S. News & World Report. Accessed March 15, 2021. https://www.usnews.com/news/politics/articles/2021-01-13/transcript-of-trumps-speech-at-rally-before-us-capitol-riot.

"In the 2016 primary campaign": Appelbaum, Yoni. "Americans Aren't Practicing Democracy Anymore." The Atlantic. September 13, 2018. Accessed March 15, 2021. https://www.theatlantic.com/magazine/archive/2018/10/losing-the-democratic-habit/568336/.

Beyond Election Reform

"Four in ten Americans say they're lonelier than ever": Pesce, Nicole Lyn. "More than 4 in 10 Americans Are Feeling Lonelier than Ever during the Pandemic." MarketWatch. April 15, 2020. Accessed March 15, 2021. https://www.marketwatch.com/story/social-distancing-has-40-of-americans-feeling-lonelier-than-ever-2020-04-15.

"A majority of American communities feel misunderstood": Pampuro, Amanda. "Poll: American Communities Feel Disconnected From Each Other." Courthouse News Service. May 23, 2018. Accessed March 15, 2021.

https://www.courthousenews.com/poll-american-communities-feel-disconnected-from-each-other/.

"Historian Yoni Applebaum": Applebaum, "Americans Aren't Practicing Democracy Anymore."

"The 2010 census found": Ibid.

"Lerner pointed out that in 2016": Foundation Funding for U.S. Democracy. Accessed March 15, 2021. https://democracy.candid.org/.

Agency

"Their study's introduction put it more bluntly": Gilens, Martin, and Benjamin I. Page. "Testing Theories of American Politics: Elites, Interest Groups, and Average Citizens: Perspectives on Politics." Cambridge Core. September 18, 2014. Accessed March 15, 2021. https://www.cambridge.org/core/journals/perspectives-on-politics/article/testing-theories-of-american-politics-elites-interest-groups-and-average-citizens/62327F-513959D0A304D4893B382B992B.

"Their central finding echoed": Page, Benjamin I., and Martin Gllens. "Critics Argued with Our Analysis of U.S. Political Inequality. Here Are 5 Ways Theyre Wrong." The Washington Post. April 18, 2019. Accessed March 15, 2021. https://www.washingtonpost.com/news/monkey-cage/wp/2016/05/23/critics-challenge-our-portrait-of-americas-political-inequality-heres-5-ways-they-are-wrong/.

"Seventy percent of Americans today believe the political system is 'rigged'": Fernandez, Marisa. "Despite Trump's Populist Promises, 70% of Americans Still Say the Political System Is Rigged." Axios. August 25, 2019. Accessed March 15, 2021. https://www.axios.com/poll-political-system-rigged-trump-c3f84eaa-7e94-441d-ba78-fb477d2b47e3.html.

"budgets are essentially 'moral documents'": Wallis, Jim. "Truth That Bears Repeating: A Budget Is a Moral Document." Sojourners. March 31, 2017. Accessed March 15, 2021. https://sojo.net/articles/truth-bears-repeating-budget-moral-document.

"ultimately helped reduce child mortality": Wampler and Mike, Brian, and Mike Touchton. "Brazil Let Its Citizens Make Decisions about City Budgets. Here's What Happened." The Washington Post. May 03, 2019. Accessed March 15, 2021. https://www.washingtonpost.com/news/ monkey-cage/wp/2014/01/22/brazil-let-its-citizens-make-decisions- about-city-budgets-heres-what-happened/?noredirect=on&utm_ term=.5e3157a189ad.

"included in its platform": "Community Control." M4BL. February 01, 2021. Accessed March 15, 2021. https://m4bl.org/policy-platforms/ community-control/.

"In December 2020, the Seattle City Council voted": Dubb, Steve. "Seattle Launches $30 Million Participatory Budgeting Process." Non Profit News | Nonprofit Quarterly. February 05, 2021. Accessed March 15, 2021. https://nonprofitquarterly.org/seattle-launches-30-million-participa- tory-budgeting-process/.

Trust

"One recent study found": "Partisan Antipathy: More Intense, More Personal." Pew Research Center - U.S. Politics & Policy. August 17, 2020. Accessed March 15, 2021. https://www.pewresearch.org/politics/2019 /10/10/partisan-antipathy-more-intense-more-personal/?utm_source= link_newsv9&utm_campaign=item_268982&utm_medium=copy.

"Another survey found": "American Democracy in Crisis: The Fate of Pluralism in a Divided Nation." PRRI. Accessed March 15, 2021. https:// www.prri.org/research/american-democracy-in-crisis-the-fate-of-plural- ism-in-a-divided-nation/.

"disdain for the opposing political party now outweighs": Ladd, Jonathan M. "Negative Partisanship May Be the Most Toxic Form Of polarization." Vox. June 02, 2017. Accessed March 15, 2021. https://www.vox.com/ mischiefs-of-faction/2017/6/2/15730524/negative-partisanship-toxic- polarization.

"'pernicious polarization'": Drutman, Lee. "How Hatred Came To Dominate American Politics." FiveThirtyEight. October 05, 2020. Accessed March 15, 2021. https://fivethirtyeight.com/features/how-hatred-negative-partisanship-came-to-dominate-american-politics/.

"Americans aren't nearly as polarized": Hopkins, Dan. "Analysis | Why Were Polarized Shows How Media, Emotion, Politicians and More Are Dividing Americans." The Washington Post. January 29, 2020. Accessed March 15, 2021. https://www.washingtonpost.com/politics/2020/01/29/why-were-polarized-shows-how-media-emotion-politicians-more-are-dividing-americans/.

"supported by more than seventy percent": Hall, Madison. "75% of Americans Support Bidens $1.9 Trillion COVID-19 Relief Bill despite Outcries from GOP Lawmakers, a New Poll Finds." Business Insider. March 10, 2021. Accessed March 15, 2021. https://www.businessinsider.com/75-americans-support-bidens-covid-19-bill-despite-gop-outcries-2021-3.

"the most isolated Democrats": Brown, Jacob R., and Ryan D. Enos. "The Measurement of Partisan Sorting for 180 Million Voters." https://www.nature.com/articles/s41562-021-01066-z.epdf

"identifies as Catholic": Oloughlin, Ed. "Ireland Takes On the Catholic Church Again. This Time It's About Schools." The New York Times. June 01, 2018. Accessed March 15, 2021. https://www.nytimes.com/2018/06/01/world/europe/ireland-catholic-church-baptism-schools.html

"In 2016, the Irish government partnered": "The Citizens Assembly behind the Irish Abortion Referendum." Involve.org.uk. July 09, 2018. Accessed March 15, 2021. https://www.involve.org.uk/resources/blog/opinion/citizens-assembly-behind-irish-abortion-referendum.

"random sample of 99 Irish citizens": "The Irish Citizens Assembly: Heinrich Böll Stiftung: Washington, DC Office - USA, Canada, Global Dialogue." Heinrich-Böll-Stiftung. Accessed March 15, 2021. https://us.boell.org/en/irish-citizens-assembly.

"after historic turnout": "Irish Abortion Referendum: Ireland Overturns Abortion Ban." BBC News. May 26, 2018. Accessed March 15, 2021. https://www.bbc.com/news/world-europe-44256152.

"Citizens' Initiative Review in Oregon": "Citizens Initiative Review." Healthy Democracy. Accessed March 15, 2021. https://healthydemocracy. org/cir/.

"Citizens' Statement": "Citizens' Review Statement of Measure 26-199, Portland Metro Region Affordable Housing Bond (2018)." https:// healthydemocracy.org/wp-content/uploads/2018-PDX-CIR-Final-Citizens-Statement.pdf.

Storytelling

"In 2014, the New York City Council passed": "Stop-and-Frisk During the Bloomberg Administration 2002-2013 (2014)." New York Civil Liberties Union. February 19, 2019. Accessed March 15, 2021. https://www.nyclu. org/en/publications/stop-and-frisk-during-bloomberg-administration-2002-2013-2014.

"'Giselle had a real, concrete effect on me'": Oh, Inae. "How A Trans Woman Inspired Real Reform Through Her Art." HuffPost. December 07, 2017. Accessed March 15, 2021. https://www.huffpost.com/entry/theatre-of-the-oppressed_n_5398405.

"Augusto Boal": "Augusto Boal." Wikipedia. March 11, 2021. Accessed March 15, 2021. https://en.wikipedia.org/wiki/Augusto_Boal.

"One example is Theatre of the Oppressed NYC": "Our Work." Theatre of the Oppressed NYC. Accessed March 15, 2021. https://www.tonyc.nyc/ our-work.

"'We want to take back the storytelling process'": Oh, Inae. "How A Trans Woman Inspired Real Reform Through Her Art." HuffPost. December 07, 2017. Accessed March 15, 2021. https://www.huffpost.com/entry/theatre-of-the-oppressed_n_5398405.

"a rebellion against all history": "A 'Wake-Up Call' For US Democracy." Texas Standard. January 07, 2021. Accessed March 15, 2021. https://www. texasstandard.org/stories/a-wake-up-call-for-us-democracy/

"just days before the 2020 election" "Join The Race 2020." Sojourn Theatre. Accessed March 15, 2021. http://www.sojourntheatre.org/join-the-race-2020

"In Manchester, England": Account, Info. "Using Theatre to Make Policies: Legislative Theatre in Manchester." People Powered. January 11, 2021. Accessed March 15, 2021. https://www.peoplepoweredhub.org/news-content/legislative-theatre-manchester.